The Proxy Century

Why Small Wars Decide Big Empires

By

Viktor Romcev

Vij Books

New Delhi (India)

Published by

Vij Books
(Publishers, Distributors & Importers)
4836/24, 3rd Floor, Ansari Road
Delhi – 110 002
Phone: 91-11-43596460
Mobile: 98110 94883
e-mail: contact@vijpublishing.com
www.vijbooks.in

ISBN: 978-81-99786-83-7 (HB)

ISBN: 978-81-99802-69-8 (PB)

ISBN: 978-81-99802-68-1 (eBook)

This book was developed using advanced writing tools to support the drafting and ideation process. All content has been thoughtfully curated, refined, and reviewed to ensure quality and relevance.

Contents

Introduction

At dawn, a convoy moves along a rutted road that does not appear on most maps. The men riding in the back are young, poorly paid, and alert to every shadow. Their rifles are not new, but they are not old either; the serial numbers have been filed away, the crates long since discarded. Somewhere far beyond the hills, officials in capital cities will deny any connection to what happens next. If the convoy is ambushed, the deaths will be local. If it reaches its destination, the consequences will not be. This is how contemporary power often travels: indirectly, anonymously, and with just enough distance to preserve the fiction of restraint.

Proxy wars are usually introduced to the public as clever solutions to difficult problems. They are framed as limited commitments, cost-effective interventions, or acts of reluctant necessity. Someone else does the fighting. Someone else absorbs the casualties. Someone else shoulders the moral and legal ambiguity. For leaders facing wary electorates, economic interdependence, and the ever-present danger of escalation, proxy warfare appears to offer the best of all worlds. Influence without occupation. Pressure without fingerprints. Power without responsibility.

Yet the bill for these supposedly modest conflicts keeps arriving, and it rarely comes in manageable instalments. It arrives as regional instability that spills across borders. As armed groups that refuse to disband when the war they were created for is over. As criminal networks, frozen conflicts, and diplomatic crises that outlive the politicians who authorised the original intervention. Again and again, wars sold as marginal prove decisive, reshaping alliances, draining treasuries, and hardening enmities for generations. The paradox at the heart of proxy warfare is not that it is messy or morally compromised. It is that small wars, precisely because they are treated as peripheral, so often end up deciding the fate of great powers.

This book begins from that paradox. It asks why states that possess formidable armies, advanced technologies, and global reach so often choose to fight through others. It asks how these relationships are built, maintained, and lost. It asks why indirect wars, meant to reduce risk, repeatedly generate forms of danger that are harder to control than the conflicts they were meant to avoid. Above all, it asks how a world of deniable violence has become the primary arena in which empires are tested, weakened, and sometimes undone.

The appeal of proxy war is neither new nor uniquely modern. Long before the language of plausible deniability and hybrid conflict entered strategic vocabularies, powerful states learned the value of fighting at arm's length. Imperial authorities funded rival chiefs on distant frontiers. Dynasties sponsored rebellions inside enemy realms. Merchants armed privateers while governments professed innocence. What distinguishes the present age is not the existence of proxy warfare but its centrality. In a world shaped by decolonisation, nuclear deterrence, mass media, and economic entanglement, direct conquest has become politically radioactive. Occupation invites resistance, scrutiny, and long-term obligations. Proxy war promises leverage without liability.

This shift has altered not only how wars are fought, but how power itself is exercised. Modern proxy conflicts are sustained by elaborate systems that connect distant patrons to local fighters: arms pipelines that cross continents, intelligence feeds stripped of identifying marks, financial networks that blend state budgets with private donations, narratives crafted to satisfy domestic audiences and international law. These systems are often invisible to those who live with their consequences. They are also poorly understood by many who authorise them. Proxy warfare is treated as a technical instrument, a tool to be deployed and withdrawn at will. In practice, it behaves more like an ecosystem, adaptive, resilient, and prone to producing unintended outcomes.

The human cost of this ecosystem is easy to overlook precisely because it is distributed. The fighters are rarely citizens of the patron state. The cities reduced to rubble are usually far from the centres of global finance and diplomacy. Refugees cross borders that seldom lead to the capitals where strategic decisions were made. Distance dulls accountability. It also breeds complacency. When a proxy offensive fails, it can be dismissed as a local setback. When it succeeds, the victory can be claimed without ownership. In both cases, the stronger structural effects accumulate quietly.

One way to understand proxy war is as a series of bargains struck under conditions of asymmetry. Patrons possess resources, diplomatic clout, and the ability to walk away. Clients possess local knowledge, manpower, and a willingness to take risks that patrons cannot. Each side believes it can manage the other. Each side underestimates how quickly interests diverge once blood has been shed and power redistributed. The relationship is neither fully contractual nor wholly ideological. It is contingent, transactional, and always vulnerable to rupture.

This book offers a framework for reading those bargains. It traces how states decide to outsource violence, how they select partners, and how they attempt to shape behaviour through money, weapons, training, and intelligence. It examines the stories leaders tell their own publics to justify these choices, and the legal arguments they advance to defend them abroad. It follows the money as carefully as the guns, showing how sanctions, illicit finance, and donor networks become instruments of war in their own right. It treats information not as a backdrop to conflict but as a battlefield, where narratives can determine legitimacy as decisively as any military engagement.

A recurring motif runs through these pages: the idea of control at a distance. Proxy warfare is built on the belief that influence can be exerted without presence, that outcomes can be shaped without exposure. Time and again, this belief collides with reality. Distance weakens oversight. Deniability erodes discipline. The very features that make proxy war attractive to patrons make it empowering for clients. Armed, funded, and legitimised, proxies acquire options. They can escalate, defect, fragment, or survive their sponsors. The line between instrument and actor blurs, then disappears.

History offers no shortage of warnings. Cold War interventions intended to be limited metastasised into regional catastrophes. Insurgencies nurtured for tactical advantage evolved into strategic threats. Alliances forged in secrecy became liabilities once exposed. What is striking is not that states repeat these mistakes, but that they continue to frame each new proxy war as an exception, a unique case where lessons do not apply. Institutional memory proves short. Political incentives reward optimism. The costs, when they arrive, are blamed on local conditions rather than structural design.

The urgency of this subject lies in the fact that proxy warfare is no longer confined to a handful of ideological battlegrounds. It has become the default mode of competition in a crowded, multipolar world. Regional powers emulate the practices of superpowers. Non-state actors learn to play patrons against one another. Private military companies market deniability as a service. New technologies, from armed drones to encrypted communications, lower barriers to entry while complicating attribution. The result is not a reduction in violence, but its diffusion.

For civilians caught in these conflicts, the distinction between proxy and principal is meaningless. What matters is who controls the checkpoint, who pays the fighters, and whether tomorrow will be quieter than today. For states, however, these distinctions shape strategy, law, and reputation. A missile strike conducted by a uniformed pilot carries different risks from one enabled by intelligence passed through intermediaries. A massacre committed by a client militia triggers different calculations from one carried out by national troops. Proxy warfare thrives in these gaps, exploiting the spaces between responsibility and consequence.

This book does not argue that proxy wars are inherently irrational or always avoidable. States face real threats. Leaders operate under constraints. Indirect methods can, in some circumstances, prevent wider wars or buy time for diplomacy. The problem is not that proxy warfare exists, but that it is habitually misunderstood. It is treated as cheaper than it is, more controllable than it proves to be, and more reversible than experience suggests. By the time these misconceptions are exposed, the structures they created are often too entrenched to dismantle.

To make sense of this world, we need better questions. Not simply who is winning on the battlefield, but who is gaining leverage over whom. Not whether a proxy is advancing, but what incentives that advance creates. Not how much money is being spent, but what forms of dependency and autonomy that spending produces. This book is organised around those questions. Each chapter examines a different layer of the proxy system, from the initial decision to outsource force to the long afterlife of armed groups once the shooting subsides.

The aim is not to provide a catalogue of conflicts, nor to moralise from a distance. It is to offer readers a way of seeing. To recognise the patterns that link a civil war in one decade to a frozen conflict in the next. To understand why similar strategies recur across regions and regimes. To appreciate how choices made in the name of prudence can generate risks that are anything but limited.

As the chapters unfold, familiar assumptions will be challenged. The idea that proxy wars are cheap will be tested against their cumulative economic and political costs. The belief that deniability reduces escalation will be weighed against the evidence of miscalculation and spillover. The notion that control can be maintained through money and training will be set beside cases where clients escaped, with consequences that reshaped entire regions. Even the concept of success will be interrogated, moving beyond battlefield outcomes to consider influence, legitimacy, and long-term stability.

The final chapters look forward, not to predict specific wars, but to map the terrain on which future proxy contests are likely to unfold. As power diffuses and technology evolves, the temptation to fight indirectly will only grow. So too will the risks. The next proxy century is unlikely to be quieter than the last. It will, however, reward those who understand how small wars accumulate into large effects.

The question, then, is not whether proxy warfare will continue. It is whether states, institutions, and citizens will learn to recognise its true costs before they are paid in full. When a distant conflict appears on the evening news, framed as marginal or manageable, what invisible systems are already in motion? Whose interests are being served, and whose futures are being mortgaged? And how many such "limited" wars can an empire fight before it discovers that the periphery has become the centre?

This book invites readers to sit with that discomfort. To look past the language of efficiency and necessity, and to see proxy warfare for what it is: a defining feature of modern power, and a quiet arbiter of imperial rise and decline.

Chapter 1

Why States Favour Proxy Wars

In the late nineteenth century, when an empire wanted to impose its will, it sent a column. Uniformed troops disembarked from ships, marched inland, raised flags, and fought battles that were meant to be seen as much as won. The violence was explicit, the chain of command unmistakable, the political ownership impossible to deny. Today, in many of the same regions, influence arrives differently. It travels through bank transfers routed via third countries, through trainers who never appear in official photographs, through militias that swear loyalty to local causes while quietly adjusting their tactics to suit distant patrons. The banners have changed. The logic has not entirely disappeared.

The shift from expeditionary warfare to proxy conflict is often described as a story of restraint, even progress. Large invasions are said to belong to a cruder age, replaced by precision, subtlety, and prudence. Yet this narrative conceals as much as it reveals. The retreat from overt conquest was not driven solely by ethical awakening or strategic sophistication. It was forced by hard constraints: the collapse of formal empires, the advent of nuclear weapons, the rise of mass politics at home, and the unforgiving glare of global media. What looks like choice is often adaptation. Proxy warfare emerged not because states lost their appetite for power, but because the old ways of exercising it became too costly to sustain.

To understand why states favour proxy wars, it is useful to linger on a simple contradiction. Governments invest enormous effort in maintaining disciplined, hierarchical armed forces, trained to obey orders and operate within formal chains of accountability. Yet when the stakes rise, many of those same governments choose to fight through actors who are irregular, fragmented, and motivated by agendas only partially aligned with their own. This is not an accident or a failure of nerve. It is a calculated response to a strategic environment in which direct confrontation threatens escalation, domestic backlash, or international isolation. Proxy warfare is not a deviation from rational state behaviour; it is one of its most revealing expressions.

The roots of this preference lie in the long retreat from empire. As colonies gained independence and nationalist movements reframed foreign troops as occupiers rather than administrators, expeditionary campaigns lost their legitimacy. Military success no longer guaranteed political control. In many cases it actively undermined it, fuelling resistance and delegitimising local elites associated with foreign rule. At the same time, the spread of nuclear weapons placed hard ceilings on interstate war among major powers. Conflicts that once might have been settled on the battlefield became exercises in risk management. Indirect action offered a way to compete without inviting catastrophe.

Domestic opinion reinforced these constraints. The twentieth century turned warfare into a mass experience, visible in newspapers, on television, and later on personal screens. Casualties ceased to be abstractions. They acquired names, faces, and political consequences. Governments that could once absorb losses in distant territories found themselves increasingly sensitive to body counts, even in conflicts framed as peripheral. Economic interdependence added another layer of caution. Wars that disrupted trade, energy flows, or financial markets carried costs that reverberated far beyond the battlefield. In this environment, proxy warfare appeared as a compromise: a means of acting without fully committing, of shaping outcomes without paying the full price.

A brief contrast makes the point. In the early twentieth century, a European power seeking to pacify a rebellious province in a strategic hinterland dispatched regular troops, established garrisons, and imposed administrative reforms at gunpoint. Decades later, facing unrest in the same region, a successor state pursued its interests through arms deliveries, intelligence sharing, and the cultivation of local militias nominally opposed to extremism. The objectives overlapped. The methods diverged sharply. What stayed the same was the desire to influence the political order. What changed was the tolerance for visibility, ownership, and long-term responsibility.

This evolution raises a deceptively simple question: what, precisely, makes a war a proxy war? The term is used loosely, often as a synonym for any conflict involving external involvement. Yet not every alliance, arms sale, or training mission qualifies. A proxy war, in its most useful sense, is a conflict in which external patrons materially shape the capabilities and behaviour of local combatants while deliberately avoiding open ownership of the fight. Influence is exercised without formal command. Responsibility is blurred rather than assumed. The proxy is neither a mere client nor a fully autonomous ally, but something in between.

Control and commitment sit at the heart of this distinction. In some Cold War conflicts, superpowers exercised near-total control over their proxies' strategic choices, embedding advisers deep within command structures and conditioning support on strict compliance. In others, backing was looser, more opportunistic, allowing local actors wide latitude in exchange for alignment on a single overriding goal. Contemporary civil wars display similar variation. Some external sponsors micromanage targeting decisions and messaging. Others content themselves with funding and occasional guidance, accepting chaos as the price of access. Whether a conflict is best understood as a proxy war depends less on the scale of support than on the nature of the relationship it creates.

Why, then, do leaders persistently choose this ambiguous middle ground instead of confronting adversaries directly? The answer lies in a cluster of incentives that reward indirection. Escalation looms large among them. Direct clashes between states risk drawing in allies, triggering treaty obligations, or crossing thresholds that are difficult to uncross. Proxy warfare allows leaders to test boundaries without committing themselves irreversibly. It offers room to probe an adversary's resolve, to apply pressure incrementally, and to retreat if signals are misread.

Alliance politics amplify this logic. In tightly woven security networks, a single overt move can reverberate unpredictably. Supporting a proxy, by contrast, creates space for ambiguity. It allows partners to calibrate their responses, to offer tacit support without public endorsement, or to maintain plausible distance when domestic constraints demand it. Media scrutiny reinforces the appeal. Indirect involvement is easier to frame as humanitarian assistance, counterterrorism, or capacity building. It buys time. It dulls outrage. It shifts debate from intent to interpretation.

Consider the familiar spectacle of aid convoys and training missions presented as neutral support for stability, even as the recipients' battlefield behaviour clearly advances one side of a conflict. The language of humanitarianism coexists comfortably with the reality of partiality. Leaders rely on this duality not because they are cynics, but because modern politics punishes candour in war. Deniability becomes a form of insulation, protecting decision-makers from the immediate consequences of their choices.

Proxies also transform how risk is calculated. By interposing local forces between themselves and their adversaries, patrons reduce the likelihood that setbacks will escalate into direct retaliation. Losses are absorbed elsewhere. Failures can be reframed as local missteps rather than national humiliations. At the same time, proxies offer a means of signalling intent. An advance can communicate resolve. A withdrawal can signal restraint. These movements acquire meaning beyond their immediate tactical value, functioning as messages in a broader strategic conversation.

This signalling function turns proxy forces into bargaining chips. Their presence or absence can shape negotiations far removed from the battlefield on which they fight. A militia's success may strengthen a patron's hand in talks over sanctions or security guarantees. Its vulnerability may invite concessions. In this sense, proxy wars are rarely about the proxy alone. They are embedded in wider contests over influence, status, and rules.

Yet the very features that make proxy warfare attractive also generate its central tension. Proxies are not pieces on a board. They are organisations composed of individuals with their own incentives, fears, and ambitions. Once armed and legitimised, they develop survival instincts that do not always align with patron preferences. Moral hazard creeps in as risks are externalised. Local rivalries intensify. Ideologies harden. What began as a tool becomes an actor.

History is replete with moments when this autonomy asserts itself violently. A client force, emboldened by battlefield success, launches an offensive its sponsor sought to avoid. A militia, fearing abandonment, strikes pre-emptively. An armed group, flush with weapons and confidence, turns against its former backer when interests diverge. These episodes are often dismissed as anomalies. They are anything but. They are structural features of indirect control.

This chapter explores why states accept these dangers. It does so not to condemn or defend proxy warfare, but to explain its enduring appeal. The preference for proxies is rooted in rational calculations made under constraint. It reflects the realities of a world where overt force is politically toxic yet strategic competition remains fierce. Understanding this preference requires looking beyond individual conflicts to the incentives that shape decision-making across time and geography.

What follows traces the evolution from expeditionary campaigns to outsourced violence, clarifies what distinguishes proxy wars from other forms of intervention, and examines the motives that drive leaders towards indirection. It also confronts the limits of this approach, introducing the problem of control that will recur throughout the book. By the end of the chapter, the reader will have a framework for recognising proxy warfare not as a marginal tactic, but as a central pillar of modern statecraft.

The questions raised here do not belong to the past. They surface whenever a government debates whether to send troops or advisers, weapons or words. They matter when conflicts are described as manageable, when costs are presented as low, and when responsibility is diffused. Why, in a world of unprecedented military capability, do states so often choose to fight through others? And what does that choice reveal about the kind of power they are trying to exercise, and the risks they are willing to accept?

The answers are rarely comfortable. They are, however, essential for understanding how small wars come to carry such large consequences.

From expeditionary wars to outsourcing

In July 1839, a British expeditionary force marched through the Bolan Pass towards Kandahar, its banners visible, its officers named, its intent unmistakable. The First Anglo-Afghan War was meant to secure India's north-western frontier by installing a friendly ruler in Kabul. It was an imperial operation in the classical sense: regular troops, explicit political ownership, and the assumption that force could reorder a distant society at acceptable cost. Three years later, in January 1842, the retreat from Kabul ended in catastrophe. Of the roughly 16,000 soldiers and camp followers who left the city, only one reached Jalalabad alive. The ledger was brutal. Empire learned, slowly.

A century and a half later, in the same mountains and valleys, foreign power returned by other means. In July 1979, the United States authorised covert assistance to Afghan insurgents resisting a pro-Soviet government. The programme, later known as Operation Cyclone, expanded after the Soviet invasion that December, channelling money, weapons, and training through Pakistan's Inter-Services Intelligence. No American battalions marched on Kabul. No flags were raised. Yet the intervention helped bleed a rival superpower, altered regional politics, and left armed movements that outlived the Cold War. Same terrain. Different method.

Count the bodies later.

The contrast between these two episodes captures a broader transformation in how states project force. Expeditionary wars, once the hallmark of imperial power, demanded visibility. They relied on the assumption that military success translated into political compliance, and that metropolitan publics would tolerate distant violence as the price of security or prestige. That assumption eroded under the combined pressure of decolonisation, nuclear deterrence, and domestic opinion. What replaced it was not pacifism but outsourcing: the deliberate use of clients, militias, and movements to achieve strategic aims without formal conquest.

Decolonisation did more than redraw maps. It delegitimised occupation as a tool of governance. Anti-colonial movements reframed foreign troops as invaders rather than administrators, turning even tactically successful campaigns into political failures. France's experience in Indochina and Algeria illustrated the point with painful clarity. Superior firepower could win battles; it could not secure consent. As new states joined international institutions, sovereignty acquired a normative weight that made overt intervention costly even when it remained militarily feasible. The presence of foreign troops became a liability, a rallying point for resistance and an embarrassment in global forums.

Nuclear weapons hardened these constraints. After 1945, direct wars between major powers carried risks that no amount of conventional superiority could neutralise. The possibility of escalation imposed a discipline on state behaviour. Competition did not cease; it moved sideways. Supporting allies and proxies offered a way to contest influence while preserving the fiction of restraint. The superpowers learned to fight without touching, to wound without striking openly. Proxy warfare became a pressure valve in a system where direct confrontation threatened annihilation.

Domestic opinion completed the triangle. As mass media brought war into living rooms, casualty figures acquired political force. The Vietnam War demonstrated how sustained losses in a distant theatre could fracture consensus at home. Leaders absorbed the lesson unevenly, but they absorbed it nonetheless. Soldiers' deaths were no longer easily absorbed as imperial overhead. They demanded justification, explanation, and, increasingly, avoidance. Outsourcing risk to non-citizens became attractive not because leaders were indifferent to foreign lives, but because domestic accountability was asymmetrical. Voters counted their own dead first.

These structural shifts did not abolish expeditionary warfare overnight. They changed its calculus. States still deploy troops abroad, but the threshold has risen, and the justifications have narrowed. When they do intervene directly, they often seek rapid exit strategies, multinational cover, or mandates that diffuse responsibility. Where such conditions cannot be met, indirect methods fill the gap. Money replaces battalions. Advisers replace commanders. Influence flows through intermediaries.

The mechanics of outsourcing are deceptively mundane. Selecting a local partner requires judgement about competence and compliance. Arms must be supplied in ways that obscure origin. Training has to impart doctrine without creating dependency that is politically embarrassing. Each decision leaves traces, behavioural rather than formal. A militia paid regularly adopts payroll rhythms. Fighters trained by foreign instructors mirror their tactics. Intelligence passed selectively shapes targets chosen and avoided. These are visible behaviours, measurable in patterns of movement, casualty ratios, and operational tempo. Outsourcing is not abstraction; it is practice.

Operation Cyclone offers a clear illustration. By routing support through Pakistan, the United States reduced its own exposure while empowering a regional ally. The Central Intelligence Agency avoided direct contact with many Afghan commanders, relying on Pakistani intermediaries to distribute funds and weapons. The arrangement limited Washington's control over which factions benefited most. Groups favoured by Islamabad gained disproportionate strength. The implication was clear at the time and clearer in retrospect: outsourcing influence also outsourced decision-making. Control diminished as deniability increased.

A different pattern appeared in Central America during the 1980s. In Nicaragua, the United States supported Contra forces opposing the Sandinista government. Here, oversight was tighter, political scrutiny sharper, and the line between covert and overt more contested. Congressional restrictions, most notably the Boland Amendments, constrained direct funding, leading to improvised financial channels that later erupted into scandal. The Iran–Contra affair revealed a limitation of outsourcing: domestic institutions do not always accept deniability as an answer. When indirect wars surface, they can corrode trust at home even as they pursue objectives abroad.

These cases underline a central point. Outsourcing violence reduces some costs while creating others. It lowers the visibility of intervention but complicates accountability. It minimises immediate casualties among patron forces but increases reliance on actors with their own priorities. It allows flexibility but weakens control. States accept these trade-offs because the alternatives often look worse. The choice is rarely between clean and dirty methods; it is between different kinds of mess.

There are, however, important counter-examples that temper any claim of inevitability. In April 1982, Argentina seized the Falkland Islands. The United Kingdom responded with a conventional task force, sailing 8,000 miles to retake the territory. The war was short, overt, and unapologetically expeditionary. Why did outsourcing not appeal here? The answer lies in alignment of stakes and legitimacy. The islands were claimed as British territory. Public support was strong. The adversary was a state, not a movement embedded in civilian populations. The political costs of inaction outweighed those of visibility. Outsourcing made little sense when ownership was essential to the outcome.

Reconciling this exception with the broader trend sharpens the analysis. States favour proxy wars not because they lack capacity for direct action, but because most contemporary conflicts do not resemble the Falklands. They are internal wars with external implications, fought among civilians, intertwined with identity and governance. In such environments, expeditionary forces risk becoming occupiers, their presence generating resistance faster than they can suppress it. Outsourcing appears as a way to influence without inflaming, to shape without standing at the centre of the storm.

The quiet motif threading through these shifts is distance. Not physical distance alone, but political and moral distance. Expeditionary wars collapsed that distance. They forced patrons to own outcomes, good and bad. Outsourced wars stretch it, sometimes to breaking point. Decisions made in capital cities ripple through local conflicts with delayed and distorted effects. By the time consequences return, the original rationale has often faded, replaced by new priorities.

Distance also alters learning. Expeditionary failures were visible, their lessons painful but hard to ignore. Outsourced failures are easier to misread. A proxy's defeat can be blamed on local incompetence. Atrocities can be disowned. Successes can be claimed selectively. This ambiguity feeds repetition. States return to indirect methods not only because they seem cheaper, but because their full costs are harder to tally. The ledger is kept in fragments.

What stayed the same between the British march on Kabul and the later covert war was the strategic impulse to shape Afghanistan's alignment without fully understanding its internal dynamics. What changed was the method and the tolerance for exposure. In 1839, empire assumed responsibility and paid dearly. In 1979, power intervened obliquely and paid later, in different currency. The trade-offs shifted; the risks did not disappear.

Outsourcing force has become a habit of modern statecraft, reinforced by institutions, technologies, and expectations. It is easier to authorise a shipment than a deployment, easier to deny a relationship than a command. Yet each act of indirection tightens a knot of dependency and resentment that can be difficult to untangle. The question that remains, and that haunts every decision to avoid an expeditionary war, is not whether outsourcing reduces immediate costs. It is whether the distance it creates will eventually demand payment, and on whose terms.

What makes a war a proxy

On 11 November 1975, as Portugal formally ended its rule in Angola, Cuban troops began arriving in Luanda. Within weeks, thousands were on the ground, flying in on Soviet aircraft, stiffening the position of the MPLA as rival movements advanced from the interior. Washington denied direct involvement. Moscow denied command. Havana insisted on revolutionary solidarity. Yet by early 1976 the outcome was clear: the MPLA held the capital, its rivals were pushed back, and Angola had become one of the Cold War's most consequential proxy battlegrounds. Flags mattered. So did fingerprints.

The Angolan war mattered because it revealed something precise about modern conflict. Power could be decisive without being explicit. Influence could be exercised through others while formal ownership was avoided. The result looked like a civil war. The engines driving it lay elsewhere. This is the core intuition behind the idea of proxy war, an intuition often blurred by loose usage but sharpened by practice.

Ownership was deliberately obscured.

At its simplest, a proxy war is not defined by who fires the weapon, but by who shapes the conditions under which it is fired. External patrons materially influence local combatants while avoiding open responsibility for the fighting. Material influence leaves traces. Weapons arrive in identifiable patterns. Training alters behaviour. Intelligence changes targeting choices.

Funding stabilises some groups and starves others. What patrons avoid is formal command and public authorship. The proxy fights under its own name, its own flag, its own grievances. The war remains, on paper, local.

This distinction matters because not all external involvement creates a proxy relationship. States sell arms to allies every day without dictating how those weapons are used. Training missions can strengthen partners without pulling them into a patron's strategic orbit. Even battlefield coordination between allies does not automatically turn a conflict into a proxy war. The line is crossed when support begins to shape not only capability but choice, when it constrains options and channels behaviour in ways that serve an external agenda.

The difference can be seen in visible decisions. A group that times offensives to coincide with foreign diplomatic initiatives is responding to external cues. A militia that refrains from striking certain targets despite local advantage reflects imposed restraint. A movement that fragments along funding lines reveals patron influence in its internal politics. These are not abstractions. They are patterns observable to commanders and civilians alike.

Cold War Angola offers a clear case of high control combined with high deniability. The Soviet Union supplied heavy weapons, advisers, and strategic direction to the MPLA. Cuba provided troops, openly but nominally independently. The United States and South Africa backed rival movements, notably UNITA, through funding, arms, and regional partners. Each patron sought to shape outcomes without triggering direct confrontation. Control varied. Moscow exerted substantial influence over MPLA strategy, while Washington's relationship with UNITA was looser, filtered through intermediaries. The implication was asymmetry. Where control was tighter, coordination improved. Where it was looser, local agendas flourished, often violently.

Contrast this with the Syrian civil war after 2011. Here, multiple external actors backed an array of local forces, often simultaneously. The United States, Russia, Iran, Turkey, and Gulf states all intervened indirectly at various stages. Support ranged from arms and training to intelligence and air power. Control varied not only between patrons but over time. Some groups operated as disciplined clients, adjusting operations to retain support. Others treated patrons as one funding source among many, switching allegiances or ignoring guidance when it conflicted with survival.

The Syrian case complicates the proxy label precisely because ownership was both avoided and, at times, embraced. Russia's intervention from September 2015 included overt air operations in support of the Assad government, reducing deniability while preserving a narrative of sovereign invitation. Iran's role blended proxy militias with formal advisers, creating layered responsibility. The United States oscillated between covert backing of opposition groups and overt operations against the Islamic State. Syria demonstrates that proxy warfare is not a binary condition but a spectrum, shaped by degrees of control and commitment.

Control is the first axis that distinguishes proxies from allies. In a classic alliance, partners coordinate but retain strategic autonomy. They share risks openly. In a proxy relationship, autonomy is conditional. Support is contingent on behaviour. Control is exercised through funding cycles, weapons compatibility, intelligence access, and political recognition. When a patron suspends aid after disobedience, that is control. When it redesigns a group's command structure through training, that is control. When it dictates who may sit at negotiating tables, that is control.

Commitment is the second axis. Proxy patrons deliberately cap their exposure. They avoid treaty obligations. They resist being seen as indispensable. Their aim is influence without entrapment. This is why proxy wars often feature hedging behaviour: diversified clients, ambiguous statements, and reversible investments. A patron that commits fully ceases to have a proxy; it acquires a partner or a liability. The proxy exists in the space between.

These axes explain why some conflicts resist the proxy label despite heavy external involvement. Consider the Korean War after 1950. While it featured massive intervention by external powers, control and commitment were explicit. Chinese forces fought under their own command. American troops operated openly. The war was internationalised, not outsourced. Calling it a proxy war obscures more than it clarifies. The same can be said of NATO's intervention in Kosovo in 1999, where direct ownership replaced indirection once the decision to act was taken.

Acknowledging these counter-examples sharpens the concept rather than weakening it. Proxy war describes a specific configuration of power, not a synonym for meddling. It is defined by deliberate distance. That distance is maintained through legal arguments, public messaging, and organisational design. It is also fragile. Leaks, battlefield evidence, and shifting politics can collapse it overnight.

The motif that threads through proxy wars is deniability, not as a legal trick but as a strategic resource. Deniability buys time. It allows patrons to test responses. It softens domestic debate. Yet it also imposes costs. The more deniable the relationship, the less enforceable control becomes. Patrons trade command for cover. Clients trade autonomy for resources. Both accept uncertainty.

Angola again illustrates the point. When Cuban forces intervened decisively, deniability narrowed but effectiveness increased. The war's trajectory shifted. In Syria, when Russia moved from covert assistance to overt air power, control over the battlefield improved, but political exposure grew. Each step towards ownership brought clarity and constraint. Each step away restored ambiguity and risk.

The practical value of defining proxy war lies in diagnosis. Mislabeling a conflict leads to faulty expectations. Treating a loosely supported militia as a controllable proxy invites surprise when it acts independently. Treating a tightly managed client as an autonomous ally obscures responsibility when it commits abuses. The label shapes how policymakers, journalists, and publics assign blame and credit.

Visible metrics help. Frequency of consultation between patron and client leaders indicates control. Conditionality clauses in funding agreements indicate leverage. Changes in tactics following external pressure indicate responsiveness. None of these require access to classified material. They are observable in outcomes. Proxy war leaves footprints even when it hides its face.

There is an unresolved tension at the heart of the concept. The more a patron shapes a war, the harder it is to deny ownership. The more it avoids ownership, the less it can shape outcomes. Proxy warfare lives in that narrow corridor. It is tempting because it promises influence without responsibility. It is dangerous because it rarely delivers both for long. The test, for any state contemplating indirect involvement, is not whether it can avoid being named, but how much control it is willing to sacrifice to remain unnamed.

Why leaders avoid direct confrontation

On 25 March 2015, Saudi Arabia announced the start of Operation Decisive Storm. Airstrikes began over Yemen within hours, launched from bases inside the Kingdom and coordinated with regional partners. The United States did not join the bombing campaign. Instead, it offered intelligence support, aerial refuelling, and expedited arms transfers, describing its role as assistance to restore stability and ease humanitarian suffering. Washington insisted it was not a party to the war. By the end of the year, thousands were dead, ports were blockaded, and the line between support and participation had blurred beyond recognition. Responsibility travelled sideways.

Leaders choose distance deliberately.

The Yemen case is not an aberration. It is a worked example of why governments, even those with overwhelming military capacity, increasingly avoid direct confrontation. The preference is not rooted in timidity. It is driven by a dense web of incentives that reward indirection and punish ownership. Escalation risks, alliance commitments, media scrutiny, casualty sensitivity, and economic interdependence combine to make overt war a last resort. Proxy methods offer an escape hatch, imperfect but politically survivable.

The first pressure point is escalation. Direct confrontation narrows options quickly. Once uniformed forces clash, retreat becomes costly, both strategically and reputationally. Adversaries respond in kind. Allies invoke obligations. What begins as a limited strike acquires momentum. Leaders know this from experience. The memory of wars that expanded beyond their authors' intentions is institutional, embedded in doctrines and briefings. Indirect methods preserve space. They allow a state to apply pressure while keeping escalation ladders intact.

This is visible behaviour, not theory. When Russia intervened in eastern Ukraine in 2014, it avoided deploying regular units openly. Instead, it relied on local militias, volunteers, and equipment without insignia. The decision preserved ambiguity at a critical moment, complicating NATO's response and buying time to consolidate gains. The implication was strategic delay. Direct intervention might have triggered immediate countermeasures. Indirection slowed the clock.

Alliance entanglements reinforce this logic. Modern security arrangements bind states together through treaties, expectations, and habits of consultation. These ties deter aggression, but they also constrain initiative. A unilateral move risks fracturing coalitions painstakingly built over decades. Supporting a proxy allows leaders to act while maintaining formal alignment. It offers something for everyone: reassurance for hawks, deniability for sceptics, and procedural cover for partners unwilling to endorse open war.

The 1980s war in Afghanistan demonstrated this clearly. By funnelling support to insurgents through Pakistan, the United States avoided direct confrontation with Soviet forces and spared its allies the burden of explicit participation. European partners could condemn the invasion while remaining insulated from operational decisions. The alliance held. The cost was ceded control over distribution and priorities to intermediaries. Leaders accepted the trade because the alternative threatened unity.

Media scrutiny sharpens these incentives. Modern conflicts unfold under constant observation. Images travel faster than explanations. Civilian casualties become headlines within hours. Direct intervention places leaders at the centre of this glare. Indirect involvement diffuses attention. It allows officials to speak in the language of assistance, partnership, and concern rather than command and culpability. This is not deception in a crude sense. It is framing under pressure.

The behaviour associated with this framing is measurable. Governments limit public statements. They classify missions narrowly. They emphasise aid figures over sortie counts. During the early years of the Syrian conflict, several Western states highlighted humanitarian funding and refugee assistance even as they supplied arms and training to selected opposition groups. The metric that mattered politically was not battlefield impact but narrative plausibility. Support had to look compatible with restraint.

Casualty sensitivity sits at the heart of this narrative management. Democracies, in particular, have learned that public tolerance for military deaths is finite and context-dependent. Losses incurred in defence of the homeland are absorbed differently from those suffered in distant, ambiguous wars. Leaders respond by shifting risk outward. Contractors replace conscripts. Local fighters take the front line. Deaths still occur, but they are statistically and politically displaced.

This displacement is visible in budget lines and force composition. After 2003, the United States dramatically increased its reliance on private contractors in Iraq and Afghanistan. By 2010, contractors outnumbered uniformed personnel in theatre, according to data compiled by the Congressional Research Service. The implication was not merely logistical. Contractor casualties attracted less sustained attention. The human cost remained. The political cost changed shape.

Economic interdependence adds another layer of caution. States deeply embedded in global markets calculate war's impact not only in military terms but in disrupted supply chains, energy prices, and investor confidence. Direct confrontation threatens these flows. Sanctions and counter-sanctions follow. Markets react. Proxy warfare offers a way to compete below thresholds that would trigger comprehensive economic retaliation.

This dynamic was evident after Russia's annexation of Crimea in March 2014. Western responses combined sanctions with indirect military assistance to Ukraine. The aim was to impose costs without rupturing economic ties entirely. Energy dependence and financial exposure shaped the tempo and scope of action. Leaders measured responses against potential blowback at home. Indirection allowed calibration.

Yet these incentives do not operate in isolation. They interact, reinforcing one another. Escalation fears make alliance management more delicate. Media scrutiny amplifies casualty sensitivity. Economic exposure magnifies the political costs of miscalculation. Proxy methods sit at the intersection of these pressures. They promise influence without rupture.

The humanitarian frame is a particularly powerful tool within this matrix. By presenting support as relief or protection rather than combat, leaders recast involvement as moral duty rather than strategic choice. In Yemen, the United States justified its role as necessary to facilitate aid delivery and defend shipping lanes. Refuelling sorties and intelligence sharing were described as enabling restraint. The visible behaviour told a different story. Without refuelling, air operations would have been curtailed. Without targeting support, accuracy would have suffered. The implication was functional participation under a humanitarian banner.

This pattern recurs. In Libya in 2011, the initial justification for intervention rested on civilian protection. As operations expanded, Western states avoided deploying ground troops, relying instead on air power and local militias. Direct confrontation with the regime was avoided until collapse made it moot. The aftermath exposed the limits of this approach. Responsibility for stabilisation was diffused. Militias filled the vacuum. Leaders had avoided the costs of occupation. They had not avoided the costs of disorder.

A credible counter-example tempers any claim that leaders always shun direct confrontation. The United States' response to the attacks of 11 September 2001 included the overt invasion of Afghanistan in October of that year. NATO invoked Article 5. Public support was broad. The rationale was explicit. Why did indirection not suffice? The answer lies in threat perception and legitimacy. The attack was direct. The target was clear. Deniability offered no political shelter. Ownership was demanded.

Reconciling this exception clarifies the rule. Leaders avoid direct confrontation when objectives are ambiguous, risks diffuse, and legitimacy contested. They embrace it when threats are concrete and publics demand visible action. Proxy warfare thrives in the grey zone between. It is a strategy of management, not resolution.

The quiet motif threading through these choices is insulation. Leaders insulate themselves from escalation, from alliance rupture, from media backlash, from economic shock. Each layer of insulation reduces immediate exposure while increasing reliance on intermediaries. The distance created is not merely spatial. It is moral and political.

That distance, however, comes at a price. Insulation weakens control. Partners pursue their own priorities. Actions taken in a patron's name but not under its command generate consequences that are hard to disown. The very features that make indirect methods attractive also make them unstable. Leaders know this. They proceed anyway.

The calculus is brutally pragmatic. Direct confrontation concentrates risk. Indirect methods spread it. The distribution favours those with the greatest capacity to absorb delayed consequences. It disadvantages civilians and client forces who bear immediate costs. This asymmetry is rarely acknowledged openly. It is built into the structure of choice.

As conflicts proliferate and interdependence deepens, the temptation to remain at arm's length will grow. The unresolved tension is whether insulation can be maintained as evidence accumulates and responsibilities entangle. At what point does support become ownership? How much distance is enough to avoid escalation without surrendering control? Leaders answer these questions case by case. The answers rarely age well.

How proxies change risk calculations

In October 1973, as Egyptian and Syrian forces crossed ceasefire lines and Israeli units counterattacked, the United States quietly raised its nuclear alert level to DEFCON 3. The signal was not directed at Cairo or Damascus. It was aimed at Moscow. Soviet matériel flowed to Arab armies; American airlifts sustained Israel. No American or Soviet troops faced each other directly on the battlefield. Yet the war brought the superpowers closer to confrontation than at any moment since Cuba. The fighting was local. The signalling was global. Risk moved without crossing borders.

This episode captures the distinctive way proxies alter strategic calculation. They allow states to act at once cautiously and aggressively, to test limits while maintaining formal restraint. Through clients, patrons probe defences, impose costs, and communicate intent without stepping fully into the line of fire. The battlefield becomes a signalling device, its advances and retreats read far beyond their immediate geography.

Risk, in this context, is not eliminated. It is redistributed.

The first way proxies change calculation is by lowering the perceived threshold for action. Direct military moves carry clear triggers for retaliation. Indirect ones blur those triggers. When a militia advances, it is easier to frame the event as local momentum rather than deliberate escalation. This ambiguity widens the menu of options available to leaders. They can authorise support that would be unacceptable if delivered by their own forces.

Visible behaviour illustrates this shift. Patrons provide weapons systems that alter balance without announcing intervention: anti-tank missiles, air-defence assets, surveillance drones. Each delivery changes what local forces can attempt. Each attempt tests how far an adversary will tolerate change before responding. The implication is incrementalism. Proxies make stepwise escalation feasible.

The Soviet and American roles in the 1973 Arab–Israeli War demonstrate this dynamic. By resupplying their respective partners, both superpowers shaped the battlefield without crossing the line into direct combat. When Israeli forces crossed the Suez Canal and encircled Egypt's Third Army, Soviet leaders signalled concern through diplomatic channels and military posture rather than troops. The United States responded in kind. The proxy war became a rehearsal for escalation management. Red lines were sketched, not crossed.

A more recent example lies along Israel's northern border. Since the mid-2000s, Hezbollah's military posture in southern Lebanon has functioned as a buffer for Iran. Tehran does not fire rockets into Israel. Hezbollah does. When rocket fire intensifies or abates, it is read as a signal not only from Beirut but from Tehran. The group's decision to escalate in July 2006 triggered a major Israeli response, while subsequent restraint has been equally communicative. Advances and pauses acquire diplomatic meaning.

This signalling works because proxies occupy contested space. They sit between patrons and adversaries, absorbing pressure that would otherwise fall directly on the sponsor. This buffer function reduces immediate vulnerability. It allows patrons to contest territory, influence, or legitimacy at a remove. The battlefield becomes a zone of managed friction.

That friction can be measured. Frequency of clashes, depth of incursions, and choice of targets all convey information. When a proxy halts short of a sensitive site, it signals caution. When it advances despite warnings, it signals resolve. These behaviours are observed, interpreted, and fed into broader negotiations. Risk calculation becomes dynamic rather than binary.

Proxies also impose costs asymmetrically. Supporting a client is often cheaper than countering one. A relatively modest investment can force an adversary to commit disproportionate resources. This logic animated much Cold War strategy. In Afghanistan during the 1980s, the United States increased the cost of Soviet occupation by supplying insurgents with increasingly effective weapons. The introduction of the FIM-92 Stinger missile in 1986 altered air operations measurably, reducing helicopter freedom and raising Soviet losses. The metric mattered. Costs rose. The implication was strategic pressure without direct engagement.

Cost imposition need not aim at victory. It often seeks distraction. A proxy conflict draws attention, manpower, and political capital away from other theatres. Leaders calculate that tying down an adversary is itself a gain. This is visible in deployment patterns and budget reallocations. When resources flow into a secondary front, they do not flow elsewhere.

Yet proxies do more than drain. They also create bargaining chips. Control over a client's actions can be traded for concessions. A patron may restrain a proxy in exchange for relief elsewhere, or allow limited escalation to strengthen its negotiating hand. The client's behaviour becomes currency.

A clear illustration can be found in eastern Ukraine after the Minsk agreements of September 2014 and February 2015. Fighting ebbed and flowed around contested towns such as Debaltseve. Ceasefire violations spiked at moments of diplomatic pressure, then subsided. The advances and withdrawals of separatist forces were read as indicators of Moscow's stance in negotiations with Kyiv and Western capitals. The battlefield spoke when official statements did not.

This mechanism depends on credibility. For signalling through proxies to work, adversaries must believe the patron can restrain or unleash the client. That belief rests on past behaviour. When a patron demonstrably curbs a proxy's actions, restraint gains meaning. When proxies act autonomously, signals blur. Risk calculation becomes noisy.

The Syrian conflict again offers contrast. Iran's network of militias allowed it to project influence across borders, from Iraq to Lebanon. Advances by these groups signalled Tehran's reach. At the same time, their occasional defiance complicated messaging. Israel's strikes on Iranian-linked targets inside Syria tested red lines repeatedly. Each response, or lack thereof, adjusted expectations. The proxy buffer absorbed blows. It also transmitted pressure.

A credible limitation tempers the apparent elegance of this system. Proxies do not always behave as intended. Autonomy, misperception, and local incentives can derail signalling. When Iraqi militias attacked United States facilities in early 2020 following the killing of Qasem Soleimani, Tehran faced a dilemma. Restraint risked looking weak. Escalation risked war. Proxy action narrowed, rather than expanded, its room for manoeuvre. The buffer threatened to ignite.

Reconciling this limitation clarifies the trade. Proxies widen strategic options only when control is sufficient and interests aligned. Where alignment frays, risk returns with interest. The very distance that allows signalling also allows misreading. Adversaries may attribute intent where none exists, or dismiss warnings as noise. The ladder of escalation remains, but its rungs are uneven.

The quiet motif running through proxy risk calculation is testing. Patrons test adversaries' tolerance. Adversaries test patrons' control. Each probe adjusts the perceived boundary. This process is continuous. It explains why proxy conflicts rarely freeze completely. Movement matters. Stillness sends its own message.

Testing also reshapes domestic calculations. Leaders can present proxy advances as organic developments, insulating themselves from blame while claiming credit indirectly. Conversely, proxy setbacks can be disowned. This asymmetry encourages experimentation. It lowers the political cost of trying and failing.

Yet every test leaves residue. Weapons remain. Fighters gain experience. Narratives harden. The buffer thickens. Over time, what began as a signalling instrument acquires its own inertia. The proxy's existence becomes a fact on the ground, constraining future choices.

Risk, then, is not simply shifted. It is transformed. Proxies convert immediate, concentrated danger into diffuse, prolonged exposure. They allow patrons to manage crises tactically while storing problems strategically. The calculation favours those with patience and resources. It punishes those who mistake delay for resolution.

The unresolved tension lies here. If proxies make escalation manageable, they also make it chronic. Each advance or retreat speaks. Each message invites reply. At what point does signalling exhaust its usefulness? When does the buffer become a trap? Leaders rarely answer these questions in advance. They discover the answers as options narrow.

The limits of indirect control

On 12 October 2000, a small boat packed with explosives rammed the USS *Cole* in the port of Aden, Yemen, killing seventeen American sailors. The attack was carried out by al-Qaeda, an organisation whose senior figures had emerged from the anti-Soviet jihad in Afghanistan during the 1980s. That earlier war had been fuelled by external money, weapons, and training, much of it channelled through regional partners with Washington's encouragement. Two decades later, the distance collapsed. A former proxy milieu struck directly at its onetime sponsor. Control had ended. Consequences had not.

This was not an accident. It was a pattern.

Indirect warfare rests on a wager: that influence can be sustained without command, and that clients will continue to act in ways broadly consistent with patron interests. The wager occasionally pays. Often, it does not. Proxies are not inert tools. They are organisations embedded in local societies, animated by ideology, rivalry, fear, and ambition. They learn. They adapt. Above all, they survive. When these imperatives collide with a patron's preferences, control frays.

Distance deceives.

The first source of slippage is moral hazard. When clients know that an external sponsor bears part of the cost of failure, their appetite for risk increases. This is visible behaviour. Militias undertake offensives they could not sustain alone. Insurgent groups resist compromise, calculating that continued fighting will attract more aid. The metric is tempo. Operations accelerate after funding injections. Restraint weakens when losses can be replaced.

In Afghanistan during the 1980s, the flow of external support altered insurgent decision-making. As assistance grew, factions splintered and competed for resources, prioritising visibility over coordination. The implication was fragmentation. Success against Soviet forces did not translate into political cohesion. When the common enemy withdrew, rival groups turned inward. The patron's objective had been achieved. The proxy's future had not been settled.

Local rivalries deepen this dynamic. Proxies fight on terrain saturated with history. Clan divisions, sectarian fault lines, and personal vendettas shape choices more reliably than distant strategy papers. External patrons often underestimate these forces, mistaking temporary alignment for durable loyalty. The result is drift.

Iraq after 2003 provides a stark illustration. Various Shi'a militias received backing from Iran to counter foreign forces and rival groups. Over time, these militias embedded themselves in neighbourhoods, businesses, and political parties. Their actions reflected local power struggles as much as Tehran's regional aims. When some groups attacked Iranian diplomatic facilities in Basra in 2018, the message was unmistakable. Patronage did not equal obedience.

Ideology compounds the problem. Belief systems do not scale neatly to sponsor objectives. A movement motivated by religious or nationalist conviction may accept external aid without internalising external restraint. Training and funding can sharpen capability without moderating intent. The behaviour to watch is target selection. When proxies strike symbols irrelevant to patron goals, ideology has outpaced control.

Al-Qaeda again offers an example. Its leadership framed the Afghan jihad not as a limited campaign but as a template for global struggle. External sponsors had sought to bleed a rival superpower. The organisation sought something else entirely. The implication was divergence. Support aimed at one enemy fertilised a campaign against another.

These failures are often dismissed as blowback, a term that implies surprise. In practice, the mechanisms are well known. Indirect control weakens as proxies accumulate resources and legitimacy. Battlefield success increases autonomy. New funding streams reduce dependence. Leaders who survive multiple campaigns develop confidence, then ambition. Each step loosens the patron's grip.

Control can be measured. Frequency of compliance with patron guidance declines. Requests are ignored or delayed. Public rhetoric shifts. When a proxy begins issuing statements that contradict sponsor messaging, alignment has eroded. When it courts alternative backers, control is already compromised.

Yet the picture is not uniformly bleak. There are cases where indirect control has been sustained for long periods. Hezbollah's relationship with Iran demonstrates this possibility. Despite moments of tension, the organisation has largely operated within parameters set by Tehran, particularly regarding escalation with Israel. The reasons are concrete. Funding is regular. Training pipelines are centralised. Command structures overlap. Ideological affinity reinforces material dependence. Control endures because incentives align.

Reconciling this counter-example clarifies the limits. Durable proxy relationships require more than money and arms. They demand institutional integration and shared strategic horizons. These conditions are rare. They are also costly. The closer a proxy comes to being controllable, the closer it comes to being an extension of the patron, eroding deniability.

This trade-off sits at the heart of indirect warfare. Patrons can have autonomy or control. Rarely both.

The quiet motif threading through these cases is drift. Not sudden betrayal, but gradual deviation. Decisions taken for local reasons accumulate. A tolerated excess becomes precedent. A forgiven disobedience becomes expectation. Over time, the proxy's centre of gravity shifts. By the time a patron recognises the change, leverage has diminished.

Efforts to arrest drift often backfire. Cutting support can push proxies towards alternative sponsors or illicit finance. Tightening control can provoke resistance. Public discipline undermines deniability. Each corrective measure carries cost.

The United States' experience with the South Lebanon Army in the 1990s illustrates this dilemma indirectly through Israel's patronage. As Israeli forces prepared to withdraw in 2000, their local ally faced collapse. Years of dependence had not produced resilience. When support ended, the proxy disintegrated within days, its members fleeing or switching sides. Control had existed only while presence remained. Distance finished the job.

What appears as control is often conditional presence.

Indirect warfare thus produces a paradox. The more a patron relies on proxies to reduce risk, the more it accepts the risk of divergence. The strategy substitutes one set of dangers for another. Immediate escalation is deferred. Long-term instability grows.

This is not a moral argument. It is a structural one. Proxies respond to incentives closest to them: survival, dominance, legitimacy in their communities. Patron preferences rank lower unless constantly reinforced. Reinforcement costs money, attention, and political exposure. Eventually, trade-offs sharpen.

The unresolved question is diagnostic. How much deviation is tolerable before a proxy ceases to serve its purpose? When does patience become complicity, and withdrawal become abdication? States rarely answer these questions cleanly. They drift as their proxies do.

The moment of reckoning often arrives abruptly, with violence directed the wrong way. By then, the distance that once protected the patron has narrowed. Control has limits. The bill arrives anyway.

Chapter 2

Patron and Client Relationships

On a winter evening in a provincial capital, a delegation waits in a half-lit room. The men at the table are not equals. One side controls access to money, weapons, and diplomatic recognition. The other controls fighters, territory, and the local legitimacy that no external power can manufacture. They speak through interpreters, but the real translation happens elsewhere: in calculations about who needs whom more, and for how long. By the time tea is poured, both sides know the meeting will end without signatures. The war will continue. The relationship will deepen anyway.

Proxy wars are sustained not by ideology alone, nor by raw coercion, but by relationships. These relationships are rarely stable, often unequal, and always conditional. They resemble contracts without courts, marriages without vows, and markets without prices. Each side believes it can manage the other. Each side is partly right, and eventually wrong. To understand why proxy wars persist, mutate, and so often escape their architects' intentions, one must understand the bargaining that binds patrons and clients together.

At first glance, the roles appear straightforward. Patrons possess resources. Clients provide force. Yet this simplicity dissolves quickly. Not all patrons are alike, and neither are their clients. A global power juggling commitments across continents bargains differently from a regional state defending its near abroad. An insurgent movement embedded in a rural hinterland brings different assets to the table than an exiled political faction fluent in international law and media. Mercenary outfits, operating for profit rather than cause, obey a logic that unsettles both categories. The proxy relationship is less a single model than a family of arrangements, shaped by power, proximity, and purpose.

This chapter opens that family album.

The first task is classification, not for neatness, but for clarity. Global powers can afford redundancy. They back multiple clients, hedge their bets, and absorb failure in one theatre without existential damage. Their strategic depth allows patience. Small states cannot do this. When they choose a proxy, they often choose one. Their margins are thinner, their exposure greater. A single client's collapse can reverberate domestically. These asymmetries shape behaviour from the outset. They influence how much autonomy is tolerated, how quickly support is escalated, and how ruthlessly it is withdrawn.

Clients, too, vary in kind. Insurgent movements trade in manpower and local knowledge, but they are constrained by ideology and internal cohesion. Exiled politicians trade access and legitimacy, but often lack fighters they can command. Militias rooted in sectarian or tribal networks bring mobilisation capacity alongside deep rivalries. Mercenary groups offer professionalism and deniability, but little loyalty beyond contract terms. Each type enters negotiations with different currencies. Each imposes different risks.

A superpower backing three factions in a fragmented civil war behaves differently from a border state supporting a single militia across the frontier. The former can threaten to reallocate resources, playing clients against one another. The latter cannot. Its leverage rests on commitment, not choice. These structural differences explain why some patrons micromanage and others tolerate chaos, why some clients accept discipline and others bristle at it. The relationship is shaped before the first weapon is delivered.

From typology, the chapter moves into bargaining, where the proxy relationship truly takes form. Support is never unconditional. It is negotiated over goals, resources, and time. Patrons seek alignment with their strategic objectives; clients seek survival and advantage. The negotiation is rarely explicit. It unfolds through demands, delays, and demonstrations of value. A client launches an operation to prove effectiveness. A patron withholds ammunition to signal displeasure. Each move recalibrates expectations.

Classic bargaining concepts illuminate this dance without draining it of human texture. Leverage is not an abstract property; it is visible in alternatives. A client with access to multiple sponsors can resist pressure. One with a single lifeline cannot. Outside options matter. Credible commitment matters more. When a patron has a history of abandoning allies, promises ring hollow. When a client has defected before, discipline tightens. Memory shapes trust, and trust shapes risk.

Consider the recurring moment when a client is asked to moderate its ideology to broaden appeal. Accept this, the patron implies, and better weapons will follow. Refuse, and support may dry up. The client faces a trade-off between purity and power. The patron faces its own compromise: tighter control reduces local legitimacy, but looser control risks deviation. The bargain struck is rarely final. It is revisited after each battlefield shift, each diplomatic turn.

Risk appetite complicates these bargains further. Patrons and clients experience the same war differently. For the patron, the conflict is one file among many, its urgency relative. For the client, it is existential. This divergence distorts incentives. Desperate clients escalate. Cautious patrons hesitate. The result is friction.

When a client launches an offensive without approval, it is not merely disobedient; it is acting on a different clock. Immediate threats loom larger than long-term strategy. Patrons respond with restraint or reprimand, but their leverage weakens once fighting resumes. The ground moves faster than the capital. This asymmetry explains why carefully calibrated proxy strategies unravel at moments of crisis. Control depends on shared perception of risk. That perception rarely aligns.

Competition among patrons intensifies these dynamics. In many modern conflicts, multiple states back rival factions, or even rival wings of the same movement. The result is not balance but distortion. Payrolls compete. Commanders shop for sponsors. Loyalty becomes transactional. Fragmentation follows.

The incentives are visible. Fighters gravitate towards units that pay reliably. Leaders split organisations to maximise revenue streams. Ideological coherence erodes as material support dictates allegiance. What appears, from afar, as irrational proliferation is often rational adaptation to patron competition. War lengthens because peace threatens income. Patron strategies collide on the bodies of clients.

This competitive environment tempts patrons to overbid, offering more resources for marginal gains. The short-term effect is influence. The long-term effect is dependency without discipline. Each patron fears losing ground to rivals. Few step back. The conflict metastasises.

Eventually, some clients escape. Control was always contingent, but certain thresholds matter. Battlefield success can embolden a client to defy orders. New funding sources reduce dependence. Ideological radicalisation hardens resolve against compromise. Leadership turnover introduces figures less invested in the original bargain. At these moments, the proxy ceases to be a means and becomes an actor.

The transformation is rarely announced. It reveals itself in tone. Orders are acknowledged but ignored. Negotiations stall. The client pursues goals that no longer align with patron interests. In extreme cases, weapons provided for one fight are turned against the sponsor's forces or allies. What began as delegation becomes confrontation.

This chapter does not treat such outcomes as anomalies. They are inherent to relationships built on unequal power and shared violence. The patron–client bond contains the seeds of its own instability. It thrives on asymmetry but resents it. It requires trust but incentivises hedging. It promises control but generates autonomy.

The relevance of this analysis extends beyond any single conflict. As proxy warfare becomes more common, so do these relationships. Governments that once managed a handful now juggle dozens, often through intermediaries. Non-state actors learn quickly, adapting their bargaining strategies to extract maximum benefit. Private military companies blur categories further, inserting market logic into political violence. The patron–client relationship becomes the basic unit of modern war.

Understanding this unit changes how we read events. A sudden offensive may reflect bargaining failure rather than strategic intent. A ceasefire violation may signal competition among patrons rather than local breakdown. A client's defection may reveal shifts in resource flows invisible to outsiders. This perspective does not excuse violence. It explains its persistence.

The chapter ahead dissects these relationships in detail, moving from types and bargains to breakdowns and escapes. It does so not to catalogue dysfunction, but to illuminate power. Proxy wars are not fought only with weapons. They are fought with promises, pressures, and perceptions. The patron–client relationship is where these forces meet.

The question that hangs over every such relationship is deceptively simple. Who needs whom more, and for how long? The answer is never static. It shifts with every battle, every negotiation, every alternative that appears on the horizon. To follow those shifts is to see proxy warfare not as a series of isolated conflicts, but as a system of relationships that shape the modern world's most consequential wars.

Types of patrons and clients

In May 1986, boxes marked as "agricultural equipment" moved through warehouses around Peshawar, Pakistan, while men with new rifles queued for instruction in camps beyond the city. The Central Intelligence Agency was not stamping its seal on those crates, and the Afghan commanders receiving them were not taking orders from Washington. Yet the flow of weapons, money, and access was already reshaping which factions could fight, recruit, and claim authority. The outcome was not subtle: within months, the introduction of the FIM-92 Stinger missile in Afghanistan altered the air war and forced Soviet aircraft to adapt their tactics, a change documented by journalists and scholars of the conflict, including Steve Coll in *Ghost Wars* (2004). A local war began to behave like a global contest.

Every patron has its limits.

The point of beginning here is simple. Proxy relationships are often discussed as if they were a single species: a powerful state "uses" a weaker actor, the weaker actor "obeys", and the war unfolds as a kind of remote-controlled chess match. Real proxy politics is messier. The patron can be a superpower or a small state with a single vulnerable frontier. The client can be a disciplined insurgency, a loose militia network, an exiled politician with no fighters at all, or a commercial outfit that sells violence as a service. Each type carries a different set of constraints and temptations. The differences matter because they determine how much control is possible, how quickly the relationship can change, and what kinds of failure are most likely.

A workable typology begins with resources, regime type, and strategic depth, not as academic labels, but as practical determinants of choice. Resources decide what can be bought and sustained: weapons, training, salaries, propaganda, safe houses, legal defence, and the unglamorous costs of logistics. Regime type shapes how openly a patron can act and how much domestic scrutiny it can tolerate. Strategic depth—geography, buffers, and the ability to absorb retaliation—determines how risky the patron can be and how easily it can retreat. These factors do not merely colour behaviour. They produce it.

Global powers sit at one extreme. Their distinctive advantage is not just wealth or technology, but redundancy. They can support several clients simultaneously, hedge across factions, and shift resources without exposing their core security. In Afghanistan during the 1980s, the United States could tolerate uncertainty in the distribution of support because the war was one theatre within a broader Cold War portfolio. If one faction disappointed, the pipeline could favour another. If a programme leaked, it could be rebranded. Global powers also possess the diplomatic reach to launder relationships through allies, international organisations, or multilateral coalitions, multiplying deniability without sacrificing capability.

This latitude changes the patron's posture. A global power tends to measure success in strategic effects—costs imposed on rivals, access gained, alliances managed—more than in territorial minutiae. Its time horizon is often longer than the client's, and its patience can be both an asset and a provocation. When support arrives in tranches, tied to conditions and reviews, it reflects not stinginess but the logic of distance: a superpower can afford to wait, because the war is rarely existential for it. The implication for clients is clear. They must compete for attention.

Regional states occupy the crowded middle. Their wars are nearer, their exposure sharper. They cannot always hide behind oceans or alliances, and they often lack the slack to run multiple clients indefinitely. Yet they have a powerful advantage: proximity. They understand local languages, clan structures, trade routes, and border economies. They can offer sanctuary, medical care, and cross-border logistics that a distant patron cannot replicate. Their influence often runs through the mundane: who gets to cross a checkpoint, which wounded fighters receive treatment, whose families receive stipends. Proximity makes control more feasible. It also makes retaliation more likely.

Regime type affects how these states operate. An authoritarian system may endure international condemnation more easily but can still fear domestic instability if proxy conflict spills back across borders. A democracy may face sharper scrutiny over covert action, but can also mobilise legitimacy through parliamentary mandates or alliance frameworks. The visible behaviour is disclosure and denial: how often officials speak, how precisely they define their role, what they classify, and what they quietly normalise. A regional state that repeatedly insists it is "only protecting the border" while expanding training programmes is not merely spinning; it is managing a domestic coalition.

Clients look equally diverse when viewed up close. Insurgent movements are the archetype. They trade in fighters, intelligence gathered from villages, and the ability to make territory ungovernable. Their internal discipline varies. Some resemble shadow states, collecting taxes and administering courts. Others are coalitions of commanders linked by convenience. Patrons prefer discipline, but discipline is expensive: it requires cohesive leadership, ideological glue, and enforcement mechanisms that often involve coercion. When patrons fund an insurgency, they are not simply buying firepower; they are subsidising an organisational form.

The choice of whom to back is therefore a choice about governance as much as combat. A patron that funds a movement with a central command can hope for predictable behaviour, but risks creating a durable political rival once the war ends. A patron that funds fractured militias can prevent any single group from dominating, but invites chaos, civilian predation, and interminable conflict. The metric is fragmentation: how often groups splinter, how rapidly commanders change allegiance, how many distinct "brigades" appear after each influx of resources. Patronage can stabilise a faction. It can also encourage multiplication.

Exiled politicians are a different species of client, and often misunderstood. They bring something that fighters cannot: a claim to legitimacy recognised in foreign capitals, the ability to speak the language of international law, and access to media platforms. They can serve as the face of a proxy strategy, allowing patrons to say they are supporting a "government in waiting" rather than a militia. Yet exile politics is notoriously brittle. Distance from the battlefield weakens credibility. Internal rivalries intensify because power is imagined more than exercised. Patrons back exiles when they want a political vehicle, not just a military instrument. The danger is that the vehicle may have no engine.

Mercenary outfits and private military companies add another twist. They are neither ideological clients nor traditional state forces. They sell training, security, and sometimes combat capability under contract, and they can be deployed with a degree of deniability that suits patrons wary of sending regular troops. Their core constraint is commercial: they must be paid, and they must manage reputational risk in a market where clients and regulators watch. This can produce disciplined performance in narrow tasks—guarding a site, training a unit—but it also encourages behaviour aimed at demonstrating value quickly, sometimes at the expense of long-term stability. The visible behaviour is contract logic made operational: prioritising visible "security" outcomes, securing resource concessions, or rotating personnel in ways that weaken institutional memory.

None of these categories is pure. That is the first limitation of typology, and it is worth stating plainly. A regional state can act like a global power in one theatre and like a vulnerable border patron in another. An insurgent movement can become a patron in its own right, sponsoring sub-factions or foreign fighters. Exiled politicians can acquire armed wings. Mercenary outfits can develop ideological narratives to secure local recruits. The purpose of typology is not to trap actors in boxes, but to clarify the constraints that shape their bargaining.

A short contrast makes the structure vivid. In Angola in 1975–76, the Cold War superpowers and their partners backed multiple clients, explicitly or covertly, across the same battlefield. The United States and the Soviet Union treated the war as part of a wider contest, and support often flowed through intermediaries and shifting arrangements. Cuba, by contrast, acted as a comparatively small state with a more singular commitment: it deployed troops primarily in support of the MPLA, accepting high exposure for a focused objective. The superpowers could diversify. Cuba could not. The result was that Cuba's commitment, precisely because it was concentrated, carried a different kind of credibility. Its lifeline was thick but narrow. The superpowers' lifelines were wide but sometimes tangled.

That metaphor of the lifeline is useful because it captures what resources really do in proxy relationships. Weapons and money are not just inputs; they are bonds. They create dependence, expectations, and bargaining power. A patron with many lifelines can cut one without collapsing its strategy. A patron with a single lifeline is vulnerable to sabotage, scandal, or the client's failure. A client with many lifelines can refuse demands. A client with one can be squeezed until it breaks. The structure of lifelines determines who can bluff.

Strategic depth amplifies these effects. A distant patron can often absorb blowback, at least initially, because the war's immediate turbulence is far away. A proximate patron cannot. Refugees cross its borders. Arms leak into its markets. Retaliation may arrive as cross-border raids, terrorism, or economic disruption. This proximity creates urgency, and urgency often creates impatience. A regional state may push its client to act quickly, even recklessly, because delay imposes costs at home. The client, living inside the war, may be even more desperate. When both clocks run fast, escalation becomes more likely.

Regime type shapes how openly these clocks can be acknowledged. Leaders in democracies must justify exposure in public terms: humanitarianism, counterterrorism, alliance obligations. Leaders in authoritarian states may speak more bluntly, but they still manage audiences—military elites, internal security services, business networks, clerical establishments. In both cases, the proxy relationship becomes a political instrument as well as a military one. That instrument must be tuned to domestic noise.

A further limitation complicates any neat understanding of patrons and clients: capacity does not always predict behaviour. There are moments when a global power behaves like a small state, committing deeply to a single client because prestige, identity, or credibility is at stake. There are moments when small states hedge, backing multiple factions because survival demands flexibility. The categories help, but they do not substitute for attention to context. Typology is a starting lens, not a verdict.

The deeper value of mapping patrons and clients lies in what it prepares us to see next: bargaining. If we know what each actor can offer and what each actor fears, we can anticipate where negotiation will tighten and where it will fail. A global power's abundance makes it more willing to trade strict control for plausible deniability. A regional patron's proximity makes it more tempted to micromanage. An insurgency's need for legitimacy makes it vulnerable to political demands. An exile's hunger for relevance makes it prone to overpromise. A mercenary outfit's contract structure makes it sensitive to visible metrics, sometimes perversely so.

The unresolved test is deceptively simple, and it can be asked of any proxy relationship before a single weapon is shipped. Who holds the lifeline, and who can live without it? The answer determines not only bargaining power, but the shape of the war that follows.

Bargaining over goals and resources

In October 2015, a new name appeared on the Syrian battlefield: the Syrian Democratic Forces. Announced in the north-east of the country, the SDF presented itself as a broad coalition, explicitly multi-ethnic and explicitly focused on fighting the Islamic State. The timing was not accidental. The United States had been searching for a partner force it could support at scale without owning the politics of Syria's wider civil war, and without appearing to back a single Kurdish militia as the face of its campaign. The rebranding did not change every reality on the ground, but it changed enough. Support deepened. Air power coordinated more closely. Territory changed hands. A label became a bargaining chip.

Nothing comes for free.

The SDF's emergence illustrates a simple truth about proxy relationships: they are negotiated, not ordained. Goals, resources, timelines, and reputations are traded like currency. A client offers battlefield performance and local legitimacy. A patron offers weapons, intelligence, money, diplomatic cover, and—often underestimated—time. Both sides try to maximise what they get while minimising what they owe. The "proxy" is not a puppet; it is a counterparty. The patron is not a benefactor; it is an investor with conditions.

Begin with what bargaining looks like when stripped of romance and rhetoric. It looks like meetings in safe houses and ministries, but it also looks like quieter decisions: which units receive ammunition, which commanders are invited to briefings, which operations are praised publicly and which are ignored. It looks like vetting lists. It looks like training syllabi. It looks like delayed deliveries meant to discipline. It looks like the sudden appearance of better weapons after a client has made a political concession. Bargaining is not confined to negotiation tables. It is written into logistics.

The core concept is leverage, and leverage is not a slogan. It is the practical ability to say no. A patron has leverage when it can suspend support without losing its strategic position. A client has leverage when it can fight, or threaten to fight, without that patron. Leverage becomes visible in outside options. The client with alternative backers—another state, a diaspora network, an illicit revenue stream—can resist pressure. The client with no alternatives cannot. The patron with multiple clients can punish disobedience by shifting support. The patron with a single client cannot credibly threaten abandonment without harming itself.

This is why bargaining begins long before any agreement is articulated. The patron chooses whether to cultivate redundancy; the client chooses whether to cultivate alternatives. Those choices may be presented as ideological—"we are independent", "we do not meddle"—but their function is strategic. They are insurance policies.

The SDF example captures bargaining over identity and legitimacy. The Kurdish YPG, which formed the backbone of the new coalition, had proven itself a capable battlefield partner. That capability was not the only variable. The YPG's political associations and the regional sensitivities they triggered constrained what a patron could openly do. By broadening the umbrella and foregrounding Arab components, the client traded a degree of ideological and organisational purity—its ability to operate solely as a Kurdish movement—for wider acceptance and deeper material support. The patron, in turn, traded strict control for local legitimacy. It accepted a partner with its own agenda and internal politics because it needed a force that could credibly hold territory, not merely take it. The implication was mutual compromise disguised as necessity.

The bargain was not merely rhetorical. It expressed itself in behaviour. A coalition identity facilitated recruitment among communities that might otherwise reject Kurdish leadership. It also created a political story a patron could sell: this was not a narrow militia, but a "local force" with broader representation. In practice, such arrangements always contain tension. Internal hierarchies persist. Command structures rarely equalise overnight. Yet the fact that the arrangement was imperfect does not make it meaningless. Proxy bargaining often operates in the space between symbolic change and material consequence. A new flag can bring new munitions.

Goals are bargained over just as identity is. Patrons often seek limited objectives: degrade an enemy, secure a corridor, obtain intelligence access, pressure a rival. Clients often seek maximal objectives: dominance, revenge, statehood, survival. The negotiated outcome is usually neither. It is a working overlap—enough shared purpose to justify support, enough ambiguity to preserve each side's freedom. Where overlap narrows, bargaining intensifies.

That intensity is visible in the most contentious commodity of all: time. Patrons like timelines because timelines imply control. Clients fear timelines because timelines imply abandonment. When a patron announces that its mission is temporary, it is speaking to domestic audiences as much as to the battlefield. When a client hears "temporary", it hears "disposable". The client responds by accelerating its own priorities: grabbing territory, settling scores, hoarding weapons, entrenching itself politically. The implication is perverse. The more loudly a patron insists on limits, the more urgently a client behaves as if limits will soon bite.

Credible commitment is the concept that explains why this cycle is so hard to break. Promises matter only when they can be believed. In proxy relationships, belief is fragile. Patrons change governments. Parliaments vote. Media scandals erupt. Strategic priorities shift. Clients know this. They have seen yesterday's "partner" become today's embarrassment. They therefore discount assurances, and their actions reflect that discounting. When a client diverts weapons, builds independent revenue streams, or resists integration into state structures, it is often responding to a rational fear: that the patron's commitment is contingent, and that survival requires preparation for withdrawal.

Patrons face their own credible commitment problem. A client may promise restraint, inclusivity, or focus on a shared enemy, then violate those promises once resources arrive. The patron can threaten to cut support, but that threat must be credible too. If the patron needs the client for a pressing campaign, it will hesitate. Clients learn the patron's thresholds quickly. They test them. Each test is bargaining by action.

A Cold War example shows the same logic operating under different banners. In the late 1970s and through the 1980s, the Soviet Union and its allies supported the People's Republic of Afghanistan against insurgents, while the United States, Pakistan, Saudi Arabia, and others channelled support to the mujahideen. The clients were not single entities. They were factions. The patrons did not merely supply arms; they shaped which factions could become dominant. Pakistan's Inter-Services Intelligence, acting as the gatekeeper for much external aid, made distributive choices that affected battlefield outcomes and post-war politics. Here, bargaining over goals and resources occurred through selection: who received rifles, who received money, who received access to training, who received introductions to foreign visitors.

The mujahideen factions bargained too. They learned to present themselves in ways that attracted support, sometimes adopting rhetoric and organisational forms that suited external sponsors. Ideological purity was not surrendered wholesale, but it was often curated. Leaders emphasised themes that resonated with patrons, suppressed those that frightened them, and competed for symbolic attention as vigorously as for weapons. The implication was not simply opportunism. It was adaptation within a market of patronage, where the "product" was credible performance and acceptable politics.

This is where outside options become decisive. Afghan commanders with independent local revenue—through taxation, smuggling, or patronage networks—could defy pressures that others could not. Patrons understood this and sometimes tried to reduce autonomy by centralising flows or insisting on unified command structures. Such efforts rarely succeeded fully. They did, however, reveal the essence of bargaining: each side tries to change the other's options.

A credible limitation sits uncomfortably inside any tidy account of bargaining. Sometimes the relationship is not truly negotiated because one side can coerce. A patron may impose conditions so strict that the client becomes little more than a subcontractor. Alternatively, a client may be so militarily indispensable that it can ignore patron demands without consequence. In these cases, the language of bargaining can mislead, suggesting mutual influence where power is one-sided.

Yet even here, control is rarely absolute. Coercive patronage often produces evasion rather than obedience. Clients comply superficially while building parallel structures. Indispensable clients can still lose support if they become politically toxic. Bargaining persists because both sides remain vulnerable: the patron to reputational and escalation costs, the client to resource deprivation and internal fracture. The form changes. The logic remains.

The most instructive bargaining is often the kind conducted without words. A patron insists on discipline by embedding trainers and requiring reporting. A client responds by reshaping its units to appear compliant while preserving informal command networks. A patron offers sophisticated weapons but restricts ammunition, creating dependency. A client responds by capturing or purchasing ammunition elsewhere, loosening the patron's grip. Each move is a proposal. Each response is a counter-proposal.

The quiet motif running through all of this is the string. Patrons pull strings. Clients cut them, knot them, or add new ones. Every delivery adds a strand. Every alternative funding source loosens one. The string is never merely material; it is also political. A patron can offer recognition, invitations, and legitimacy in exchange for moderation. A client can offer the appearance of broad representation in exchange for deeper support. The string is an exchange rate between violence and respectability.

Return to the Syrian north-east and the SDF's coalition identity, and the motif becomes concrete. By changing what it was called, by changing who it claimed to represent, the client offered a political texture that a patron could defend. In return, the patron offered more consistent backing. Neither side got everything. The client could not compel its sponsor to adopt its full political project. The patron could not compel the client to abandon its long-term ambitions. What emerged was a bargain that functioned in the short term precisely because it left long-term questions unresolved.

That unresolved quality is not a flaw. It is often the point. Proxy bargaining thrives on ambiguity because ambiguity postpones hard choices. It allows a patron to say it supports stability without defining a final political order. It allows a client to take weapons without declaring permanent subordination. The danger is that postponed choices do not disappear. They accumulate.

The forward test, for any patron contemplating such arrangements, is not whether a client can be bought. Most can, at least temporarily. The test is whether the strings being tied today will still be pullable tomorrow—after the client has won battles, acquired alternatives, and discovered that the patron's promises, like its denials, have an expiry date.

Managing divergent risk appetites

On 21 January 2018, Turkish forces and allied Syrian factions launched Operation Olive Branch against the Kurdish-held enclave of Afrin. The United States had troops embedded with Kurdish-led forces elsewhere in Syria and had urged restraint. There was no approval. The offensive went ahead regardless. Within weeks, Afrin fell, tens of thousands fled, and a partner force that Washington had armed and trained was forced to retreat without meaningful external support. The message was unambiguous: local urgency had outrun distant caution.

Risk looks different from the ground.

Proxy relationships strain most visibly not over goals or resources, but over danger itself. Patrons and clients inhabit the same war yet experience it through incompatible clocks. For the patron, the conflict is one variable among many, calibrated against alliance cohesion, escalation thresholds, and domestic tolerance. For the client, the conflict is immediate and existential. Homes are shelled. Rivals mobilise. Leaders calculate survival in weeks, not election cycles. When these risk appetites diverge, control becomes brittle.

The first divergence arises from threat perception. Patrons tend to see threats in relative terms. They compare theatres, weigh adversaries, and assess whether a loss in one place can be offset elsewhere. Clients see threats absolutely. A lost town may mean extinction. A delayed response may mean encirclement. This asymmetry drives behaviour. Clients escalate because delay is lethal. Patrons hesitate because escalation multiplies costs.

This difference becomes visible in operational tempo. Clients push for offensives when windows open. Patrons counsel patience. When a client advances despite caution, it is not recklessness; it is a rational response to a narrowing horizon. The patron reads the same move as irresponsible risk-taking. Each side believes the other misunderstands reality.

The Syrian conflict provides repeated examples. Kurdish forces, facing hostile neighbours and internal displacement pressures, often prioritised territorial consolidation over diplomatic sensitivity. Their sponsors, balancing relations with NATO allies and regional powers, prioritised de-escalation. When Turkish pressure mounted, the gap widened. The result was not merely a policy dispute but a clash of survival strategies.

Time horizons deepen this gap. Patrons plan in phases: degrade an enemy, stabilise a front, transition responsibility. Clients plan in battles. Their legitimacy, recruitment, and internal cohesion depend on momentum. A prolonged stalemate erodes authority. Fighters drift. Rivals whisper. An offensive, even a costly one, can restore confidence. Patrons, seeking to avoid headlines and escalation, often miss this internal logic.

The behaviour that signals this mismatch is unauthorised action. When a client launches an operation without approval, it is asserting its own clock. In 2008, Georgian forces moved against South Ossetia, calculating that delay favoured separatists and their Russian backers. Western partners had urged caution. The offensive triggered a swift Russian response, overwhelming Georgian forces and reshaping the region's strategic balance. The patron's restraint was rendered moot by the client's urgency.

Risk divergence also runs in the opposite direction. Sometimes patrons are willing to gamble where clients prefer caution. A regional power may see opportunity in chaos, while a local force bears the immediate cost. Iran's encouragement of militia expansion in Iraq after 2014 exposed local groups to backlash and internal fracture. For Tehran, pressure on rivals was a strategic gain. For local commanders, it meant operating under constant threat from airstrikes and rival factions. The patron's tolerance for risk exceeded the client's.

Metrics reveal this imbalance. Patrons measure acceptable loss in political capital and diplomatic fallout. Clients measure loss in fighters and territory. A patron may accept a spike in violence if it yields leverage elsewhere. A client may resist because the spike empties villages and fuels desertion. These are not abstract preferences. They are ledger entries kept in different currencies.

Efforts to manage divergent appetites usually involve restraint mechanisms. Patrons impose conditions: rules of engagement, approval chains, intelligence throttling. Clients respond by adapting. They fragment units to maintain plausible deniability. They reclassify operations as defensive. They exploit grey zones where oversight thins. Each adaptation widens the gap between formal control and actual behaviour.

A credible counter-example tempers this picture. In Lebanon after 2006, Hezbollah largely observed constraints aligned with Iranian preferences, avoiding major escalation with Israel despite provocation. Here, risk appetites aligned more closely. The organisation's leadership calculated that survival and legitimacy required restraint, mirroring Tehran's assessment. Alignment was reinforced by integrated command structures and shared ideological framing. Divergence was managed because clocks synchronised.

Reconciling this exception clarifies the rule. Managing risk divergence requires more than leverage; it requires shared perception. Where patrons and clients interpret threats similarly, restraint holds. Where they do not, mechanisms fail. Training and funding cannot substitute for alignment of horizons.

The quiet motif threading these cases is the ticking clock. Patrons hear a slow, measured tick, spaced by briefings and elections. Clients hear a rapid one, marked by funerals and shortages. Each decision is taken to the sound the decision-maker hears. Proxy relationships falter when those sounds diverge too sharply.

As wars drag on, divergence often widens. Patrons tire. Clients radicalise or fracture. The initial overlap of interests narrows. Risk appetites drift apart. At this stage, restraint imposed from afar becomes increasingly symbolic. The ground decides.

The unresolved test is practical and uncomfortable. When a client's survival calculus demands action that a patron fears, whose clock governs? Delay may preserve alliances but doom the proxy. Action may save the client but drag the patron closer to confrontation. Proxy warfare thrives in this tension. It rarely resolves it.

Patron competition within the same conflict

In September 2014, General Khalifa Haftar announced "Operation Dignity" from eastern Libya and set out to crush Islamist-leaning militias. In Tripoli, rival armed groups and politicians rallied under what became the Government of National Accord. Within a year, Libya's war had become a contest not only between Libyan factions but between their backers: the United Arab Emirates and Egypt increasingly aligned with Haftar; Turkey and Qatar leaned towards forces tied to Tripoli. Arms, drones, advisers, and money flowed despite a United Nations embargo. The front lines moved. So did loyalties. By 2019, Haftar's assault on Tripoli had turned the proxy contest into a grinding siege, and by June 2020 the offensive had failed, leaving Libya more militarised, more fragmented, and more dependent on outside patrons than before.

Money has a gravity.

Patron competition is often discussed as if it were simply geopolitics projected onto a local map: one sponsor backs one faction, another sponsor backs its rival, and the war becomes a tidy proxy duel. Reality is harsher. When multiple patrons enter the same conflict, they alter incentives inside armed groups, not only between them. Competition does not just fund war. It changes its social chemistry. It rewards fragmentation, encourages splintering, and turns commanders into brokers who negotiate less over strategy than over payroll.

The mechanism begins with a basic observation. A militia is not a nation. It is a coalition of armed men who must be paid, fed, equipped, and persuaded that tomorrow will not be worse than today. When two patrons offer support to similar actors, or offer competing packages to different wings of the same movement, the war acquires a market. In markets, actors compare. They choose. They defect. The supposed "client" becomes a price-sensitive supplier of violence.

This is easiest to see when the commodity is wages. A patron's most immediate tool is not a missile system; it is a regular payment. Pay on time, and a commander can keep fighters under control. Pay late, and discipline dissolves. The visible behaviours are mundane but decisive: desertions, looting, checkpoint rackets, sudden shifts in unit allegiance, and the quiet migration of fighters to the faction with a better stipend. Patron competition turns those behaviours into bargaining signals. If one payroll falters, another patron can buy influence overnight.

Libya after 2014 offers a grim laboratory. Rival sponsors delivered different mixes of cash, equipment, and political cover. Some groups became quasi-regularised under ministries in Tripoli, drawing salaries while retaining autonomous command. Others in the east tied themselves to Haftar's emerging command structure, receiving external backing in parallel with local patronage networks. The implication was not simply that foreign money sustained combat. It rewired local incentives: commanders learned that maintaining a distinct brand—an emblem, a name, a "brigade" identity—could attract a dedicated stream of external support. Unity became less profitable than differentiation.

This is the first way multi-patron competition prolongs war. It makes peace economically irrational for the people with guns. A ceasefire threatens revenue streams, access to smuggling routes, and the privileges of armed administration. When patrons compete, those streams can multiply. A commander can promise to "stabilise" an area for one sponsor while quietly keeping channels open to another. The war becomes not a failure of politics but a system of income.

The second way patron competition prolongs war is through strategic incoherence. Different sponsors often pursue overlapping but not identical aims. One wants a friendly government. Another wants a weakened rival. A third wants access to ports, bases, or resources. Their clients absorb these mixed signals and translate them into mixed strategies. A faction may fight hard in one region to satisfy one patron while restraining itself elsewhere to avoid angering another. The battlefield becomes patchwork, not front line. Civilians experience this not as geopolitics but as unpredictability: a town changes hands not because of local sentiment, but because payrolls and patrons shifted.

The Syrian opposition in the early and mid-2010s illustrates the same dynamic with different actors. Multiple states supported different factions, sometimes under the same rhetorical umbrella of "moderate opposition", while also competing to shape post-war political influence. Reports by journalists and researchers chronicled how groups split, rebranded, and merged in response to shifting external support. The visible metric was organisational churn: a brigade name would disappear, only to reappear under a new banner with a new sponsor's imprimatur. The implication was fragmentation that outpaced strategy. Fighters learned to treat identity as negotiable.

Competition can occur not only between patrons backing rival camps, but within a camp. When different sponsors back different wings of the same coalition, or route support through different intermediaries, they create internal rivalries with real firepower behind them. A movement that might have developed a coherent chain of command instead develops competing procurement channels, competing propaganda lines, competing "legitimate" representatives. Patron competition turns internal politics into a security dilemma: each wing fears being outbid, so each wing arms up, recruits more, and resists compromise.

The logic resembles an auction, and the currency is loyalty. The quiet motif here is the payroll again: who pays whom, for what, and how reliably.

Competing payrolls do not merely increase violence. They reshape the internal constitution of armed groups. Command becomes transactional. Discipline becomes conditional. Ideology becomes a brochure.

This is not to romanticise ideological purity; it is to note what changes when money becomes the primary axis of cohesion. A movement held together by shared belief can fracture, but it fractures slowly, through debates and defections that carry social cost. A movement held together by stipends fractures quickly. A commander can take his men and his weapons and become a new "faction" before sunrise. Patron competition makes that manoeuvre attractive. It also makes it common.

A Cold War example reveals the same incentive structure in a different idiom. During the Soviet–Afghan War, the United States, Saudi Arabia, and others provided support to the Afghan mujahideen, much of it channelled through Pakistan's Inter-Services Intelligence. Steve Coll's *Ghost Wars* (2004) describes how external support interacted with factional rivalries and gatekeeping decisions. The point here is not to relitigate who did what, but to observe what multi-sourced patronage did to local politics. Rival commanders competed for access to the pipeline. Those who secured it gained strength; those who did not splintered or sought alternative patrons. The implication was a war effort rich in fighters and poor in unity, an imbalance that became catastrophic when the common enemy withdrew and the patron coalition's priorities shifted.

It is tempting to treat patron competition as merely the externalisation of rival national interests. That is true, but incomplete. Competition also produces information problems. Patrons rarely see the battlefield clearly. They depend on intermediaries—intelligence services, liaison officers, political fixers—who have their own incentives. In a multi-patron environment, these intermediaries become traders in narrative. They exaggerate threats to solicit more aid. They claim victories to justify continued funding. They denigrate rivals within the same camp to capture resources. The result is distorted decision-making in capitals and distorted strategy on the ground.

Trust becomes a decision, not a feeling. A patron shows trust by providing weapons without tight end-use monitoring, or by sharing sensitive intelligence. A client shows trust by accepting constraints: target vetting, operational approvals, public messaging guidelines. In a multi-patron setting, both sides trust less. Patrons tighten control because they fear diversion to rivals. Clients hedge because they fear abandonment. The observable behaviours are duplication and secrecy: parallel procurement channels, hidden stockpiles, off-the-books units, and "unofficial" operations that allow plausible denial even within the alliance.

There is, however, a credible limitation to the claim that patron competition inevitably fragments clients and prolongs war. Sometimes multiple patrons coordinate effectively, imposing a hierarchy rather than a market. Where a dominant sponsor sets rules and others subordinate their support to those rules, the incentives change. A coalition can act like a single patron if it centralises funding, standardises training, and makes access to resources conditional on compliance with unified command arrangements. The violence remains violent. Yet fragmentation slows.

One can see a version of this in the international support to the Afghan government after 2001, particularly in the training and equipping of certain national units under coordinated programmes led by the United States and NATO partners. The coordination was never perfect, and Afghanistan ultimately demonstrated the limits of external state-building. Still, the structure differed from competitive patronage. The aim was to concentrate authority in a recognised chain of command rather than to bid for militia loyalty. The implication is that patron plurality is not destiny. Governance of patronage matters.

Reconciling this limitation brings us back to what competition truly does: it changes payoffs. When patrons compete, they reward fragmentation because splinter leaders can offer differentiated loyalty. When patrons coordinate, they reward cohesion because access to resources depends on unified behaviour. The same commander who would split his unit to attract a second sponsor may instead accept discipline if all sponsors speak with one voice. The difference lies less in culture than in incentives.

Yet coordination among patrons is difficult precisely because their interests diverge. Even when they share an enemy, they rarely share a desired political end state. A state that wants an allied government with strong institutions will find itself at odds with a state that prefers a pliable client regime, and both may be undermined by a sponsor primarily interested in access to ports or influence over migration routes. Patron competition reasserts itself because it is rooted in real strategic disagreements.

The war, meanwhile, becomes a conveyor belt of intermediaries. Arms move through cut-outs. Payments move through front companies. Political recognition is granted in fragments. Each fragment creates a constituency that benefits from continued conflict. That constituency is not abstract. It consists of commanders who can pay their men, businessmen who profit from contracts, officials who manage access, and politicians who trade on the language of resistance or sovereignty. Patron competition expands these constituencies. It thickens the war economy.

The motif of payroll returns because it is the simplest diagnostic. When you observe a proliferation of armed groups with overlapping ideologies and shifting names, ask a blunt question: who pays them? When you see repeated splintering after a new sponsor enters the theatre, follow the wages. When you find that ceasefires collapse not at moments of ideological crisis but at moments of funding disruption, you are watching a patronage market at work.

Patron competition also changes how wars end. Negotiations require parties that can commit. In fragmented environments, commitment is scarce. A leader can sign an agreement and still fail to deliver compliance because a rival wing answers to a different sponsor—or to a different payroll. Patrons may then respond by backing new "spoiler-proof" factions, which further fragments the landscape. The peace process becomes another arena for bidding, with seats at the table treated as assets.

The forward test is uncomfortable because it forces clarity. When multiple patrons enter a war, are they willing to subordinate their rivalry to a shared discipline of support, or will they treat the conflict as a marketplace in which influence is bought and sold through other people's guns? If the answer is the latter, the bidding war does not merely reflect the conflict. It becomes the conflict.

When clients escape control

In the summer of 2014, fighters of the Islamic State swept across northern Iraq and eastern Syria, seizing Mosul in June and declaring a caliphate days later. The organisation had not emerged from a vacuum. Its senior cadres traced their lineage through earlier insurgent networks that had, at various points after 2003, received tacit tolerance, selective funding, or indirect benefit from regional actors pursuing narrower aims in Iraq and Syria. By July 2014, those calculations lay in ruins. A group that had once operated as a local instrument against rivals had become an autonomous force commanding territory, resources, and global attention. Control had not merely slipped. It had inverted.

Every proxy relationship contains an expiry date, even if no one knows when it will arrive.

Clients escape control not in dramatic leaps but through accumulations. Orders go unanswered. Guidance is reinterpreted. Requests for restraint are acknowledged, then ignored. At some point, the patron realises that what it assumed was influence has become habit, and habit has become memory. The client no longer needs to ask. That moment—the tipping point—is what distinguishes a proxy from an independent actor.

The first pathway to escape is success. Battlefield victories change incentives faster than any ideological manifesto. When a client captures territory, recruits surge, tax bases expand, and local legitimacy hardens. Each gain reduces dependence on external support. Fighters paid from local revenues are harder to discipline than fighters paid from abroad. The visible metric is substitution: salaries shift from patron-funded stipends to locally extracted income; weapons captured from enemies replace deliveries. The implication is autonomy built on momentum.

The Islamic State's early expansion offers a brutal illustration. Its capture of oil facilities, banks, and military depots generated revenues that dwarfed any previous reliance on outside channels. Estimates varied, but contemporaneous reporting by organisations such as the Financial Action Task Force in 2015 documented millions of dollars in monthly income from oil, taxation, and extortion. The precise figure mattered less than the effect. External leverage collapsed. Patrons could no longer credibly threaten withdrawal because withdrawal no longer mattered.

A second pathway runs through alternative funding. Even without territorial conquest, clients can escape by diversifying income: diaspora donations, criminal enterprises, resource smuggling, or sponsorship from rival states. Each new stream dilutes control. Patrons often underestimate how quickly such diversification occurs because it is deliberately opaque. Fighters who collect "taxes" at checkpoints or skim aid deliveries are not merely corrupt; they are building independence. The behaviour is visible in procurement patterns. Ammunition appears that was never supplied. Vehicles change. Communications upgrade. The client's operational tempo becomes less sensitive to the patron's budget cycle.

This dynamic played out repeatedly in Lebanon's civil war from 1975 to 1990. Militias initially dependent on external backing developed independent revenue through ports, checkpoints, and illicit trade. Patrons retained influence, but control weakened as groups learned to finance themselves. The war's longevity was not simply ideological. It was fiscal.

Ideology provides a third route to escape, often underestimated because it is less tangible. When a client's worldview radicalises beyond what the patron can tolerate, compliance becomes morally costly. Orders to moderate are reframed as betrayal. Guidance becomes interference. The visible sign is rhetoric: public statements grow absolutist, enemies multiply, compromise disappears from the lexicon. Once this shift occurs, material leverage alone rarely suffices to restore control.

Al-Qaeda's evolution after the Afghan jihad illustrates this pattern starkly. What began as a network focused on supporting a specific conflict reframed itself into a transnational movement with a universalist agenda. External sponsors who had once found the group useful against a common enemy discovered that its ambitions now encompassed them. Ideological radicalisation severed the psychological basis of patronage. Control did not merely weaken; it became impossible.

These pathways often reinforce one another. Success brings funding. Funding sustains ideology. Ideology justifies defiance. By the time a patron recognises the convergence, the client has crossed a threshold. Attempts to reassert control through conditionality or pressure tend to fail because the client's calculus has shifted from dependence to dominance.

A fourth, quieter factor is organisational learning. Clients observe how patrons behave under stress. They notice which threats are credible and which are not. They catalogue precedents. If a patron tolerates disobedience once, it establishes a baseline. Over time, clients internalise the patron's red lines and operate just beyond them. This is not rebellion. It is calibration.

Calibration becomes escape when patrons themselves become constrained—by domestic politics, alliance management, or reputational risk. A client may defy an order precisely because it knows the patron cannot respond without exposing itself. The patron's restraint becomes the client's opportunity. The behaviour is telling: clients escalate at moments when patrons are distracted elsewhere or publicly committed to de-escalation. Control proves contingent on the patron's freedom of action.

There are cases where control persists despite these pressures, and they deserve attention because they clarify what escape is not. Hezbollah's relationship with Iran again offers a counter-example. Despite battlefield success, diversified funding, and strong ideology, the organisation has generally remained within strategic parameters set by Tehran. The reasons are concrete. Command structures overlap. Financial channels remain centralised. Strategic narratives align. The implication is not that escape is inevitable, but that preventing it requires sustained investment and integration that few patrons are willing or able to maintain indefinitely.

Reconciling this exception highlights the cost of control. It demands constant attention, political risk, and deep entanglement. The more a patron invests to prevent escape, the less deniable the relationship becomes. Control and deniability pull in opposite directions. Most patrons compromise. They accept partial control to preserve distance. That compromise creates space for escape.

The moment when a client adopts a new patron crystallises the process. Switching allegiance is rarely instantaneous. It begins with quiet contacts, parallel negotiations, and trial deliveries. The patron notices only when the switch is advanced enough to matter. By then, leverage has eroded. The client's message is implicit: your support is no longer indispensable.

This occurred repeatedly among armed groups in Yemen as the conflict deepened after 2015. Factions recalibrated relationships as battlefield fortunes shifted and external backers reassessed priorities. Groups that once operated as reliable proxies began to hedge, then defect, aligning with whichever sponsor promised survival. Control dissolved not because of betrayal, but because the war's structure rewarded flexibility.

The quiet motif threading these stories is gravity. Patrons believe influence flows outward. In practice, gravity shifts. As clients accumulate mass—fighters, territory, money, legitimacy—they bend the relationship around themselves. The patron's pull weakens. At some point, the client orbits independently.

Escape is often diagnosed only after violence turns the wrong way. Weapons appear in the hands of former enemies. Training methods are repurposed. Intelligence flows reverse. These are not aberrations. They are the logical end of relationships built on contingent alignment rather than shared fate.

The unresolved test for patrons is stark. How much autonomy can be tolerated before influence becomes illusion? Tighten control, and risk exposure and escalation. Loosen it, and risk irrelevance or blowback. There is no stable midpoint. Control is always contingent, and the conditions that sustain it erode with every success a proxy achieves.

Chapter 3

Building and Supplying Proxy Forces

In a scrubby training ground far from any front line, a small group of men practise the same drill again and again. Their weapons are mismatched, some old, some unfamiliar. An instructor corrects their spacing, then their posture, then the way they move as a unit. The men are few, disciplined, and carefully chosen. Elsewhere in the same country, a much larger force waits—poorly organised, politically influential, and hungry for arms. The patron backs the smaller group first. It looks like caution. It is, in fact, design.

Proxy wars are not improvised. They are built.

If Chapter 2 explored relationships as bargains and tensions, this chapter turns to the machinery that makes those relationships operational. Proxy warfare lives or dies not on declarations, but on logistics: who is selected, who is trained, what is supplied, how it moves, and what happens when control frays. These choices are often presented as technical, even bureaucratic. They are not. They encode political priorities, moral trade-offs, and long-term risks that outlast any single campaign.

The central paradox of proxy-building lies at the beginning. Patrons want fighters who can win, but they also want fighters who will listen. These two qualities rarely coincide. The most capable groups tend to be the most autonomous, embedded in local power structures that resist external direction. The most compliant groups are often smaller, less rooted, and less immediately effective. Early selection decisions therefore shape everything that follows. They determine not only battlefield performance, but the degree of leverage a patron will retain months or years later.

Choosing a proxy from scratch is an act of prediction. It requires judging leadership character under pressure, estimating how organisations will grow, and deciding which internal fractures are manageable and which are fatal. Vetting is never perfect. Patrons rely on intermediaries, defectors, local elites, and intelligence fragments. They look for discipline, ideological compatibility, and the absence of reputational liabilities. They also look for hunger. A group that needs support badly is easier to mould—at least at first.

This is why patrons often begin with small, tightly controlled factions rather than mass movements. A compact unit can be trained, monitored, and embedded more easily. Its leaders can be cultivated. Its failures can be contained. A larger, unruly force brings immediate manpower but limited control. Backing it early may secure relevance, but it also locks the patron into someone else's politics. The initial preference for discipline over scale is not moral. It is instrumental.

Once a partner is chosen, supply becomes the language of the relationship. Weapons are not neutral objects. They carry signals. A patron that provides light arms communicates caution; one that provides advanced systems communicates commitment. Every shipment recalibrates expectations on both sides. The question is not only what is supplied, but how. Deniability is preserved through indirection: older equipment that cannot be easily traced, weapons captured from previous conflicts, items routed through third countries or commercial cut-outs. The aim is ambiguity, not invisibility.

Arms pipelines develop their own geographies. Certain corridors become familiar lifelines, reused across decades and conflicts. Borders that appear porous on maps become arteries in practice. Some governments tolerate this traffic because it serves their interests; others monetise it, renting airspace, ports, or warehouses while maintaining official distance. These arrangements are rarely static. Routes shift as scrutiny increases or alliances change. The same rifle can move through multiple wars, accruing stories along the way.

Training is the next layer of construction, and here doctrine matters as much as skill. How a proxy is taught to fight shapes not only its effectiveness but its political footprint. Patrons who emphasise strict rules of engagement, civilian protection, and command accountability are attempting to limit blowback as much as to win battles. Patrons who prioritise aggression and speed accept higher short-term gains at the cost of reputational damage and future instability. These choices surface later, when civilian harm becomes a diplomatic liability or when indiscipline corrodes command.

Doctrine travels quietly. It appears in training manuals, in the presence or absence of embedded advisers, in the kinds of operations that are praised or ignored. Over time, it becomes habit. A proxy trained to clear areas methodically will behave differently from one trained to shock and intimidate. The battlefield outcome may look similar in the moment. The political consequences will not.

Yet no supply system is closed. Leakage is inevitable. Weapons are sold, traded, stolen, or lost. Low pay encourages diversion. Poor tracking systems compound it. Black markets thrive on surplus, and surplus is endemic in proxy wars. What begins as a tightly managed pipeline becomes a diffuse ecosystem. Arms reappear in unexpected places, sometimes pointed back at the original patron's own forces or allies. The long tail of supply is often longer than the war itself.

This chapter examines these processes not as a checklist but as a sequence of decisions under uncertainty. Building a proxy force involves continual trade-offs between speed and control, effectiveness and deniability, discipline and scale. Supplying that force extends those trade-offs across borders and time. Each choice narrows some risks while widening others.

The modern relevance is obvious. As states seek to avoid large deployments while still shaping outcomes, the demand for proxies grows. So does the complexity of managing them. Technologies proliferate. Surveillance improves. Attribution becomes easier in some domains and harder in others. Yet the fundamentals remain stubbornly consistent. The same questions that confronted patrons decades ago recur in new guises. Who can be trusted? What can be supplied without being owned? How much training is enough? When does deniability collapse into exposure?

A recurring image runs through this chapter: the supply line as both lifeline and fault line. It sustains the proxy, but it also marks the point of vulnerability. Cut it too abruptly, and the proxy may fragment or defect. Maintain it too generously, and the proxy may outgrow control. Every patron walks this line, often without realising how thin it is.

The sections that follow trace this arc in detail. They begin with the earliest moments of proxy creation, when selection and vetting set trajectories that are hard to reverse. They move through the shadow world of arms pipelines and clandestine routes, where deniability is engineered rather than assumed. They examine training as a political act, not merely a military one. They end with the consequences of leakage and diversion, where the costs of earlier decisions return, sometimes years later, in unexpected forms.

The promise of proxy warfare is efficiency. The reality is accumulation. Weapons accumulate. Skills accumulate. Grievances accumulate. This chapter does not argue that proxies are inherently unmanageable. It shows why managing them requires constant attention to the mundane details that rarely make headlines. The wars that decide empires are often built one shipment, one training course, one compromise at a time.

By the end of this chapter, the reader will not see supply chains as neutral conduits, or training camps as mere technicalities. They will appear instead as the hidden architecture of modern conflict—structures that shape outcomes long after the guns fall silent, and long after the patrons who authorised them have moved on.

Building a proxy from scratch

In late October 2014, a handful of fighters crossed the Tigris River near the Syrian town of Kobane under American air cover. The group was small, disciplined, and obscure. It was not the largest force opposing the Islamic State in northern Syria, nor the most politically connected. It was, however, organised, responsive, and willing to coordinate. The United States chose to work with it anyway. Within months, that decision had reshaped the map of the war in the north. Scale had lost to structure.

This is where proxy wars begin: not with mass movements, but with selection.

Building a proxy force from scratch is an exercise in constrained choice. Patrons rarely encounter a blank slate. They enter landscapes already crowded with militias, factions, warlords, and political entrepreneurs. Each offers something different. Some bring numbers. Others bring discipline. Others bring local legitimacy, or access to trade routes, or a reputation for ruthlessness. The patron's first decision—whom to back—locks in a trajectory that is difficult to reverse.

That decision is not simply about ideology or alignment. It is about control. A proxy that can fight well but cannot be steered may deliver short-term gains and long-term damage. A proxy that listens but struggles on the battlefield may preserve deniability while bleeding credibility. Patrons are forced to choose which risk to accept first.

The initial screening process often looks technical: background checks, leadership profiles, past behaviour. In practice, it is interpretive. Vetting relies on partial intelligence, local intermediaries, and incentives that skew reporting. Leaders present themselves strategically, emphasising discipline to attract support or exaggerating strength to appear indispensable. Patrons read these signals through their own biases, often overestimating their ability to reshape organisations once support begins.

Visible behaviour matters more than declared intent. Patrons watch how units move, how commanders enforce orders, how fighters treat civilians. They measure responsiveness: how quickly a group adapts after feedback, how reliably it reports losses, how it handles setbacks. These observations form the basis of trust, which in proxy-building is never moral. It is operational.

Trust has a price.

Early support is therefore often cautious and narrow. Patrons back small units precisely because they are easier to observe and discipline. A compact force can be trained intensively, its leadership cultivated, its failures contained. If it collapses, the damage is limited. This preference for manageability explains why patrons sometimes bypass large, politically influential movements in favour of marginal groups with little public profile. The choice looks counterintuitive. It is not.

The trade-off between effectiveness and compliance emerges immediately. Larger movements can mobilise fighters quickly, control territory, and claim representation. They are also harder to direct. Their leaders answer to constituencies beyond the patron's reach. Smaller groups lack reach but offer pliability. Patrons betting on the long game often choose the latter, hoping to grow capacity under controlled conditions rather than inherit complexity.

This was the logic behind the early American partnership with select Kurdish units in northern Syria rather than with broader opposition coalitions. The chosen groups were not universally popular, but they were coherent. They could absorb training, integrate intelligence, and execute combined operations. Their scale could be increased later. Their behaviour could not be retrofitted if it went wrong.

Organisation is the next layer of construction. A proxy is not simply a collection of fighters; it is a system. Command hierarchies, reporting lines, recruitment rules, and disciplinary mechanisms all shape how force is applied. Patrons often attempt to impose organisational templates: unified command, standard ranks, centralised logistics. These templates reflect the patron's own military culture more than local realities.

The friction appears quickly. Local fighters may be loyal to commanders rather than institutions. Authority may flow through kinship or ideology rather than rank. Patrons face a choice: adapt structures to local norms, or insist on conformity. Adaptation preserves buy-in but dilutes control. Conformity strengthens control but risks resistance or desertion. Each path carries cost.

The behaviour to watch is enforcement. When a commander punishes looting or insubordination despite losing fighters, discipline is real. When violations are ignored to preserve numbers, discipline is cosmetic. Patrons learn this early. They reward enforcement with support. They tolerate lapses when alternatives are scarce. These micro-decisions accumulate into organisational character.

Leadership vetting is particularly fraught. Charismatic leaders mobilise loyalty but often resist oversight. Technocrats manage systems but struggle to inspire. Patrons frequently prefer leaders who appear pragmatic and unideological, believing them easier to steer. This can be a misreading. Ideology sometimes enforces discipline more effectively than contracts. The absence of belief does not guarantee compliance.

A credible limitation complicates the picture. Occasionally, patrons back large, unruly movements from the outset because no alternative exists. In Iraq after 2014, the urgency of countering the Islamic State pushed external actors to work with sprawling militias whose internal politics were opaque. The immediate threat outweighed long-term concerns. The implication was acceptance of reduced control in exchange for rapid mobilisation. The costs appeared later, as militias entrenched themselves politically and resisted integration.

Reconciling this limitation clarifies the conditions under which small beats large. Where time allows, patrons favour discipline. Where time collapses, they accept scale. Proxy-building is therefore shaped not only by preference but by tempo. The faster the crisis, the more compromises are made upfront.

Another factor shaping early choices is reputational risk. Patrons are acutely aware that the first proxy they back becomes their face in the conflict. Atrocities, indiscipline, or ideological extremism rebound quickly. A smaller, tightly managed group offers reputational insulation. Its actions can be monitored. Its messaging can be aligned. If it fails, it can be quietly sidelined. A mass movement cannot be hidden.

This reputational calculus explains why patrons sometimes endure accusations of bias or exclusivity by backing niche factions. The alternative—owning the behaviour of a broad, volatile coalition—is worse. The proxy relationship begins as much in the information space as on the battlefield.

The quiet motif threading through these decisions is pruning. Patrons prune options to reduce uncertainty. They trim scale to cultivate control. They narrow leadership to manage behaviour. Each cut simplifies the picture while limiting potential. The art lies in pruning without stunting growth.

Over time, successful proxies attract recruits. Growth tests the original design. New fighters dilute training standards. New commanders challenge authority. Patron oversight stretches. The very success that validates early choices undermines them. This is the paradox of proxy-building: the qualities that make a group attractive at inception are hardest to preserve as it expands.

Some patrons attempt to manage this by tiered growth, expanding units slowly and embedding advisers to transmit norms. Others accept that growth will erode control and plan accordingly, shifting from command to influence. Both approaches recognise the same reality. Building a proxy is not a one-off act. It is a continuous process of selection and adjustment.

The closing tension is unavoidable. If patrons choose small and disciplined partners, they risk irrelevance if the war demands mass. If they choose large and unruly ones, they risk losing control before objectives are met. There is no stable equilibrium. Proxy-building is a gamble on trajectory: betting that the organisation a patron creates or cultivates will grow in the right direction faster than it drifts away. The opening move matters most, but it never decides the end.

Weapons supply chains and deniability

In March 2013, journalists examining rebel-held territory in northern Syria photographed crates of FN FAL rifles and 7.62×51mm ammunition bearing markings linked to Yugoslav-era stockpiles. The weapons were decades old, incompatible with the Syrian Arab Army's standard kit, and conspicuously unsuited to a modern battlefield. Their presence answered a question without settling it. Someone had supplied them. No one would admit who. Within two years, variants of the same weapons appeared again—this time in Libya, and later in Yemen—circulating through conflicts that were officially unconnected. The rifles had travelled further than any diplomatic statement.

Arms move quietly.

Proxy warfare depends on supply, but it survives on ambiguity. Weapons supply chains are designed not merely to deliver firepower, but to blur authorship. The success of a proxy campaign is often measured not by how many weapons arrive, but by how difficult it is to prove where they came from. Deniability is not an afterthought. It is engineered into the pipeline.

The first principle of deniable supply is distance. Patrons rarely ship arms directly to clients. Instead, they route matériel through intermediaries: allied states, intelligence services, commercial brokers, or cut-out organisations. Each handoff adds a layer of separation. Each invoice, licence, or transfer document becomes an opportunity to mislabel or obscure origin. The visible behaviour is paperwork that technically complies while substantively misleads. A shipment becomes "surplus". A destination becomes "end user pending". The trail cools.

Older equipment plays a central role here. Cold War-era weapons circulate precisely because they are ubiquitous. An AK-pattern rifle or a Soviet-calibre mortar tells little about its last owner. Patrons favour such matériel because it resists attribution. Newer systems, by contrast, carry signatures—serial numbers, distinctive components, manufacturing quirks—that investigators can trace. The implication is perverse. Obsolescence becomes an asset.

Captured stocks offer another route. Weapons seized from defeated forces can be redistributed with minimal explanation. The patron can claim, with technical accuracy, that it did not supply the arms; the proxy simply captured them. This explanation holds even when the capture was enabled by patron intelligence or air support. The distinction satisfies lawyers and complicates journalists. It also muddies propaganda. Adversaries struggle to prove complicity when the weapons in question once belonged to someone else.

The Syrian conflict again provides a clear example. As government arsenals fell in the early years of the war, opposition groups displayed captured tanks, artillery, and small arms. External backers could plausibly point to battlefield capture rather than supply. Over time, however, the mix shifted. Non-Syrian weapons appeared in greater numbers, routed through regional allies. The combination of captured and imported arms created a fog in which attribution became a matter of interpretation rather than evidence.

Intermediaries are not passive conduits. They shape the flow. Intelligence services, in particular, act as filters, deciding which groups receive what and when. This gatekeeping allows patrons to manage risk indirectly. If a proxy misbehaves, deliveries slow. If it performs, deliveries resume. The patron maintains influence without public fingerprints. The intermediary absorbs blame when things go wrong.

Commercial brokers add another layer of deniability. Arms dealers operate in grey markets where legality varies by jurisdiction and enforcement is uneven. They can source weapons from decommissioned stockpiles, private sellers, or state arsenals looking to offload surplus. Transactions are fragmented into smaller shipments, routed through free ports and re-export zones. Each fragment reduces visibility. The behaviour is systematic: small loads, multiple routes, inconsistent documentation.

This system creates efficiency at the cost of control. The more intermediaries involved, the harder it becomes to track end use. Weapons leak. They are resold, stolen, or repurposed. Patrons accept this risk because the alternative—direct supply—is politically costlier. Deniability trades precision for insulation.

A striking example of resurfacing weapons underscores this trade. During the Balkan wars of the 1990s, vast quantities of small arms entered circulation. Decades later, investigators documented Balkan-manufactured weapons in Middle Eastern conflicts, including Syria and Iraq. Reports by organisations such as Conflict Armament Research traced serial numbers and manufacturing marks, demonstrating how arms migrated across theatres and decades. The implication was unsettling. A weapon supplied for one war could reappear in another, stripped of context but heavy with consequence.

This circulation complicates propaganda for all sides. Adversaries accuse patrons of direct supply; patrons deny, pointing to black markets and historical legacies. Both claims can be partially true. The weapon's journey becomes a narrative battleground. Attribution is no longer binary. It is probabilistic.

Deniability also relies on timing. Patrons often delay delivery until political conditions shift. A shipment arriving after a ceasefire collapses can be framed as defensive necessity. A shipment arriving before negotiations can be described as deterrence. The same weapons, moved weeks apart, carry different political meanings. Timing becomes a tool.

The quiet motif running through these practices is laundering. Not of money, but of responsibility. Each step in the supply chain cleans the weapon of its last owner. By the time it reaches the proxy, its origin is ambiguous enough to sustain denial. This laundering does not erase reality. It reframes it.

A credible limitation deserves attention. Deniability has eroded in some domains. Digital imagery, open-source intelligence, and forensic analysis have made it easier to trace weapons and expose supply routes. Social media posts reveal serial numbers. Satellite imagery shows air bridges. Investigative groups publish detailed reports. The margin for plausible denial has narrowed.

Reconciling this limitation reveals adaptation rather than abandonment. Patrons respond by shifting methods. They favour systems harder to trace, reduce volumes per shipment, or rely more heavily on training and intelligence rather than hardware. They also exploit information overload. When evidence proliferates, certainty diminishes. Deniability survives not by hiding everything, but by contesting interpretation.

The risk calculus remains. Direct supply invites accountability. Indirect supply diffuses it. Patrons continue to choose diffusion even as tracing improves, because the political cost of exposure is often lower than the cost of ownership. A leaked report can be dismissed. A declared intervention cannot.

For proxies, these supply chains shape behaviour. Groups adapt to what they receive. Older weapons demand different tactics. Inconsistent supply encourages hoarding and black-market trading. Units prioritise capturing enemy equipment to reduce dependence. These adaptations feed back into the war's character, often increasing brutality as groups seek matériel by force rather than patience.

The unresolved question is whether deniability still buys what it once did. When every conflict is documented, when weapons can be traced across continents, and when narratives circulate faster than arms, does ambiguity still protect patrons from consequence? Or does it merely delay reckoning, allowing supply chains to grow longer and more entangled before they are exposed?

Weapons will continue to move. The question is not whether they can be hidden forever, but whether the structures that hide them outlast the wars they fuel.

Training, doctrine, and discipline

On a dusty training range outside Taji, north of Baghdad, in July 2007, American advisers halted a live-fire exercise midway through the drill. An Iraqi unit had advanced too quickly, firing without positive identification. The correction was immediate. The exercise restarted. The rules were restated. Civilian harm was the constraint, not an afterthought. The message was blunt and repetitive: firepower mattered, but control mattered more. Years later, units trained under those standards behaved differently from those that were not. Doctrine had left a residue.

Training writes habits.

Proxy forces do not merely receive weapons; they absorb ways of fighting. Training camps, manuals, and advisers transmit more than tactics. They encode assumptions about risk, authority, and restraint. Over time, these assumptions shape battlefield outcomes and political consequences alike. A proxy's doctrine becomes its signature, visible to civilians, adversaries, and international observers long after the trainers have left.

The first claim is straightforward. Training determines behaviour under stress. Show it in practice. When a unit is drilled to pause, identify, and clear before firing, civilian casualties tend to fall. When a unit is trained to advance aggressively and exploit shock, collateral damage rises. Name it. This is doctrine: a set of principles guiding action when orders run out. Explain it. Doctrine fills the gap between command intent and individual decision. Implication follows. Patrons who choose doctrine choose reputation.

Training environments reveal patron priorities early. Camps emphasising discipline devote time to marksmanship, communication, and restraint. They enforce hierarchy. They punish violations. Camps prioritising aggression compress timelines, reward initiative, and tolerate indiscipline if it yields momentum. Both produce fighters. They produce different wars.

The visible behaviour that signals this choice is curriculum time. Hours spent on escalation control displace hours spent on rapid assault. Manuals that stress proportionality crowd out those that glorify speed. Embedded instructors who intervene during operations shape outcomes more than distant funding ever could. These are measurable decisions, not abstractions.

A clear contrast sharpens the point. During the height of the Iraq conflict, US-led training programmes emphasised rules of engagement, civilian protection, and reporting. Violations risked suspension of support. The intent was not altruism alone. It was strategic. Civilian casualties fuelled insurgency and eroded domestic backing. By contrast, Iranian training of certain Iraqi militias during the same period prioritised resilience, decentralised command, and offensive capability against rival forces. Civilian harm was a secondary concern. Both approaches produced capable fighters. They produced different political footprints.

Doctrine also shapes command relationships. Proxies trained in hierarchical systems tend to centralise authority. Orders matter. Deviations are punished. Proxies trained in mission-type tactics decentralise. Initiative is rewarded. This affects control. Patrons seeking leverage favour hierarchies. Patrons seeking deniability tolerate decentralisation. The trade-off is visible. Hierarchies slow adaptation. Decentralisation invites autonomy.

Discipline is where doctrine meets enforcement. It is one thing to teach rules. It is another to make them stick. Discipline depends on pay, promotion, and punishment. Patrons influence all three. Units paid regularly and promoted predictably are easier to discipline. Units paid irregularly rely on loot and patronage, undermining restraint. The implication is uncomfortable. Financial systems are moral systems by proxy.

A five-word sentence belongs here. Discipline is expensive.

The counter-example complicates the story. Hezbollah's training regime, heavily influenced by Iranian doctrine, combines strict discipline with aggressive tactics. The organisation enforces internal rules rigorously while pursuing confrontational strategies externally. Civilian harm is managed selectively rather than minimised universally. The reconciliation lies in intent. Discipline does not guarantee restraint; it guarantees obedience. Doctrine determines what is obeyed.

Training also affects battlefield effectiveness in less obvious ways. Units drilled to coordinate fires and manoeuvre coherently outperform numerically superior opponents. This was evident in northern Syria, where Kurdish-led forces trained by Western advisers executed combined-arms operations despite limited heavy equipment. Their effectiveness derived from procedure as much as materiel. The behaviour was visible: coordinated advances, disciplined withdrawals, reliable reporting. The implication extended beyond the battlefield. Such performance justified continued support.

Embedded advisers amplify doctrine. Their presence during operations reinforces norms. They correct deviations in real time. They also become conduits for intelligence and logistics. The decision to embed is therefore consequential. It increases influence but raises exposure. Patrons who embed accept greater ownership. Patrons who do not accept drift.

Manuals matter too. Written doctrine travels when people do not. Manuals standardise behaviour across units and time. They also fossilise assumptions. A proxy trained on outdated doctrine may fight yesterday's war. Updating manuals requires sustained engagement. Many patrons do not stay long enough. The result is doctrinal lag.

The quiet motif threading this section is the drill square. What happens there repeats under fire. Movements practised in calm reappear in chaos. Corrections made early echo later. Patrons who neglect the drill square cede the battlefield to habit.

Political reputation flows from these habits. Civilian harm attracts scrutiny. Scrutiny constrains policy. A proxy trained to minimise harm preserves patron flexibility. A proxy trained to maximise aggression accelerates escalation. This is not theoretical. Media footage of undisciplined proxies has ended programmes and forced withdrawals. Doctrine can collapse a strategy.

There is a limit. Training cannot override local incentives indefinitely. Fighters embedded in communities respond to local pressures. When survival or revenge dominates, doctrine erodes. Patrons can mitigate this through continued engagement, but never eliminate it. Training is a multiplier, not a shield.

The forward test remains unresolved. As conflicts shorten and patrons rotate faster, can doctrine be transmitted deeply enough to matter? Or will proxies increasingly fight as they always have, absorbing techniques but discarding constraints? The answer will decide not only how wars are fought, but who owns their consequences.

Third-country and clandestine routes

In January 1966, US aircraft struck targets along the Laotian panhandle, far from the declared battlefield in South Vietnam. The aim was not symbolic. It was logistical. The Ho Chi Minh Trail—an evolving web of paths, roads, river crossings, and depots running through Laos and Cambodia—had become the artery sustaining North Vietnamese forces. It was not a single road, and it did not belong to a single war. For more than a decade, it absorbed bombs, rerouted traffic, and continued to function. Geography, quietly weaponised, had outlasted policy.

Routes decide wars.

Proxy warfare depends on movement through space that is politically inconvenient. Arms, money, trainers, and fighters must pass somewhere. Rarely is that somewhere the patron's own territory. Third countries therefore become stages, buffers, and markets. Some cooperate openly. Others look away. A few sell access with the precision of a service industry. The map of proxy war is less about front lines than about corridors.

The core claim is simple. Control of routes shapes control of proxies. Show it in practice. A proxy with secure access to supply corridors can resist pressure. One dependent on fragile routes remains pliable. Name it. Geography is leverage. Explain it. Routes determine tempo, volume, and survivability of support. Implication follows. Patrons invest as much in transit politics as in battlefield tactics.

Third countries host these routes for reasons that are rarely ideological. The visible behaviours vary. Some governments provide staging bases, allowing training camps, warehouses, or airfields to operate just inside their borders. Others permit air bridges—ostensibly civilian flights that move matériel under diplomatic cover. Still others tolerate maritime routes, where small vessels shuttle between ports with limited oversight. Each arrangement reflects a calculation.

That calculation turns on cost and benefit. Turning a blind eye can bring aid, security guarantees, or diplomatic favour. Renting territory can generate revenue and influence. Even denial has value. A government can plausibly claim ignorance while quietly shaping outcomes. The decision is rarely binary. It shifts over time as pressure mounts or opportunities arise.

The Ho Chi Minh Trail remains the archetype because it illustrates endurance. North Vietnam exploited the political constraints of Laos and Cambodia, states unable or unwilling to seal their territory fully. The trail adapted constantly: routes multiplied, storage dispersed, camouflage improved. US bombing campaigns increased cost but never severed flow. The implication was stark. Once a corridor embeds itself in terrain and politics, removing it requires escalation most patrons wish to avoid.

This pattern repeats. In the 1980s, Pakistan's tribal areas served as the principal staging ground for support to Afghan mujahideen. Training camps operated with varying degrees of oversight. Arms flowed through Karachi and onward by road. The Pakistani state balanced domestic risk against strategic gain, tolerating activity it could later claim exceeded its intent. The corridor's existence shaped the war's outcome and the region's future. Geography again proved sticky.

Air bridges offer a different logic. They compress distance and increase control but raise visibility. Flights require permissions, manifests, and infrastructure. Patrons use them when speed matters or when maritime routes are contested. The behaviour to watch is scheduling. Irregular flights suggest deniability. Regular ones suggest commitment. The metric is frequency, not capacity.

Maritime routes thrive where borders are porous and coastlines long. Small craft move at night. Cargoes are split to reduce loss. Ports with weak customs regimes become hubs. Governments tolerate this traffic when enforcement costs exceed political benefits. Crackdowns occur when exposure rises. The sea offers deniability through noise.

A credible counter-example tempers the argument. Some states refuse corridor roles despite pressure. Jordan, for example, tightly controlled its borders during phases of the Syrian conflict, balancing alliance demands against domestic stability. Support still moved, but at higher cost and lower volume. Reconciling this limitation clarifies the rule. Corridors exist where state interests align with tolerance. Where they do not, geography constrains strategy.

The quiet motif threading this section is the hinge. Corridors act as hinges between wars and regions. They allow conflicts to swing open or closed without formal entry. Once installed, they creak but rarely break.

These routes also accumulate history. A corridor used in one conflict becomes known, mapped, and resourced. Networks persist. Smugglers, fixers, and officials remember. When a new war erupts, old paths reopen. The Balkans, the Sahel, the Levant—all bear scars of reused routes. Weapons and people follow familiarity. Attribution grows harder as layers pile up.

Patrons understand this accumulation and exploit it. They choose routes with memory. They revive dormant networks rather than build anew. This reduces startup cost and increases deniability. It also imports legacy problems: criminality, factionalism, and loss of control. Geography gives, then takes.

For proxies, routes shape autonomy. A group controlling a corridor can bargain harder. It can tax traffic, divert supplies, and cultivate alternative patrons. Control of movement becomes power. Patrons respond by fragmenting routes, diversifying access, or embedding monitors. Each response raises cost.

The unresolved tension sits ahead. As surveillance improves and borders harden selectively, will corridors shrink or simply shift? Will states continue to rent ambiguity, or will the price rise beyond tolerance? The answer will determine not just how proxy wars are supplied, but which states become indispensable—and which become battlegrounds without ever declaring war.

Leakage, black markets, and diversion

In June 2014, as Iraqi security forces collapsed in Mosul, fighters from the Islamic State overran bases stocked with US-supplied weapons. Within days, images circulated of captured rifles, armoured vehicles, and ammunition—equipment intended to stabilise a partner force now repurposed against it. The outcome was concrete and immediate. Firepower changed hands. Within months, those same weapons appeared in attacks against Iraqi units and their allies. Supply had become boomerang.

Leakage is not an accident.

It is the predictable by-product of proxy warfare conducted at speed, at scale, and under pressure. Weapons leave warehouses with an intended user in mind, but they do not remain loyal. They move along incentives. Where pay is irregular, oversight thin, and tracking rudimentary, arms slip their chains. Once free, they feed black markets, empower rivals, and reshape conflicts far from their point of origin.

The first claim is empirical. Leakage follows incentives. Show it in behaviour. Fighters sell weapons when wages arrive late. Commanders divert stocks to reward loyalty or fund operations. Guards swap rifles for cash. Name it. This is diversion: the reallocation of arms away from authorised users. Explain it. Proxy forces operate in environments where state capacity is weak and survival costs are high. Weapons become currency. Implication follows. Control that ignores incentives fails.

Corruption accelerates this process. When supply chains are opaque and accountability fragmented, opportunities multiply. Intermediaries skim. Paperwork lies. Audits lag reality. The visible behaviour is mismatch: inventories that never reconcile, serial numbers that vanish, depots that empty faster than operations justify. Each discrepancy widens the market.

Low pay matters more than ideology. A proxy that fights for wages will trade when wages falter. Even ideologically motivated groups contain members with families to feed. The decision to sell a rifle is often less about betrayal than arithmetic. Patrons who underfund salaries while overfund hardware create precisely the conditions for leakage.

Tracking systems promise remedy but rarely deliver it fully. End-use monitoring requires access, time, and political leverage. Proxies resist intrusive checks. Patrons hesitate to press too hard, fearing defection. The behaviour that signals weak tracking is tolerance: missing items explained away as battlefield loss, follow-up deferred, sanctions avoided. Each tolerance compounds risk.

The Mosul case illustrates the downstream effects. Weapons captured there did not remain in one place. Investigations by Conflict Armament Research documented US-manufactured arms moving across Iraq and Syria in subsequent years, some traced by serial number to earlier transfers. The implication was not that supply was reckless, but that once introduced, arms circulated through networks beyond any single patron's reach.

A second example sharpens the point. During the 1980s, large quantities of weapons supplied to Afghan mujahideen entered regional markets. Decades later, similar systems resurfaced in South Asia and the Middle East. The time lag obscured responsibility but did not erase consequence. Arms endure. Policies rotate.

Black markets thrive on predictability. They expand where conflicts overlap and routes persist. Dealers specialise. Prices adjust. The metric is availability. When weapons appear consistently, markets stabilise. Stability invites expansion. Leakage thus transforms episodic supply into permanent infrastructure.

This infrastructure feeds rival factions. Arms sold to criminals find their way to militias. Weapons diverted from one proxy arm another. The behaviour is substitution. Groups lacking external support buy what others leak. The implication is strategic irony. A patron's effort to tilt a balance may simply redistribute force, prolonging war.

A credible counter-example tempers the argument. In some tightly controlled programmes, leakage has been limited. Where patrons embedded monitors, enforced payment discipline, and restricted advanced systems, diversion fell. Reconciling this exception clarifies conditions, not guarantees. Control reduces leakage; it never eliminates it. The cost of control is sustained engagement, which many patrons resist.

The quiet motif threading this section is the echo. Weapons echo across conflicts, returning in altered hands. The echo may be delayed, distorted, or amplified. It is rarely silent.

Leakage also corrodes legitimacy. Civilians recognise weapons. When arms supplied for protection appear in criminal violence, trust erodes. Patrons face reputational damage. Proxies lose standing. The political cost often exceeds the tactical gain of initial supply.

There is a feedback loop. As leakage increases, patrons tighten restrictions. Proxies respond by hiding losses. Transparency falls. Trust erodes further. The system becomes brittle. At some point, a scandal breaks the loop, forcing withdrawal or redesign. By then, weapons have already moved on.

The most unsettling consequence is blowback. Arms return not just as symbols but as threats. In Iraq and Afghanistan, forces encountered weapons originally supplied to partners now used by adversaries. The source did not matter to the bullet. The implication is stark. Supply choices write future risk.

The forward test remains unresolved. Can patrons design supply systems resilient enough to limit leakage without smothering proxies? Or is diversion the price of indirect war, payable later with interest? Each new conflict answers partially, then moves the question elsewhere.

Chapter 4

Intelligence and Covert Support

At dawn on a winter morning in eastern Ukraine, a small artillery unit adjusted its fire after a single ranging shot. The correction was precise. Too precise. Observers on the ground noticed that the shelling now tracked movements that could not be seen from the unit's position. Within hours, the opposing force abandoned the area. No aircraft had flown overhead. No satellites were mentioned. No advisers were visible. Yet something unseen had tilted the fight. The battlefield had acquired eyes.

Intelligence rarely announces itself. It leaves traces instead—sudden improvements in timing, uncanny accuracy, confidence where uncertainty should reign. In proxy wars, these traces are often the most consequential form of support, and the most carefully concealed. Weapons can be photographed. Fighters can be interviewed. Intelligence works in silence, shaping decisions before they are made and erasing its own footsteps as it goes.

If previous chapters examined the visible architecture of proxy warfare—relationships, arms, routes—this chapter turns to the invisible scaffolding. Intelligence and covert support sit at the intersection of capability and denial. They allow patrons to shape outcomes without crossing thresholds that trigger retaliation or domestic backlash. They are also the easiest form of support to underestimate, precisely because they leave so little behind.

The central paradox is this: intelligence is most valuable when it is least attributable. A patron wants a proxy to know more, see further, and react faster, but not to know exactly why. The patron, in turn, wants results without ownership. This mutual preference for opacity produces a distinctive ecosystem of anonymised feeds, cut-outs, selective tips, and deliberately incomplete sharing. Information arrives just in time, stripped of context, framed as opportunity rather than instruction.

Sharing intelligence without fingerprints requires design. Raw imagery is sanitised before release. Signals intercepts are translated into actionable hints rather than transcripts. Targeting data is passed through intermediaries who appear to be local analysts or allied services. The proxy experiences a leap in awareness without a clear source. Adversaries sense outside involvement without proof. This ambiguity is the point.

Such arrangements alter behaviour quickly. Units move with greater confidence. Ambushes succeed more often. Supply convoys avoid danger they could not otherwise detect. Observers notice patterns. So do journalists. A sudden run of successful operations raises questions, even when no evidence answers them. Intelligence support announces itself through effect.

Advisers complicate this picture. They occupy the grey space between information and command. At one end of the spectrum are occasional visits: trainers who arrive briefly, assess performance, and depart. Their influence is indirect, filtered through manuals and after-action reviews. At the other end are embedded liaison teams who sit alongside commanders, shaping plans, synchronising logistics, and translating political intent into operational choices. The difference is not cosmetic. It determines who really decides.

Conflicts with minimal adviser presence tend to produce looser alignment. Proxies interpret guidance creatively. Operations diverge from patron preferences. This distance preserves deniability but weakens control. Where advisers embed deeply, coordination improves and outcomes become more predictable. The cost is exposure. Embedded officers leave footprints—on bases, in communications, in captured documents. Patrons must decide how much influence is worth how much risk.

The digital turn has expanded this dilemma. Cyber operations and digital enablers allow patrons to compensate for weak local infrastructure without physical presence. Secure communications platforms reduce interception. Surveillance tools map networks. Hacking operations disrupt adversary logistics or expose plans. These capabilities travel faster than weapons and require fewer people on the ground. They also blur the line between intelligence and action.

A proxy that adopts encrypted messaging, for example, can outmanoeuvre state security forces reliant on compromised channels. Coordination improves. Arrests decline. The balance shifts. From the outside, this looks like organisational maturation. From the inside, it is often the product of quiet technical assistance. The patron remains invisible. The effect is unmistakable.

Information support does not stop at the battlefield. Media, disinformation, and influence tools form another layer of covert assistance. Funding sympathetic outlets, coordinating talking points, and amplifying certain atrocities while minimising others shape the political environment in which proxy wars unfold. Narratives determine which groups receive sympathy, which face sanctions, and which interventions are tolerated. In some cases, a single viral video does more to constrain policy than months of fighting.

These information campaigns are rarely centralised. They operate through networks of activists, journalists, and platforms with varying degrees of coordination. Patrons seed content and watch what spreads. Proxies learn which stories resonate and adjust behaviour accordingly. The feedback loop tightens. Reality competes with representation, and representation often wins.

The risk, again, is exposure. Leaks happen. Battlefield evidence accumulates. Journalists connect dots. At some point, deniability collapses. Patrons face a choice: retreat, double down on secrecy, or go overt. History shows that when the political cost of denial exceeds the cost of admission, governments often choose visibility. What began as covert backing becomes open alliance. The transition is rarely smooth. It redefines stakes, invites retaliation, and changes domestic narratives overnight.

This chapter traces that arc. It begins with the mechanics of sharing intelligence without fingerprints, moves through the human presence of advisers and planners, explores the expanding role of cyber and digital tools, and examines the information battles that run parallel to kinetic ones. It ends at the threshold where covert becomes overt, and secrecy gives way to strategy.

A subtle motif runs throughout: illumination. Intelligence illuminates the battlefield for some while keeping others in the dark. It also illuminates responsibility unevenly, revealing enough to influence outcomes but not enough to assign blame. As technologies spread and scrutiny intensifies, maintaining this selective illumination becomes harder. Light leaks.

The stakes are high. Intelligence and covert support often decide proxy wars faster than weapons do. They shape tempo, confidence, and perception. They also carry the greatest risk of miscalculation. A tip misread, a signal misinterpreted, a cyber operation attributed prematurely—each can escalate a conflict patrons intended to keep contained.

The pages that follow do not treat intelligence as a technical specialty. They treat it as a political instrument, wielded under constraints and with consequences that extend beyond the immediate fight. The reader is invited to look for intelligence not where it is declared, but where outcomes suddenly shift. To notice the quiet hand that steadies a proxy's aim, sharpens its vision, and sometimes pushes it further than intended.

By the end of this chapter, covert support will no longer appear as a shadowy adjunct to proxy warfare. It will stand revealed as one of its central pillars: decisive, deniable, and increasingly difficult to keep unseen.

Sharing intelligence without fingerprints

On 9 November 2001, the Northern Alliance entered Mazar-i-Sharif, breaking the Taliban's grip on Afghanistan's north and opening a supply corridor that would reshape the war. The victory looked, in photographs, like a local triumph: bearded fighters on battered vehicles, celebratory gunfire, a city taken by men who knew its streets. Yet accounts published later, including Gary Schroen's *First In* (2005), describe CIA teams working with the Alliance in the weeks before the fall, blending cash, relationships, and intelligence with American air power. The most telling change was not a new weapon in a fighter's hands, but a new certainty in his movement. Someone else was watching them.

That is what intelligence does in proxy war when it is done well. It alters behaviour while concealing authorship. It makes a force see further than its eyes, hear more than its radios, and strike with a confidence that would otherwise look reckless. The battlefield changes texture. Ambushes become anticipatory. Targets appear at the right time. Losses fall. Opponents begin to suspect a hidden hand, even if they cannot prove it.

The craft lies in fingerprints—specifically, in removing them.

Start with what is being shared. Imagery is the most intuitive: satellite pictures, drone feeds, aerial reconnaissance. Signals intercepts matter as much: communications captured, locations inferred, patterns of movement extracted from radio traffic and mobile networks. Targeting data sits at the sharp end: coordinates, routes, schedules, vulnerabilities. These products can be decisive for a proxy with limited surveillance and weak command-and-control. They are also politically dangerous for a patron, because they imply participation, not merely sympathy.

The first method of sharing without fingerprints is sanitisation. Patrons strip intelligence down to a usable core while removing indicators of source and method. A precise intercept becomes a vague warning: a convoy will move tonight, not how that was learned. An image becomes a simple map overlay, not a time-stamped satellite frame that could be traced to a particular platform. The proxy receives an answer, not the workings. The visible behaviour is the proxy's improved timing without improved sensors. The implication is deniability preserved through asymmetry: the proxy knows *what* but not *how*.

This is not mere secrecy for its own sake. It protects capabilities. It also protects policy. If a proxy can show journalists an unredacted satellite image, the patron's role becomes harder to deny. If the proxy can only say, honestly, "we received a tip", the story remains contestable. Contestability is the political asset.

A related practice is compartmentalisation. Patrons rarely give a proxy the full picture. They provide selective tips rather than comprehensive intelligence. This reduces the proxy's ability to infer sources, but it also preserves patron control. A proxy that receives only what it needs cannot easily act in ways the patron does not want. The behaviour is constraint by information: operations cluster around the targets the patron highlights. The implication is subtle power. Guidance becomes invisible steering.

The second method is the cut-out. Patrons often share intelligence through intermediaries—another state's service, a private contractor, a liaison cell, or a multinational fusion centre—so that the immediate source appears local or allied rather than the true patron. Cut-outs are not only shields; they are filters. They decide what passes and what does not. In Afghanistan in 2001, the CIA's early work with the Northern Alliance, as described in memoirs and subsequent reporting, relied heavily on personal liaison, cash, and information flows that did not resemble formal military command. The Alliance could plausibly claim it was acting on its own initiative. The patron could plausibly claim it was not directing the fight. Yet the battle rhythm suggested coordination.

Cut-outs are especially useful when patrons want to deny not only involvement but intent. A tip passed through an allied service can be framed as routine cooperation, even when it is calibrated to shape a proxy's operational choices. This is one reason intelligence alliances matter in proxy wars. They provide bureaucratic cover: information "shared" in a way that looks procedural rather than strategic. The proxy sees help. The public sees partnership. The patron sees insulation.

The third method is anonymised feeds. Instead of handing over raw intelligence, patrons sometimes provide a stream of warnings or target packages without attribution, delivered through secured channels that reveal little about origin. The proxy learns to trust the feed because it works. Trust here is not an emotion. It is an operational decision. Units that once moved cautiously begin to move confidently. They strike more often at night. They choose routes that avoid ambush. They converge on locations at oddly precise moments. Opponents notice the pattern and suspect external surveillance, but proof remains elusive.

At this point, intelligence changes the war not only materially but psychologically. A proxy that believes it is being watched over fights differently. It takes risks it would otherwise avoid. It becomes bolder, sometimes too bold. This is where fingerprints can reappear—not in documents, but in overconfidence that exposes the patron's hidden hand through outcomes: improbably accurate strikes, uncanny anticipations, sudden reversals of fortune.

A second checkable example shows how this works in a different theatre. In Kosovo in 1999, NATO's air campaign relied on extensive surveillance and targeting processes, while the Kosovo Liberation Army operated on the ground with limited heavy capability. The relationship was not a classic proxy arrangement in every respect—NATO owned its air war openly—but the interaction illustrates the logic of intelligence-enabled local force. When air power and ground action begin to align in timing and effect, observers infer coordination even if command relationships are formally denied. The behaviour is convergence: attacks on the ground coincide with air strikes in ways that suggest shared awareness. The implication is that intelligence, even when not publicly described, becomes legible through synchronisation.

This legibility is the patron's constant problem. Intelligence wants to be used. Use creates pattern. Pattern invites attribution.

Patrons therefore manage not only what they share, but how a proxy is allowed to act on it. One common technique is to require "local corroboration". A proxy may be told, implicitly or explicitly, to validate a target through its own scouts before acting. This protects the patron from blame if the intelligence is wrong and reduces the proxy's ability to present the patron as the direct source of action. It also slows tempo. The visible behaviour is a lag: intelligence arrives, then a pause, then action. The implication is risk management disguised as caution.

Another technique is to package intelligence as defensive. Warnings about imminent raids, locations of mines, or likely ambush points can be presented as humanitarian or protective rather than offensive. Yet defensive intelligence can be strategically offensive. A proxy that avoids losses retains momentum. A force that survives becomes a political actor. The patron can claim it is saving lives while still shaping outcomes. This is the moral grammar of deniable intelligence support: protection as participation.

There is, however, a credible limitation to the promise of fingerprint-free intelligence. The first is technical. Modern forensics, captured devices, and open-source investigators can reconstruct patterns of support. A proxy's secure radios, encryption protocols, or targeting methods may reveal external training. A captured laptop with coordinate lists can suggest a level of sophistication beyond local capacity. The second limitation is organisational. Proxies talk. They boast. They leak. Commanders use alleged intelligence links to increase prestige or intimidate rivals. Deniability can be undermined by the very client it is meant to protect.

Reconciling these limitations reveals an uncomfortable truth: deniability is not a state; it is a moving threshold. Patrons do not aim for perfect invisibility. They aim for enough ambiguity to prevent decisive retaliation or domestic backlash. If involvement can be plausibly denied in official terms, the strategy has breathing room. If evidence becomes so clear that denial looks contemptuous, the strategy collapses into scandal or escalation.

This is why patrons sometimes keep intelligence support deliberately imperfect. Perfect intelligence creates perfect pattern. Pattern creates traceability. Traceability creates political cost. A patron may therefore ration the sharpest feeds, offer only partial targeting data, or route intelligence through multiple layers to blur origin even at the expense of speed. The proxy may complain. It may also learn to operate within the constraints, filling gaps with its own reconnaissance. The implication is a calibrated inefficiency—an odd feature of proxy warfare that makes sense only when deniability is treated as a strategic resource.

Fingerprints also appear in the errors. When intelligence is wrong, the consequences can be spectacular and politically toxic. A strike based on faulty intercepts that hits civilians does more than harm innocents; it exposes the patron's presence through outrage and investigation. This risk pushes patrons towards cautious sharing, yet caution can frustrate clients and tempt them to improvise. Improvisation, in turn, increases the chance of atrocity or failure, which rebounds on the patron anyway. Intelligence support sits inside a trap: the safer it is politically, the less effective it can be; the more effective it is, the harder it is to deny.

The quiet motif running through this problem is the shadow. Intelligence operates in shadow not because it is inherently secretive, but because its value depends on asymmetry. The proxy must see more than the adversary. The patron must be seen less than the proxy. When the shadow thickens too much, the proxy cannot act. When it thins too much, the patron is exposed.

Return, finally, to the tell-tale moment that begins many proxy campaigns: the sudden improvement in battlefield awareness. A force that once stumbled into ambushes now avoids them. A commander who once guessed now arrives early. A militia that once fought blind now fights as if it has a second set of eyes. Observers argue about training, morale, or luck. Sometimes those explanations fit. Sometimes they do not. When the change is abrupt and sustained, intelligence is often the missing piece.

The unresolved test for patrons is not whether they *can* share intelligence without fingerprints. They can, for a time. The harder question is whether they can do so without creating a proxy that becomes dependent on unseen sight—or worse, a proxy that uses that sight to pursue objectives the patron never intended to illuminate.

Advisers, planners, and embedded officers

On 30 September 2015, Russia began air operations in Syria, declaring it was acting at the request of the Assad government. Within weeks, the Syrian Arab Army and allied militias began retaking ground in patterns that suggested more than just air support. Offensives synchronised with strikes. Logistics improved. Units that had been hollowed out by years of war moved with new purpose. Reports from the period, including accounts by journalists and analysts tracking the intervention, described Russian officers present at command posts and coordination centres. The campaign's rhythm changed. Someone was planning.

Five words belong here. Presence becomes power quickly.

Advisers are the hinge between indirect support and operational control. They are how patrons translate money, weapons, and intelligence into decisions under fire. The same rifle in a proxy's hands can be wasted or decisive depending on how it is used; advisers exist to shape that use. Yet advisers also carry the greatest risk to a patron's deniability. A shipment can be denied. A dead adviser cannot. This tension shapes the entire spectrum of advisory involvement, from occasional training visits to embedded liaison teams that effectively direct campaigns.

The spectrum matters because it describes different bargains. At one end are episodic trainers who arrive, teach, and leave. Their influence is mediated through manuals and habits. At the other end are embedded officers sitting beside commanders, shaping plans, approving targets, and managing logistics. Their influence is immediate, personal, and often decisive. The distance between these endpoints is not a matter of degree alone. It changes who owns outcomes.

Show the difference in observable behaviour. A proxy that receives occasional training may improve marksmanship and unit cohesion yet continue to operate opportunistically, with inconsistent coordination and uneven discipline. A proxy with embedded advisers tends to move in synchrony, execute phased operations, and maintain supply discipline. The metric is coherence: the degree to which disparate units act as one, and the regularity with which operations align with patron priorities.

Name what advisers actually do. They shape operations by translating intelligence into action, by designing campaigns that sequence objectives, and by introducing planning processes that proxies may not possess. They shape logistics by building supply schedules, maintenance routines, and casualty evacuation systems. They shape political messaging by advising leaders on what to say, what not to say, and how to frame victories and losses. Explain why this matters. Logistics and narrative are force multipliers. They sustain fighting capacity and legitimacy. The implication is that advisers influence the war's political economy as much as its tactics.

Consider Syria as an example of deepening presence. Russia did not simply bomb; it helped organise. Air support without coordination can scatter enemy forces without enabling capture of territory. When Syrian government units began to exploit air strikes systematically—advancing along axes consistent with phased planning—the likely explanation was integration at the level of command. This is the tell-tale sign of embedded advisers: when operations stop being merely reactive and become cumulative.

Contrast this with a conflict where adviser presence was deliberately limited. In the early years of the US campaign against the Islamic State in Iraq and Syria, American officials repeatedly emphasised that there would be “no boots on the ground” in a combat role, while simultaneously deploying advisers to train and assist local forces. In practice, the advisory footprint expanded over time, but the initial constraint shaped outcomes. Local forces often advanced unevenly, constrained by their own internal politics and command limitations. Progress was achieved, but it depended heavily on air power and incremental training rather than fully integrated operational planning. The implication is not that limited presence fails, but that it produces a different kind of war: slower, less controllable, and more vulnerable to local divergence.

Advisory presence is not only a military choice. It is a political one. Patrons calibrate adviser numbers and proximity to combat according to domestic tolerance and escalation risk. This calibration is visible in how advisers are described. They are “trainers”, “liaison”, “support”, “non-combat”. Language does not change the battlefield, but it shapes what patrons believe they can sustain. Advisers operate inside this linguistic architecture, sometimes constrained by it, sometimes making it fiction.

The mechanics of advisory influence are intimate. Advisers build relationships with commanders. They cultivate trust through competence and shared risk. They become interpreters of patron intent and proxy reality. This is why embedded teams are so effective: influence moves through proximity. A plan delivered by email is optional. A plan discussed face-to-face at midnight, with maps spread across a table, becomes harder to ignore.

Yet intimacy brings dependency. Proxies can become reliant on advisers for planning, intelligence interpretation, and logistical coordination. When advisers withdraw, performance often drops sharply. This is a measurable pattern. Operations slow. Casualties rise. Units fragment. The implication is strategic fragility: success built on embedded expertise can collapse when that expertise leaves.

A credible counter-example complicates this, and it matters. In some cases, limited advisory presence has been sufficient because the proxy already possessed strong institutions. The US relationship with certain partner militaries that had professional command structures required fewer embedded advisers than relationships with newly assembled militias. Where local forces already plan and sustain operations, advisers can remain peripheral and still matter. Reconciling this clarifies the rule. Advisers compensate for institutional weakness. The weaker the proxy, the more advisers are needed; the more advisers are used, the harder withdrawal becomes.

Advisers also shape discipline and civilian harm. Patrons that insist on strict rules of engagement often enforce them through advisers who monitor behaviour, correct targeting processes, and withhold support when violations occur. The visible behaviour is constraint: operations paused for verification, targets dropped from lists, units reprimanded. Patrons that prioritise aggression may embed advisers who focus on speed and shock, tolerating higher civilian risk to achieve rapid gains. The implication is reputational. Civilian harm is not merely a moral issue; it becomes a strategic liability that can constrain a patron's freedom of action.

The advisory relationship also affects internal proxy politics. Advisers become gatekeepers to resources. Units that cultivate adviser relationships receive more support. Units that resist may be sidelined. This creates incentives for compliance but also for internal rivalry. Commanders compete for access. Advisers inadvertently shape factional dynamics. The war becomes, in part, a contest over proximity to the patron's representatives.

Here the quiet motif is the chair at the table. Who gets to sit beside the adviser? Who is invited to briefings? Who receives the secure radio? Those seats confer power. They redefine leadership. In proxy environments, the chair can be as valuable as the rifle.

Exposure remains the patron's central dilemma. Advisers can be killed, captured, or publicly revealed. Each incident collapses deniability. Patrons therefore build layers of separation: advisers operate in protected bases, behind front lines, or under cover of allied uniforms. Some work through contractors. Some appear as "technical specialists". These are not cosmetic choices. They are risk management.

Yet even when advisers are not physically on the front line, their influence can be operationally direct. Planning centres, liaison cells, and deconfliction channels allow advisers to shape tempo and target selection from a distance. Modern communications make this easier. A proxy commander can receive guidance in near-real time without a foreign officer standing beside him. This reduces exposure while preserving influence. It also creates new vulnerabilities, including interception and attribution.

Advisers inevitably affect political messaging. Proxies learn what their patrons can tolerate. They adjust rhetoric accordingly. They adopt slogans about counterterrorism or national unity, sometimes sincerely, sometimes tactically. Advisers encourage this because legitimacy is a weapon. A proxy that speaks in internationally palatable terms attracts more support and faces fewer constraints. The implication is that advisory work blends operational planning with narrative engineering. War is fought with statements as well as with shells.

The forward test is uncomfortable because it forces a choice patrons often postpone. How close must an adviser sit to make a proxy effective, and how far must he stand to keep the patron safe? Too close, and the war becomes owned. Too far, and the proxy becomes autonomous, for better or worse. Advisers exist in that narrow space where influence is most significant and deniability most fragile. The question is whether that space is shrinking as exposure grows—and whether patrons, faced with the cost of presence, will accept the cost of distance instead.

Cyber operations and digital enablers

In September 2015, the messaging application Telegram announced that it had surpassed sixty million monthly users. Within weeks, analysts tracking the Islamic State in Iraq and Syria noticed a shift. Propaganda channels migrated. Operational chatter thinned on older platforms. Security forces that had relied on intercepting phone calls and unsecured social media feeds found themselves chasing shadows across encrypted channels. The place was Syria and northern Iraq. The organisation was Islamic State. The outcome was measurable: arrests based on intercepted communications declined, while coordinated attacks became harder to disrupt.

Encryption changed the fight.

This was not a story about sophisticated hackers or bespoke military systems. It was about off-the-shelf digital tools, adopted quickly and unevenly, reshaping the balance between state surveillance and insurgent coordination. Cyber operations and digital enablers now sit alongside weapons and training as core components of proxy support. They matter because they compress time, flatten hierarchies, and compensate for weaknesses that would otherwise cripple irregular forces.

Show the problem first. Many proxy forces operate with poor infrastructure, limited training, and fragile command chains. Radios are scarce or compromised. Physical couriers are slow and vulnerable. Intelligence arrives late, if at all. Digital tools address these gaps. Secure messaging allows dispersed units to coordinate without fixed command posts. Commercial satellite imagery, even at low resolution, provides situational awareness once reserved for states. Simple databases track fighters, payments, and losses. The visible behaviour is speed: decisions taken in minutes rather than days.

Name the mechanism. Digital enablers reduce friction. They lower the cost of coordination and the skill threshold required to act coherently. Explain why this matters. War punishes delay. Groups that can move information faster than their opponents can act out of proportion to their size. The implication is strategic levelling: technology narrows the gap between weak actors and strong ones, especially when patrons quietly facilitate access.

Patrons rarely need to build bespoke cyber capabilities for proxies. More often, they curate access. They recommend platforms, provide training in basic operational security, and occasionally supply hardware that is harder to trace. This can include encrypted radios, secure smartphones, or access to anonymised data feeds. The key is plausibility. A messaging app downloaded from a public store leaves fewer fingerprints than a military system shipped across borders.

Return to the Islamic State example, not as a model to admire but as a case to understand. Researchers such as J.M. Berger documented how the group used Telegram channels after 2015 to disseminate instructions, coordinate media releases, and signal operations. The adoption did not require deep technical skill. It required discipline. Members were instructed to migrate, to avoid metadata leaks, and to trust the platform. The effect was not perfect security, but improved resilience. Security services adapted, but with delay. That delay mattered.

Contrast this with a second, more explicitly patron-linked case. During the conflict in eastern Ukraine after 2014, separatist forces backed by Russia demonstrated rapid improvements in coordination and information sharing. Open-source investigations by organisations such as Bellingcat documented the use of secure communications, digital mapping tools, and real-time targeting coordination that exceeded what local militias could plausibly generate alone. The visible behaviour was integration: artillery strikes aligned with drone feeds; units manoeuvred with shared situational awareness. Explain the link. Digital enablers, supported by a technologically capable patron, compensated for gaps in local training and infrastructure. The implication was battlefield effectiveness without overt command.

Cyber support also includes offensive actions, though these are usually limited in scope for proxies. Hacking can disrupt adversary communications, deface websites, or leak documents. More often, proxies benefit indirectly from patron cyber operations that distract or degrade opponents while leaving the proxy's hands ostensibly clean. The metric here is confusion: delayed responses, contradictory orders, and public embarrassment.

Yet digital tools cut both ways. A credible limitation tempers the story. Encryption protects content but not always metadata. Secure platforms can be infiltrated through human error, compromised devices, or poor discipline. Islamic State itself suffered from this. As the conflict progressed, security services learned to map networks, exploit operational mistakes, and seed channels with disinformation. The same tools that enabled coordination also created records. Reconciling this shows the pattern. Digital enablers amplify capability, but they also amplify the cost of mistakes. Technology raises the ceiling and the floor at the same time.

Patrons understand this and adjust their support. They emphasise basic cyber hygiene rather than complex techniques. They prioritise platforms with large user bases, where proxy activity blends into civilian noise. They accept that perfect security is impossible and focus instead on resilience: the ability to recover quickly when channels are compromised. This is visible in redundancy. Multiple platforms. Frequent migrations. Short-lived accounts.

The quiet motif here is the channel. Channels open. Channels close. Control flows through them. In proxy warfare, the channel often matters more than the headquarters. Whoever shapes the channel shapes behaviour.

Digital enablers also alter internal power dynamics. Leaders who control communication platforms gain influence. Fighters who lack access are marginalised. Patrons may quietly favour certain factions by granting better tools or training. This can stabilise a proxy or fracture it, depending on how it is managed. The implication is political. Technology redistributes authority inside armed groups, sometimes unintentionally.

Civilian harm and reputation are affected as well. Improved coordination can reduce indiscriminate violence by enabling more precise operations. It can also enable rapid mobilisation for repression. The outcome depends on doctrine and oversight, discussed elsewhere in this book. What matters here is that digital tools magnify intent. They do not determine it.

A second counter-example sharpens the point. In some conflicts, state security forces have regained the upper hand by investing heavily in cyber surveillance and legal access to platforms. Where governments can compel companies or exploit infrastructure, encryption offers less protection. Proxies operating in such environments gain less from digital enablers. The reconciliation is geographic and political. The value of cyber tools depends on jurisdiction, enforcement capacity, and the willingness of platforms to cooperate.

Patrons therefore choose where to invest. In weak states, digital support yields high returns. In strong surveillance states, it may not. This selectivity is itself a strategic choice, shaping where proxy wars are fought and how long they last.

The adoption of encrypted messaging altered balances not because it made proxies invincible, but because it shifted the tempo of contest. It forced states to adapt, to invest, and to accept gaps. It also tied proxies more closely to patrons who could help them navigate the digital terrain.

The unresolved tension lies ahead. As platforms tighten controls and states extend digital reach, will proxies lose this advantage, or will new tools restore it? For patrons, the test is sharper still. How much digital capability can be shared before fingerprints become unavoidable, and how much dependence can be created before control slips away through the very channels designed to manage it?

Media, disinformation, and influence tools

On 17 August 2016, the Aleppo Media Center released a short video from the al-Qaterji neighbourhood in Aleppo, Syria. It showed a dazed boy, Omran Daqneesh, seated in the back of an ambulance after an airstrike, his face dusty, his gaze blank, his small hand lifting to touch blood he did not yet seem to understand. The clip travelled at the speed of outrage. Within hours it was on the front pages and evening bulletins across Europe and North America. Within days, governments that had been speaking in the language of "complexity" found themselves pressed to speak in the language of guilt.

The camera became a weapon.

This is the information side of proxy support: not simply persuading people, but constraining them. A viral image can narrow a patron's options more effectively than an enemy battalion. It can force a defensive posture, accelerate a policy shift, or make deniability feel like cynicism. In proxy wars, narratives do not merely accompany violence. They structure how violence is understood, which forms of violence become politically usable, and which become politically toxic.

The mechanics are less glamorous than the slogans. Patrons fund media outlets and content producers. They subsidise "civil society" organisations whose work is partly documentary and partly advocacy. They provide equipment, training, and access. They coordinate talking points across embassies, ministries, and friendly commentators. They amplify certain atrocities while minimising others, not always by lying, sometimes simply by choosing what to notice. The result is an uneven moral landscape in which some victims become symbols and others become statistics.

Start with the most basic form of influence: attention. A proxy's survival depends on being seen in the right light by the right audiences. Attention unlocks donations, recruits, diplomatic meetings, and weapons. Attention also shapes the patron's domestic politics. A government cannot sustain support indefinitely if its public believes it is backing criminals, or if it is accused of indifference to suffering. The proxy relationship therefore includes an implicit media bargain: the client promises to provide a story the patron can live with, and the patron helps that story travel.

This bargain is visible in behaviour. Proxies establish press offices, spokespersons, and social media teams. They stage interviews and manage access to front lines. They learn to film their operations and curate footage. Patrons, in turn, offer soft power resources: introductions to journalists, training in messaging discipline, sometimes direct funding for outlets that carry sympathetic narratives. None of this requires a formal order. Incentives do the work.

Name what disinformation adds. It is not simply "falsehood"; it is strategic confusion. Disinformation aims to degrade trust in any account of events, to make audiences uncertain enough to disengage, or polarised enough to retreat into camps. A patron may not need the world to believe its proxy is innocent; it may only need the world to doubt that anyone can be sure. Doubt buys time. Time buys policy space.

Explain why this matters in proxy wars specifically. Proxy warfare thrives on ambiguity. Ambiguity protects patrons from retaliation and scandal. The information environment is therefore not a side theatre; it is the armour that makes indirect war sustainable. When that armour cracks—when a story becomes too vivid, too consistent, too widely shared—patrons face a sudden exposure that weapons shipments alone rarely create.

The Omran Daqneesh video illustrates the mechanism cleanly. The clip did not prove who launched the strike or why, and it did not offer a comprehensive account of the war in Aleppo. It did something more politically potent: it established a frame. A child, an ambulance, and a quiet horror that required no translation. Once that frame lodged in public consciousness, it became harder for external patrons—whether supporting government forces or opposing them—to maintain a neutral posture. Silence began to look like complicity. Denial began to sound rehearsed.

A second checkable example shows how patrons and clients attempt to capture such frames, and how the contest can harden into parallel realities. In July 2014, Malaysian Airlines Flight MH17 was shot down over eastern Ukraine near Hrabove, killing 298 people. Within hours, competing narratives flooded the information space. Russian state media and affiliated channels offered alternative explanations, cast doubt on evidence, and accused Ukraine and its backers. Western governments and investigative bodies moved in the opposite direction, emphasising attribution and responsibility. The point here is not to adjudicate the facts—which have been addressed by official investigations—but to observe the influence logic. When a proxy conflict produces an event that cannot be ignored, patrons race not only to win the battlefield, but to win the meaning of the battlefield.

Influence tools operate at three levels: production, amplification, and suppression. Production is the creation of content: videos, testimonies, reports, satellite imagery analysis, photo essays, documentaries. Proxies often lack capacity for professional production, so patrons or aligned organisations fill the gap with equipment, training, and sometimes editorial guidance. Amplification is the distribution of that content through networks: media partnerships, social media campaigns, sympathetic influencers, diaspora communities, and diplomatic messaging. Suppression is the attempt to bury competing accounts—through censorship where possible, through flooding the zone with alternative narratives where censorship is impossible.

The behaviour is measurable. Production yields regular, high-quality content with consistent branding. Amplification yields spikes in visibility: hashtags trending, clips replayed, quotes echoed across multiple outlets in a short period. Suppression yields either silence—stories that never surface—or noise—stories drowned in controversy. These are not mysteries. They are patterns.

Patrons favour these tools because they are cheap relative to military interventions and because they scale. A modest investment in a media operation can generate international pressure that substitutes for weaponry.

A well-placed narrative can legitimise sanctions, unlock arms sales, or attract coalition partners. Even when a patron does not directly fund an outlet, it can nurture it by granting access, providing security, or offering insider briefings that shape coverage. Influence is often purchased with proximity.

Proxies quickly learn to perform for this environment. They tailor operations to produce compelling footage. They prioritise symbolic targets. They schedule announcements to coincide with diplomatic meetings. They cultivate spokespeople who can speak in internationally palatable terms. The danger is that the war becomes partly choreographed around narrative value rather than strategic necessity. Atrocities become content. Suffering becomes currency.

This is where moral hazard reappears in an information form. If a proxy believes that images of victimhood will increase patron support, it may expose civilians to risk, or at minimum fail to prioritise their protection. Conversely, a patron may prefer a proxy that generates sympathetic content even if its battlefield performance is mediocre. The implication is grim: narrative success can outcompete military competence.

Disinformation complicates this further by turning authenticity into a weapon. When audiences become accustomed to staged content, genuine documentation can be dismissed as propaganda. Patrons exploiting this dynamic do not need to prove their version of events; they need only to poison the well. This is visible in rhetorical habits: obsessive demands for "proof" coupled with refusal to accept any proof, selective scepticism applied only to inconvenient facts, and rapid shifting of explanations as each is challenged. The aim is exhaustion.

A credible limitation must be faced. Influence is not omnipotent. Viral content can backfire. A patron's obvious manipulation can provoke backlash, strengthening the opposing narrative. Audiences are not blank slates; they interpret content through identity, ideology, and trust in institutions. Moreover, the more actors attempt to weaponise information, the more the environment becomes saturated, and the harder it becomes for any single story to dominate.

Reconciling this limitation clarifies the real function of influence tools. They do not reliably convert opponents. They consolidate supporters, stiffen alliances, and reduce uncertainty among fence-sitters. They keep coalitions together by providing moral and strategic justification. Even when they fail to persuade universally, they can succeed politically by sustaining commitment among those who matter.

This is why patrons invest in "talking points", a phrase that sounds trivial until one watches it shape policy. Talking points are pre-approved frames that allow officials to respond quickly under media pressure. In proxy wars, speed matters. A patron that controls the first credible narrative often shapes subsequent debate. Proxies understand this and coordinate with patrons to ensure that events are framed promptly and consistently. The behaviour is synchronisation: statements from different officials echo the same phrases, condemning the same acts, praising the same partners, dismissing the same allegations. This is not always conspiracy; it is often bureaucratic discipline. Its effect, however, is real.

Funding media outlets is the most direct form of influence support, and it is also the riskiest. Money leaves trails. It can be exposed by audits, leaks, or investigative reporting. Patrons therefore often prefer indirect funding: grants through foundations, contracts through development agencies, support channelled via third countries, or the provision of equipment and training rather than cash. These methods preserve plausible deniability while still shaping output. The proxy receives a megaphone, and the patron can claim it merely supports "independent media".

The quiet motif running through this section is the frame. Frames decide what is seen and what is ignored. Frames turn a strike into "self-defence" or "massacre", a militia into "freedom fighters" or "terrorists", a civilian death into "collateral damage" or "war crime". Frames are not mere semantics. They determine legal arguments, alliance cohesion, and domestic consent.

Frames also determine escalation. When a viral video galvanises public outrage, it can force a patron to act—or to stop acting. The Omran Daqneesh clip did not compel a direct intervention by itself, but it contributed to a climate in which restraint required constant justification. It narrowed the rhetorical room in which policy could operate. That narrowing is a form of power.

The forward test for any patron is therefore not only whether a proxy can be supplied or advised, but whether it can be narrated. Can the patron sustain a moral and political story that survives inevitable atrocities, inevitable errors, and inevitable adversary propaganda? Can it keep its own fingerprints off the most manipulative tools while still benefiting from them? And can it predict which images will become symbols—those that widen options by generating support, and those that constrict options by triggering scandal?

Proxy wars are fought in villages and deserts. They are also fought in feeds and headlines. The weapons that decide empires are sometimes made of steel. Sometimes they are made of light.

When covert support becomes overt

On 24 February 2022, Vladimir Putin announced a "special military operation" and Russian forces crossed into Ukraine from multiple directions, including towards Kyiv. Whatever had been argued, denied, or artfully obscured in earlier years, the act itself was unambiguous. Tanks do not do deniability. By lunchtime, the vocabulary of "plausible" had evaporated; governments, markets, and publics responded to a war that had stepped into the open.

The mask had slipped.

Covert support rarely becomes overt by accident alone. It becomes overt when secrecy stops paying its rent—when the political cost of denial, the operational cost of half-measures, or the reputational cost of being caught outstrips the benefits of remaining in shadow. States do not abandon deniability because they suddenly grow honest. They abandon it because the balance sheet changes.

A five-word sentence matters here. Exposure forces a decision fast.

Proxy warfare thrives in the half-light: arms without flags, intelligence without insignia, advisers who do not exist on paper. But half-light is unstable. It demands constant maintenance. It requires disciplined messaging, careful routing of support, and, above all, a public that can be kept uncertain. Over time, three forces corrode that uncertainty: leaks, evidence, and choice.

Leaks are the most familiar. They arrive through whistleblowers, investigative journalism, parliamentary oversight, or simply the carelessness of participants. They are rarely decisive on their own. A single leak can be dismissed; a pattern cannot. The visible behaviour is defensive choreography: officials issuing narrow denials, refusing details, calling reports "unverified" while quietly adjusting policy. Each leak forces a patron to spend political capital defending the very idea of secrecy. When that spending becomes constant, covert programmes start to feel like a domestic liability rather than a strategic tool.

Battlefield evidence is harder. Weapons are photographed. Serial numbers are traced. Communications are intercepted and published. Soldiers are captured. Graves are dug. Unlike leaks, evidence accumulates in public view and often comes from multiple directions, including adversaries, open-source investigators, and international organisations. The more an external patron shapes operations—through advanced weapons, distinctive munitions, or tight coordination—the more distinctive the signature becomes. Deniability is easiest when support is low-tech and dispersed. It becomes brittle when support is sophisticated and central.

The third force is deliberate choice. Sometimes patrons decide to go overt not because they are exposed, but because they want the advantages that visibility brings: deterrence, alliance cohesion, domestic mobilisation, legal cover, and bargaining power. Covert support is useful for nudging a conflict. It is less useful for ending one decisively. At certain moments, patrons judge that the war has become important enough to own.

The Russian trajectory in Ukraine illustrates how these forces interact, though not in a neat sequence. In February 2014, unidentified armed men in unmarked uniforms—soon dubbed "little green men"—appeared in Crimea. Russia initially denied they were its troops. In April 2014, conflict erupted in the Donbas; Moscow denied directing the fighting even as evidence of external involvement became a central international dispute. Over time, denial grew more costly. Captured soldiers, equipment sightings, and later admissions in Russian public discourse eroded the plausibility of strict non-involvement. Then came 24 February 2022, when the ambiguity that had once served strategic aims became a hindrance. Open war allowed open coercion.

Show what changes when covert becomes overt. The first change is legal posture. Covert support lives in grey zones: plausible deniability, informal understandings, and carefully worded mandates. Overt involvement invites formal declarations, parliamentary debates, alliance consultations, and—crucially—clearer triggers for retaliation. A patron that remains covert can often skirt direct confrontation because the adversary cannot justify escalation to its own audiences. A patron that goes overt removes that restraint.

The second change is operational tempo. Covert support is constrained by secrecy. Weapons arrive in batches. Advisers rotate quietly. Intelligence is sanitised. Overt involvement permits scale: sustained logistics, formal basing, overt training pipelines, and public coordination. The visible metric is regularity. Supply becomes predictable. Command becomes more coherent. This can make a decisive difference in a conflict's trajectory, which is why patrons sometimes accept exposure to gain speed.

The third change is narrative control. Denial requires constant credibility management. Every photograph becomes a threat. Every death becomes a scandal. Overt involvement reframes the story: what was once "meddling" becomes "commitment"; what was once "interference" becomes "defence". This reframing does not convince everyone, but it stabilises domestic messaging. The patron can speak plainly to its own public and institutions, which can be strategically valuable even when international opinion remains divided.

These dynamics are not unique to recent wars. The Vietnam War offers a classic contrast between limited advisory involvement and overt escalation. For years, the United States expanded its advisory and support role in South Vietnam while insisting it was not fighting a war in the conventional sense. Then, after the Gulf of Tonkin incident in August 1964 and the passage of the Gulf of Tonkin Resolution, American involvement accelerated dramatically. On 8 March 1965, US Marines landed at Da Nang. The mask did not merely slip; it was discarded. Denial had become implausible, and half-measures had become insufficient for the aims Washington had adopted.

Name the underlying bargaining shift. In both Ukraine and Vietnam, the patron's objectives grew larger than covert tools could reliably deliver. Covert support can sustain a proxy, destabilise an adversary, or keep options open. It struggles to impose a decisive political outcome against determined resistance. When a patron decides it must either win or avoid humiliation, overt action becomes tempting.

Explain the implication. This is where proxy war stops being a way to manage risk and becomes a way to invite it. Overt involvement clarifies stakes. It also clarifies targets. The adversary no longer needs to guess who is responsible. Escalation ladders shorten.

Yet not every exposure leads to overt ownership. Here lies the credible limitation. Some patrons remain formally deniable even when their role is widely understood, because the benefits of continued ambiguity still exceed the costs of admission. Iran's long-term relationship with Hezbollah, for example, has been widely reported and analysed for decades, and yet the relationship retains a degree of official vagueness that serves both sides.

Full overt ownership would invite clearer legal and military consequences. Partial ambiguity preserves room to manoeuvre.

Reconciling this limitation makes the threshold clearer. Going overt is not about being "found out" in some absolute sense. It is about the *marginal* value of secrecy. When ambiguity still dampens retaliation, protects alliances, or limits domestic scrutiny, patrons cling to it—even if most informed observers are not fooled. When ambiguity ceases to dampen anything, and instead becomes a source of ridicule or constraint, patrons pivot.

That pivot often begins with a semi-overt phase. Patrons test how much they can admit without triggering backlash. They move from denial to euphemism: "advisers", "volunteers", "limited support", "technical assistance". They allow controlled leaks that normalise involvement. They use official visits and photo opportunities to signal commitment while maintaining some legal distance. The behaviour is incremental disclosure, calibrated to domestic tolerance.

At times, the pivot is forced by a specific shock: a captured operative, a leaked document, a dramatic battlefield loss that cannot be explained away. A proxy collapses. A rival escalates. A humanitarian catastrophe becomes politically intolerable. In such moments, the patron faces an awkward choice between admitting what it has been doing or accepting that its previous denials will be exposed as fiction. Some choose admission to salvage credibility. Others double down and accept the reputational hit.

Credibility is not moral; it is strategic. A patron whose denials become laughable loses influence with allies and clients alike. Allies doubt its judgment. Clients doubt its staying power. Adversaries doubt its red lines. When denial damages credibility more than admission would, going overt becomes a form of reputation management.

There is also a subtler reason patrons sometimes embrace publicity after years of denial: bargaining power at the negotiating table. Covert patrons can exert influence, but they often struggle to claim formal seats in negotiations without exposing themselves. Overt patrons can demand seats, shape ceasefire terms, and lock in arrangements. Visibility becomes leverage. This is one reason why some interventions, once openly acknowledged, quickly develop diplomatic tracks that were previously unavailable.

The motif worth holding onto is the mask. It is worn for protection. It is removed for authority. Keeping it on too long can make a patron look weak; removing it too early can make a patron look reckless. The problem is that the battlefield does not wait for a tidy moment to decide.

What does this mean for proxy wars as a broader phenomenon? It means that deniability is never a permanent condition; it is a phase. Support pipelines, intelligence sharing, advisers, and influence campaigns create footprints. Technology and investigation make footprints easier to see. Domestic politics makes them harder to justify. Eventually, patrons confront a choice: retreat into smaller, safer forms of support, or step into overt ownership.

The forward test is the one patrons prefer not to ask aloud. If the proxy fails—or succeeds too messily—will the patron still be able to keep its mask on? Or has it built a relationship and a footprint so deep that, when the moment comes, overt alliance will be the only way to keep control of the story and the war at once?

Chapter 5

Narratives And Political Cover

On 11 September 2001, while smoke still rose from lower Manhattan, political language began to harden into categories that would govern wars for decades. Words were chosen quickly and then repeated until they felt inevitable. Allies were named. Enemies were labelled. Actions taken far from home were framed as necessities at home. In the months that followed, support for armed groups abroad was not presented as intervention but as defence, not as choice but as obligation. The battles that mattered first were not fought in mountains or cities, but in speeches, headlines, and legislative chambers.

Wars need stories before they need soldiers.

Proxy warfare, more than any other form of conflict, depends on narrative cover. Because the violence is indirect, the justification must be direct. Leaders must explain why money, weapons, and intelligence are flowing to distant actors whose names most citizens cannot pronounce and whose motives are often opaque. Or they must succeed in ensuring that no explanation is required at all. This chapter sits at the heart of that task. It examines how states construct the political shelter that allows proxy wars to continue without collapsing under domestic or international scrutiny.

The paradox is simple and enduring. Proxy wars are meant to be quiet. Democracies are not. Modern states operate under constant observation, not only from rivals and journalists but from their own citizens. The more governments rely on indirect force, the more they must master indirect persuasion. Narrative becomes infrastructure. Without it, the pipeline fails.

The need for justification does not arise only in open societies. Authoritarian regimes also curate narratives, though they do so with different tools and fewer constraints. They appeal to sovereignty, historical grievance, or civilisational threat. They suppress competing accounts and punish dissent. Yet even here, narrative matters. Elites must be reassured. Security services must be aligned. The public must be kept passive or mobilised. No state is free from the politics of explanation.

This chapter begins where those explanations usually start: at home. Leaders rarely describe proxy support in blunt terms. They do not speak of arming militias or shaping foreign conflicts. They speak instead of humanitarian concern, counterterrorism, stability, alliance credibility. These frames are not chosen at random. Each connects an external action to an internal value. Each offers citizens a reason to care without asking them to look too closely. Over time, these frames become familiar enough to pass unchallenged, until an event forces a reckoning.

Returning fighters, leaked documents, or a single catastrophic failure can collapse years of careful understatement. What had been peripheral suddenly becomes personal. What had been secret becomes news. Governments then scramble to reconcile the story they told with the reality now visible. Some succeed by narrowing admissions and widening distractions. Others fail and are forced into abrupt reversals that reshape policy and politics alike.

Narrative cover does not stop at national borders. International law and norms provide a second layer of protection, one that is deliberately ambiguous. Concepts such as sovereignty, self-defence, and non-intervention are invoked with confidence and interpreted with flexibility. The same act—supplying weapons, sharing intelligence, training fighters—can be described as lawful assistance by one patron and unlawful aggression by another. This is not hypocrisy so much as strategy. Legal language becomes another arena of proxy conflict, a place where states contest legitimacy rather than territory.

What matters here is not which interpretation is correct in some abstract sense, but how ambiguity is used. States exploit the gaps between law as written and law as enforced. They rely on precedent selectively. They argue urgency when it suits them and restraint when it does not. International institutions become stages on which these arguments are rehearsed, not courts in which they are resolved. For proxy wars, this grey zone is not a flaw in the system. It is the system.

Language also determines who may be supported at all. The labels attached to armed groups—*freedom fighters*, *rebels*, *terrorists*—carry material consequences. They shape access to funding, weapons, training, and diplomatic recognition. They influence which banks will process transactions and which media outlets will grant interviews. These labels are not fixed. They shift with alliances, with battlefield behaviour, and with political convenience. A group can move from pariah to partner without changing its core identity, simply because its utility has changed.

Patrons understand this and work to fix labels early. They lobby international organisations. They brief journalists. They frame violence in ways that align with existing moral categories. Once a designation hardens, it becomes difficult to reverse, which is why so much effort is invested before it does. For proxies, narrative alignment can be as valuable as military success. A group that wins battles but loses its label may find itself isolated and unsustainable.

The fragility of narrative cover is most apparent during scandals. Covert programmes are exposed not only by enemies but by insiders: whistleblowers, disillusioned officials, or rival factions. Journalists follow money trails and weapon serial numbers. Parliamentary committees demand answers. At such moments, governments face a familiar set of choices. They can deny broadly and risk later humiliation. They can admit narrowly and sacrifice a programme or an individual. Or they can reframe the entire activity as an unfortunate necessity carried out with the best intentions.

The techniques recur with striking regularity. Blame is shifted to implementation rather than intent. Oversight failures are acknowledged while strategic goals are defended. Investigations are launched with mandates carefully drawn to protect core decisions. The aim is not to persuade everyone, but to persuade enough people, for long enough, to preserve freedom of action. Proxy wars survive not because scandals are avoided, but because they are managed.

Oversight bodies occupy an uneasy position in this process. Legislatures, parliaments, and congressional committees are charged with scrutinising activities that are deliberately hidden from public view. They rely on classified briefings, selective disclosures, and informal understandings. Some assert themselves aggressively, constraining executive action and forcing changes in behaviour. Others defer, citing national security or institutional trust. The difference between these approaches has lasting consequences. Where oversight is weak, proxy programmes proliferate and metastasise. Where it is strong, they tend to be fewer, more tightly controlled, and more politically resilient.

This chapter does not argue that narratives are mere deception. They are also how societies make sense of force. Citizens need stories to evaluate risk, morality, and interest. The problem arises when stories become substitutes for accountability rather than gateways to it. Proxy wars are especially prone to this substitution because their very design seeks to separate cause from effect, action from responsibility.

A quiet motif runs through what follows: the courtroom. Not the formal courtroom of judges and verdicts, but the permanent trial of public opinion in which states prosecute their case for intervention and defend themselves against charges of complicity and excess. Evidence is partial. Jurors are distracted. Proceedings never end. In this courtroom, narrative skill can outweigh factual precision, and timing can matter more than truth.

The urgency of this subject is difficult to overstate. As military tools become more deniable and information environments more saturated, the temptation to govern by narrative grows stronger. States that cannot justify direct war increasingly justify indirect war instead. Citizens who would reject invasion are persuaded to accept assistance. Legal systems designed to restrain force are repurposed to explain it. The result is a world in which violence persists not because it is openly embraced, but because it is continuously narrated.

The pages ahead will unpack these mechanisms in detail. They will show how leaders talk their way into proxy wars and how they talk their way out of trouble when those wars become inconvenient. They will examine the legal arguments that travel alongside weapons and the labels that determine who may be armed at all. They will trace the lifecycle of scandals and the limits of oversight. Above all, they will reveal how political cover is built, maintained, and sometimes stripped away.

The question that lingers, and that this chapter will not resolve too easily, is whether democratic accountability can survive a century of deniable war. When force is indirect and stories are carefully curated, where does responsibility finally land? The answer matters, because in proxy wars, the first casualty is often clarity—and without clarity, restraint rarely follows.

Justifying intervention to home audiences

On 12 January 2002 in Islamabad, President Pervez Musharraf appeared on national television and announced a ban on several militant organisations, including Lashkar-e-Taiba and Jaish-e-Mohammed. He spoke in the language of discipline and national interest, insisting that Pakistan would not allow "terrorism" to be carried out in its name. The speech was framed as a sovereign correction. Yet it also functioned as an admission, however carefully phrased: a recognition that forces long treated as strategic instruments had become a domestic liability. Fighters once celebrated as auxiliaries for conflicts beyond the border were now part of the security problem within it.

The reckoning had come home.

For years, the public story had been simpler. Support for militant causes could be presented as moral solidarity, strategic necessity, or not presented at all. When those causes produced blowback—violence, polarisation, international pressure—the state needed a new story, one that preserved strategic flexibility while claiming domestic authority. Musharraf's speech marked one moment in a longer process: the moment when proxy relationships, previously kept at arm's length in public discourse, became impossible to ignore because the people shaped by those relationships began to circulate back into the patron's own society.

The script always runs first.

States do not wage proxy wars only in foreign valleys and ruined cities. They wage them in front of their own audiences. That audience may be voters, party cadres, security elites, business interests, or a mixture of all three. The proxy itself can be effective, the weapons pipeline efficient, the intelligence clean—and still the project fails if it cannot be narrated at home. Domestic justification is not window dressing. It is operational enabling. It determines budgets, legal cover, elite cohesion, and the tolerance of scandal.

In democracies, justification is often overt and rhetorical. In authoritarian systems, justification may be quieter, conveyed through controlled media, selective repression, and elite bargains. Yet both face the same problem: proxy warfare creates a moral and political gap between what a state does and what it says it is. Leaders must close that gap or learn to live with it. Most try to close it.

They do so with frames that sound familiar because they have been rehearsed for decades. Humanitarian concern offers the gentlest cover. It allows leaders to claim they are supporting "the people" rather than a faction, alleviating suffering rather than shaping power. Counterterrorism offers the hardest cover. It turns proxy support into self-defence, making scepticism appear naïve or dangerous. Alliance obligations offer the most institutional cover. They present indirect war as responsible membership in an international order, a form of burden-sharing rather than adventurism.

Each frame solves one domestic problem while creating another. Humanitarian rhetoric demands moral consistency, which proxy wars rarely deliver. Counterterrorism rhetoric tends to expand targets and timelines until "limited" commitments become open-ended. Alliance rhetoric can blunt domestic opposition, but it also imports external controversies and entangles policy with partners' agendas. These are not abstract trade-offs. They show up in parliamentary votes, budget lines, cabinet resignations, and press scandals.

Humanitarian framing works best when violence is visually legible and morally one-sided—conditions that proxy wars almost never satisfy. It begins with images: a bombed hospital, a line of refugees, a child pulled from rubble. Leaders describe support as *protection* rather than intervention. Weapons become "defensive". Training becomes "capacity-building". Intelligence becomes "situational awareness". The behaviour that accompanies this rhetoric is careful calibration: assistance designed to look like aid even when it has tactical effect.

A patron may insist that it is merely enabling local actors to defend civilians. Yet the very act of choosing which local actor to support is a political decision with military consequences. Domestic audiences are rarely asked to follow that logic in detail. They are asked to accept the moral headline. The implication is that humanitarian frames can sustain proxy support precisely because they compress complexity into a single emotional claim: that inaction would be worse.

Counterterrorism framing is different. It thrives on proximity, even when the war is distant. The message is that threats travel. A militant group in one theatre is treated as a node in a network that reaches the patron's streets. This frame is powerful because it connects foreign support to domestic safety, often bypassing traditional debates about sovereignty or imperial ambition. It is also elastic. Once a conflict is described as counterterrorism, the definition of "terrorist" becomes the policy lever: broaden the label, broaden the war.

The behaviours that mark a counterterrorism frame are operational. Target lists appear. Training programmes focus on raids and intelligence exploitation. Public messaging emphasises plots disrupted rather than territory taken. The patron's role is described as technical and defensive even when it is strategically transformative. The implication is that domestic audiences are invited to evaluate proxy war as policing rather than politics.

Alliance framing offers yet another route. Here the leader's argument is not primarily moral or fearful but institutional: we must act because our partners expect it, because stability requires it, because the credibility of commitments is itself a form of security. The behaviour is coalition-building. Parliamentary debates focus on solidarity and burden-sharing. Military support is justified as "standing with allies" rather than controlling outcomes. The implication is subtle but significant: responsibility is distributed, and with it, blame.

These frames do not operate in isolation. They are layered and switched depending on events. A proxy campaign may be sold as humanitarian in its early phase, reclassified as counterterrorism when violence becomes messy, and defended as alliance maintenance when public patience thins. The same policy can wear different domestic masks over time. This is not necessarily deception in the crude sense. It is adaptive narrative management in a political environment where no single justification can survive the full moral and strategic complexity of proxy war.

The Pakistan example shows what happens when the mask tears. For decades, Pakistani policy towards militant groups in Afghanistan and Kashmir combined state influence, tolerated mobilisation, and deniable support. The public story oscillated between moral solidarity and strategic silence. After 2001, with international pressure and domestic instability rising, the state faced a new constraint: the category of "terrorism" was being globalised, and groups once treated as assets began to look like liabilities even to sympathetic audiences. Musharraf's 12 January 2002 address, delivered in Islamabad, was a domestic pivot point. It attempted to redraw the boundary between legitimate proxy use and unacceptable blowback.

The underlying trigger was not rhetorical fatigue. It was the movement of fighters and tactics back into Pakistan's own social and security space. The state could manage deniability as long as violence remained externalised. When militants and radicalised networks became entangled with domestic sectarianism and attacks, the argument that these were "foreign policy tools" became harder to sustain. The proxy had stopped being a distant instrument and become a domestic actor. At that point, justification had to evolve into containment.

A credible limitation should be acknowledged. Not every returning fighter forces a public reckoning. Some states absorb returnees quietly through surveillance, amnesties, or informal co-optation. Some suppress discussion, keeping the story sealed. Others simply maintain enough fear and censorship that reckoning never becomes politically necessary. The absence of a public debate does not mean the absence of blowback; it may only mean the absence of permission to discuss it.

Reconciling this limitation clarifies what "home audiences" really are. They are not merely the general public. They include elites who must be kept aligned: security chiefs, party powerbrokers, major donors, influential media owners. A government can survive public scepticism if elite cohesion holds. It cannot easily survive elite fracture. Proxy narratives are therefore often written as much for insiders as for voters, signalling competence, restraint, and strategic purpose.

This insider dimension shapes how governments "hide" proxy support. Hiding is not only secrecy; it is also *segmentation*. The public receives an edited version of events. Select committees receive classified briefings. Coalition partners receive private assurances. Each audience is given a different slice of the truth, calibrated to sustain consent without provoking backlash. The behaviour is compartmentalisation: different scripts for different rooms. The implication is that accountability becomes fragmented by design.

When these compartments leak into one another, crises erupt. A leaked memo, an exposed shipment, a photographed weapon, a returning fighter arrested at an airport—these events collapse the segmentation. The government must then reconcile multiple narratives at once. It may claim that actions were limited and lawful, that oversight existed, that mistakes were isolated. It may sacrifice a programme or an individual. The goal is not to reveal everything but to restore a stable story.

This is why the framing devices of proxy war tend to be so resilient. They are not chosen because they are true in every detail. They are chosen because they are survivable. Humanitarian language survives because it appeals to empathy. Counterterrorism survives because it appeals to fear and duty. Alliance language survives because it appeals to institutional identity. Each can be defended even when evidence is messy, because each rests on a value the audience already accepts.

The motif worth carrying forward is the domestic stage. Proxy wars are performed there, continually, under shifting lighting. Leaders revise lines as scandals break and threats evolve. Proxies themselves sometimes become actors in this performance, producing propaganda or behaving in ways designed to sustain patron narratives. When they cannot, patrons quietly downgrade them, rebrand them, or abandon them. The domestic story is not merely about persuasion; it becomes a form of strategic selection.

The unresolved test is uncomfortable, and it cuts to the heart of proxy warfare's political economy. How much distance can a government maintain between the violence it sponsors and the society it governs? The more it relies on proxies, the more it must rely on stories. Yet the more it relies on stories, the more brittle its legitimacy becomes when the war's consequences—fighters, weapons, radicalised networks, moral compromise—circulate back across the border. When that circulation accelerates, the state faces a choice: double down on narrative, or confront the reality it has been narrating around.

International law, norms, and grey zones

On 27 June 1986, the International Court of Justice delivered its judgment in *Military and Paramilitary Activities in and against Nicaragua*. Sitting in The Hague, the Court found that the United States had breached international law by supporting the Contra rebels through training, financing, and logistical assistance. Washington rejected the ruling, arguing that its actions constituted collective self-defence against a hostile regime. Managua described the same conduct as unlawful aggression. One set of actions. Two legal stories. Both claimed legitimacy.

The case did not end proxy war. It clarified something more unsettling. International law could name the behaviour, but it could not compel agreement on its meaning. That gap has since become one of the most heavily trafficked spaces in global politics. States operate there deliberately. It is the grey zone.

Law is supposed to draw lines. Proxy warfare lives by smudging them.

The modern legal architecture governing force is spare and austere. The UN Charter prohibits the use of force against the territorial integrity or political independence of states, while preserving an inherent right of individual or collective self-defence. Non-intervention is elevated to a core principle. Sovereignty remains the organising concept. Yet proxy war persists because these rules regulate *overt* force more clearly than indirect influence. The law speaks loudly about invasion. It whispers about assistance.

The result is not legal chaos but legal ambiguity. That ambiguity is not accidental. It is cultivated.

The first move in any legal argument about proxy support is definitional. Is the patron using force, or merely enabling another actor's use of force? Is the supported group a legitimate representative of a people, or an unlawful armed faction? Is the assistance decisive, or marginal? Each question appears technical. Each carries political weight. The behaviour that follows is careful calibration: enough involvement to shape outcomes, not enough to trigger consensus condemnation.

Sovereignty sits at the centre of these arguments, invoked by all sides and satisfied by none. A state accused of backing proxies insists that it respects sovereignty because it has not crossed borders with its own troops. The target state insists that sovereignty has been violated because its internal political balance has been forcibly altered. Both positions have doctrinal support. Neither resolves the dispute.

Self-defence offers the most flexible justification. Article 51 of the UN Charter preserves it explicitly, and subsequent state practice has stretched it generously. Patrons argue that proxy support is a defensive measure against armed attacks, imminent threats, or hostile encirclement. The visible behaviour often includes public references to intelligence assessments, intercepted communications, or prior incidents. Rarely are these materials disclosed in full. The implication is that the legal claim rests on information the claimant controls.

In the Nicaragua case, the United States argued that its support for the Contras was a response to Nicaragua's own assistance to insurgents in El Salvador. The Court rejected this, finding that the threshold for collective self-defence had not been met and that arming and training rebels constituted unlawful intervention. The judgement drew a distinction between providing weapons and logistical support, which it deemed illegal, and mere political backing, which it did not. That distinction has haunted international law ever since, because it invites exploitation. Patrons read it as a map of what to do indirectly.

A credible limitation must be acknowledged. The Nicaragua ruling did not settle the law conclusively. The United States had withdrawn from the Court's compulsory jurisdiction, and enforcement mechanisms were weak. Subsequent conflicts have generated different interpretations, especially after the expansion of counterterrorism doctrines following 2001. Some scholars argue that the threshold for self-defence has shifted. Others insist the core principles remain intact. The disagreement itself is the point. Legal uncertainty has become a strategic asset.

Norms complicate the picture further. Even when law is indeterminate, norms exert pressure. Non-intervention, civilian protection, proportionality, and accountability shape how states justify themselves rhetorically, even when behaviour strains those ideals. Norms matter because they structure legitimacy. A patron may violate a norm quietly, but it will still speak as if the norm applies. Silence is rare. Performance is constant.

This is where the grey zone becomes operational. States learn to speak the language of law without committing to its discipline. They invoke sovereignty while eroding it. They claim self-defence while denying authorship. They condemn proxies backed by rivals while excusing their own as organic movements. The same rocket, the same rifle, the same training camp is described differently depending on the speaker.

A useful contrast can be drawn from the Syrian conflict after 2011. Various external states supported armed groups opposing the Assad government. Some described their actions as assistance to a legitimate uprising or as collective self-defence against terrorism spilling across borders. Russia and Iran described their own intervention as support for a recognised government exercising its sovereign right to request help. Western states framed that same intervention as aggression propping up repression. Each side selected a different legal hook. Each accused the other of bad faith. The battlefield outcomes did not settle the argument. They entrenched it.

The abstraction of "non-intervention" becomes tangible when paired with behaviour. Training camps located just across a border. Weapons delivered by intermediaries rather than state arsenals. Funds routed through intelligence services rather than defence ministries. Each choice is designed to preserve a claim that the patron has not intervened directly. The metric is deniability, not legality. The implication is sobering: compliance is judged by appearance as much as substance.

Counter-examples matter. There are moments when states choose clarity over ambiguity. Open alliances, treaty-based interventions, and formal invitations remove the legal fog. The 1990–91 Gulf War, authorised by the UN Security Council, stands as a case where force was justified openly and collectively. Yet such moments are rare precisely because they are constraining. Proxy war offers freedom of action at the cost of legal precision. Many leaders prefer the freedom.

Reconciling this limitation helps explain why grey zones persist even when norms harden. The law does not fail because it is weak. It fails because it is permissive under pressure. It was written to prevent wars of conquest, not to regulate wars of influence. Proxy support sits uncomfortably between those categories.

The quiet motif threading this discussion is the line that cannot be drawn cleanly. Every time a state insists that its support is lawful, it reveals where it believes the line lies. Every time a rival denounces that support, it reveals a different map. These competing cartographies coexist, overlapping without resolving. International law becomes a language for argument rather than a mechanism for closure.

Legal advisers inside governments understand this well. They do not ask whether proxy support is clearly legal. They ask whether it is *defensible.* Can a plausible case be made? Can allies be persuaded to accept it? Can institutions be delayed or divided? The answers shape policy. Law becomes part of strategy, not merely a constraint upon it.

The implication for norms is corrosive but not fatal. Repeated invocation of self-defence and humanitarian necessity risks hollowing out those concepts. Yet it also keeps them alive. A state that bothers to justify itself acknowledges that legitimacy still matters. The alternative would be brute assertion. That remains rare.

The unresolved test is stark. As proxy warfare proliferates, can international law adapt without dissolving into rhetoric? Or will the grey zone expand until the distinction between defence and aggression becomes purely positional, defined only by who speaks first and loudest? The answer will not be found in a single judgement or treaty. It will be revealed, slowly, in whether states continue to feel compelled to argue their case at all.

Labelling actors as freedom fighters or terrorists

On 23 December 2009, the United States designated Tehrik-i-Taliban Pakistan (TTP) as a Foreign Terrorist Organization. The announcement was bureaucratic in form, but it was also a boundary drawn in ink: a signal to banks, airlines, charities, donors, and allied governments about what was permissible. A few years earlier, networks overlapping with Pakistan's militant milieu had been treated by segments of the state and its sympathisers as instruments of strategic depth. By 2009, after a string of attacks inside Pakistan and growing international pressure, the label "terrorist" had become not merely a moral judgement but an operating instruction.

A label can close doors.

In proxy warfare, labels do not describe reality so much as authorise relationships with it. To call a group "freedom fighters" is to grant it potential legitimacy and access; to call it "terrorists" is to criminalise contact and make support politically toxic. The battle over labels is therefore a battle over pipelines: money, weapons, training, sanctuary, and diplomatic cover. It is also a battle over time, because labels harden into law and institutional habit, making later policy pivots expensive.

Show how quickly a label moves from speech to structure. Once a group is designated under terrorism sanctions regimes—whether by the United Nations, the United States, the European Union, or individual states—transactions become punishable, assets can be frozen, travel restricted, and associations stigmatised. Banks adopt risk-averse compliance practices that often go beyond legal requirements. Charities become cautious. Diaspora fundraising chills. Even journalists and humanitarian negotiators may face legal risk. The behaviour is visible: cancelled accounts, closed payment channels, refusal letters from insurers, and sudden reluctance among intermediaries who once operated confidently. The implication is that designation is not a headline; it is a strangling mechanism.

Now show the opposite. A group treated as legitimate can receive assistance openly: training missions, public visits, aid packages, and arms deliveries justified as support for "partners". The media treats its statements as political commentary rather than propaganda. Diplomats meet its representatives without scandal. The behaviour is official: press conferences, memoranda of understanding, photo opportunities. The implication is that legitimacy multiplies capacity by reducing friction.

Labels are therefore strategic instruments, not mere adjectives. Patrons know this. They invest heavily in controlling nomenclature long before the public notices. Lobbying takes place in capitals and international organisations. Briefings are given to journalists and think tanks. Reports are commissioned. The goal is not only to persuade audiences but to lock policy in place through law and institutional inertia.

The most revealing aspect of labelling is that it often changes while the group remains broadly the same.

Consider the Palestine Liberation Organization (PLO) as a checkable example of designation changing over time. In 1974, Yasser Arafat addressed the United Nations General Assembly in New York after the UN had granted the PLO observer status. In 1975, the General Assembly recognised the PLO as the representative of the Palestinian people (Resolution 3236 of 1974 is central here; the broader recognition followed in subsequent UN practice). Western governments that had treated the PLO primarily through the lens of terrorism and hijackings gradually moved towards engagement as geopolitics and diplomacy shifted, culminating in the Oslo Accords in 1993 and the mutual recognition between Israel and the PLO. The PLO did not become saintly overnight. The label changed because the strategic context changed. The implication is that designation is, at least partly, a political verdict about usefulness.

A second, more contemporary example underscores how designation shapes what patrons can do openly. In Syria, the organisation known as Jabhat al-Nusra was designated by the United States as a Foreign Terrorist Organization in December 2012 (as an alias of al-Qaeda in Iraq, later al-Qaeda's Syrian affiliate). For various external actors supporting the Syrian opposition, this designation created sharp constraints. Support had to be routed away from groups linked to Nusra to avoid legal and reputational fallout, even when Nusra-affiliated forces were militarily effective against the Assad government. The behaviour that followed was fragmentation: patrons sought "vetted" factions; factions split and rebranded; alliances shifted to maintain access to support. The implication is that a label can reshape a battlefield by reshaping funding and weapons flows.

Labelling is not only imposed by patrons. Proxies actively seek labels that widen their options. They moderate rhetoric, adjust tactics, and adopt language that aligns with patron narratives. They create political wings. They produce codes of conduct. Sometimes these shifts are substantive; often they are performative. The point is not purity. It is admissibility.

Admissibility is measured in meetings. A group learns quickly what it must do to gain access to embassies, conferences, and coalition briefings. It learns which symbols to suppress, which leaders to present, which slogans to avoid. When external patrons praise "moderation" or "responsible conduct", proxies treat those phrases as operational guidance. The implication is that labels become behavioural incentives, shaping not only how groups are perceived but how they act—at least in public.

There is a credible limitation here, and it matters. Designations can be blunt instruments. They may criminalise engagement that could be necessary for humanitarian access or ceasefire negotiation. They can also be used opportunistically, with states labelling opponents "terrorists" to justify repression or delegitimise dissent. This is not a theoretical concern. The term "terrorist" is often deployed to collapse political complexity into moral certainty, allowing patrons to avoid uncomfortable distinctions among armed actors.

Reconciling this limitation requires precision. The existence of abuse does not mean labels are meaningless. It means labels must be understood as political tools with legal consequences. A designation can reflect genuine threats and atrocities. It can also reflect rivalry and convenience. Often it reflects both at once. The task for any analyst is to ask what the label *does* in practice: which pipelines it opens, which it closes, which actors benefit, and which become stranded.

Patrons use labels to manage domestic politics as much as international ones. A government can support a "partner force" without triggering public outrage; it struggles to support a "terrorist group" without scandal. Even covert support becomes harder when a group carries a toxic label, because leaks become more damaging. The behaviour is bureaucratic. Aid agencies demand assurances. Defence ministries require legal memos. Politicians insist on distance. The implication is that labels function as political immunisation: they protect the patron from association with some actors while enabling association with others.

Labels also structure alliances. When coalition partners disagree on designations, coordination fractures. One state's "resistance movement" is another state's "terrorist organisation". This divergence can become a proxy conflict within the proxy conflict, shaping which groups receive support and which become targets. The battlefield becomes an index of diplomatic disagreement.

The quiet motif threading this section is the stamp. Once stamped, a group carries a mark that travels across borders and institutions. Removing the stamp is harder than applying it. It requires political justification, legal changes, and a public story that can withstand scrutiny. Proxies therefore pursue not only battlefield victories but reputational manoeuvres that might, one day, allow them to shed the stamp.

The stamp, however, is not permanent. History is full of rebrandings and rehabilitations, some deserved, many opportunistic. Groups change names. They splinter. They create new fronts. Patrons sometimes accept these manoeuvres because they need partners and the old labels are inconvenient. This is where ambiguity becomes policy. A patron may avoid officially endorsing a group while tacitly tolerating support through intermediaries. The label remains, but the relationship continues in shadow.

That shadow is the grey zone of narrative cover. States condemn publicly while enabling privately. They sanction one wing while courting another. They insist on "no contact" while meeting "civil society representatives" who happen to be linked to armed actors. The behaviour is compartmentalisation. The implication is deniability preserved through semantics.

The forward test is uncomfortable because it exposes a contradiction at the heart of proxy warfare. If labels can change when strategy changes, what do they mean as moral categories? Yet if labels cannot change when behaviour changes, what do they mean as tools of accountability? Patrons oscillate between these poles, sometimes insisting that designations are principled, sometimes treating them as flexible. Proxies, watching closely, learn the real lesson: on the battlefield, weapons win ground; in diplomacy, names decide who may keep it.

Managing scandals, leaks, and denials

On 3 November 1986, the Lebanese magazine *Ash-Shiraa* reported that the United States had secretly sold weapons to Iran, a country it officially treated as an adversary, and that proceeds were being diverted to support the Contra rebels in Nicaragua. The place was Beirut; the date was precise; the effect was immediate. Within weeks, President Ronald Reagan addressed the nation, denying key elements of the story before later conceding parts of it. Congressional investigations followed. Careers ended. Yet the broader strategic posture of the United States in Central America and the Middle East endured. A programme burned. A strategy survived.

Scandals are not interruptions to proxy warfare. They are part of its operating environment.

The exposure of covert support triggers a familiar choreography. First comes denial, then narrowing, then substitution. Patrons rarely abandon the underlying objective that motivated the covert programme. They abandon the specific *mechanism* that has become politically radioactive. The behaviour is not improvisational. It is rehearsed across decades and political systems.

The initial response is almost always a denial calibrated to the evidence already public. Officials contest phrasing. They deny intent rather than action, authorisation rather than awareness. The goal is temporal: buy time. The visible behaviour is semantic. "No direct support." "No knowledge of misuse." "No authorisation at senior levels." Each clause is chosen to survive later revision. The implication is that denial is less about persuasion than about positioning for the next stage.

When evidence accumulates, denial narrows. Admissions become technical. A shipment becomes a "transfer". Advisers become "trainers". Funds become "humanitarian assistance". Responsibility shifts downward. Rogue operators appear. Oversight failures replace policy choices. The behaviour is bureaucratic distancing. Memos are cited. Chains of command are emphasised. The implication is insulation: protect the political centre by sacrificing the periphery.

Blame shifting follows a predictable gradient. Contractors are blamed before officials. Officials are blamed before ministers. Ministers are blamed before heads of government. Where possible, foreign partners are implicated. Local proxies are portrayed as unreliable or deceitful. The pattern is visible in press briefings and testimony. "They exceeded their mandate." "They misled us." "They acted independently." Each statement reframes the scandal as a management problem rather than a strategic one.

Process investigations are the final stabiliser. Commissions are convened. Inspectors general are empowered. Parliamentary or congressional hearings begin. These processes perform several functions at once. They demonstrate seriousness. They absorb public attention. They create a timeline that stretches beyond the immediate crisis. The implication is delay with dignity. By the time findings are released, the political temperature has often cooled.

The Iran-Contra affair illustrates the full sequence. After initial denials, the Reagan administration acknowledged arms transfers while disputing their purpose. The Tower Commission was established in December 1986. Lieutenant Colonel Oliver North became the focal point of blame. Senior officials avoided criminal conviction. The administration's broader anti-communist posture remained intact. Support for proxies did not end; it changed form.

A second example, different in context but similar in logic, can be seen in Pakistan's experience with militancy in the post-2001 period. For years, Pakistani officials denied or minimised links between elements of the state and certain militant groups operating in Afghanistan and Kashmir. Journalistic investigations, battlefield evidence, and international pressure made blanket denial untenable. The response was selective admission paired with strategic reframing. Some groups were reclassified as threats; others were described as beyond state control. Military operations were launched against certain factions, while others were marginalised rhetorically. The behaviour was differentiation. The implication was continuity through redefinition.

Scandals matter because they threaten the core asset of proxy warfare: plausible deniability. Once deniability collapses, the costs of indirect action approach those of overt intervention. Patrons therefore treat scandal management as a form of strategic maintenance.

One abstraction dominates this terrain: credibility. Credibility is not restored by truth alone. It is restored by coherence. Audiences tolerate revelations if the story that follows appears controlled and purposeful. This is why narrow admissions are so common. They suggest mastery rather than chaos. They imply that the state still knows what it is doing.

Another abstraction is accountability. Accountability in these episodes is often symbolic. A programme is terminated. A unit is dissolved. An official resigns. The behaviour is sacrificial. The implication is containment. By offering visible consequences, the patron seeks to draw a line under the affair without revisiting the strategic logic that produced it.

There is a credible counter-example worth addressing. Sometimes scandals do force genuine retrenchment. The US Congress's passage of the Boland Amendments in the early 1980s constrained executive support for the Contras. Intelligence oversight regimes in several democracies tightened after high-profile abuses in the 1970s. Reconciling this limitation sharpens the argument rather than weakening it. Constraints emerge when scandals align with broader political fatigue or institutional rivalry. They rarely arise from exposure alone.

Most of the time, patrons adapt. They change intermediaries. They alter funding channels. They rebrand programmes. They rely more heavily on allies. The behaviour is substitution. The implication is resilience.

The quiet motif threading this section is the firebreak. When a scandal erupts, the patron's objective is to prevent the blaze from reaching the strategic core. Firebreaks are created by compartmentalisation, legal distinctions, and personnel changes. They do not extinguish the fire; they limit its spread.

Media dynamics shape how effectively firebreaks hold. Investigative journalism can puncture official narratives, but attention is finite. Patrons exploit this. They release information strategically. They cooperate just enough to avoid appearing obstructive. They allow certain details to dominate coverage while others fade. The behaviour is agenda setting. The implication is that scandal management is as much about information control as policy adjustment.

Leaks complicate this calculus. Whistleblowers bypass official sequencing. They release documents that collapse ambiguity. The response is often legalistic. Leakers are prosecuted. Motives are questioned. National security is invoked. The implication is deterrence: discourage future leaks even if the immediate damage is done.

Battlefield discoveries present a different challenge. Captured weapons, dead advisers, or intercepted communications can make denial impossible. In such cases, patrons sometimes pivot faster to partial acknowledgement, reframing exposure as necessity. "Circumstances changed." "We responded to events." The implication is inevitability: the patron was compelled, not reckless.

The decision to sacrifice a programme is often calculated. Programmes are chosen for termination based on visibility, not importance. Those easiest to explain away are cut first. Others continue under different guises. This triage reflects a hard truth: in proxy warfare, mechanisms are disposable; objectives are not.

The unresolved tension lies in oversight. Democracies pride themselves on transparency and accountability, yet proxy warfare depends on secrecy and discretion. Scandals expose this contradiction but rarely resolve it. Each episode produces reforms calibrated to the last failure, not the next one.

The forward test is uncomfortable. As investigative tools improve and information travels faster, can patrons continue to rely on the old choreography of denial, narrowing, and substitution? Or will the cost of scandal eventually outweigh the benefits of indirect action? History suggests adaptation rather than abandonment. But adaptation itself leaves traces. The next leak will test whether the firebreaks still hold.

Parliamentary, *congressional*, and public oversight

On 27 January 1975, the United States Senate voted to establish the Select Committee to Study Governmental Operations with Respect to Intelligence Activities, soon known simply as the Church Committee. Its chair was Senator Frank Church. Its location was Washington, DC. Its mandate was sweeping. Within a year, the committee's hearings exposed decades of covert action, surveillance, and proxy relationships that had unfolded with minimal legislative scrutiny. Some programmes were terminated.

New reporting requirements were imposed. The intelligence community was reshaped.

Oversight intervened. But only after damage accrued.

That sequence captures the core dilemma. Oversight bodies almost always arrive late. Proxy warfare thrives in the space between what executives know and what legislatures are permitted to see. The gap is structural, not accidental.

Five words matter here: secrecy resists democratic timing.

Legislatures are asked to supervise activities designed to remain hidden. The visible behaviour of oversight therefore centres on process rather than substance: classified briefings, restricted hearings, redacted documents, and informal assurances. The implication is asymmetry. Executives control information flow. Legislators react within it.

Classified briefings are the most common instrument. Ministers or officials appear before select committees, outline objectives, and summarise activities. Questions are asked. Answers are partial. Notes are limited. Members are bound by secrecy. The behaviour is ritualised disclosure. The implication is containment: information is shared, but only within a narrow channel that limits political spillover.

Reporting requirements attempt to formalise this exchange. In the United States, the Intelligence Oversight Act of 1980 required the executive to keep congressional intelligence committees "fully and currently informed" of covert actions. The phrase is elastic. What counts as "fully"? When does "currently" begin? These ambiguities are not drafting errors. They are design features that preserve executive discretion.

The contrast between legislatures that constrain and those that defer is instructive. After the Church Committee, the US Congress imposed significant checks. Covert action findings required presidential authorisation. Budgetary oversight expanded. The House and Senate intelligence committees gained permanence. The behaviour was institutionalisation. The implication was friction: covert programmes became harder to launch and easier to contest.

Compare this with the United Kingdom's approach during much of the late twentieth century. Parliamentary oversight of intelligence was informal and deferential. Ministers briefed party leaders privately. Committees lacked statutory authority. During the Northern Ireland conflict, support to local forces and auxiliary units operated largely within executive control. The behaviour was trust-based oversight. The implication was latitude: the executive retained wide room to manoeuvre.

This is not a claim about virtue or vice. It is a claim about structure. Legislatures that invest in expertise, continuity, and enforcement tools can constrain proxy activity. Those that rely on convention and discretion tend to defer.

Oversight effectiveness correlates with three measurable factors. First, access to information. Committees with independent staff and subpoena power see more. Second, continuity of membership. Legislators who serve long enough to recognise patterns ask better questions. Third, political incentives. Oversight tightens when opposition parties see advantage in exposure.

Public oversight operates differently. Voters do not read classified annexes. They respond to narratives. Casualty figures, financial costs, and moral framing shape opinion. The behaviour is episodic attention. The implication is volatility: public pressure spikes after scandals and dissipates quickly.

Executives understand this rhythm. They often time disclosures to minimise impact. Bad news is released late on Fridays. Reports are buried in technical language. The goal is not persuasion but exhaustion.

A credible counter-example complicates the picture. In some parliamentary systems, coalition politics amplify oversight. Smaller parties extract concessions in exchange for support. Germany's Bundestag, for instance, has exercised comparatively robust control over foreign deployments and intelligence cooperation since the Cold War. Reconciling this does not negate the argument. It refines it. Oversight strengthens when political fragmentation raises the price of secrecy.

Informal understandings are the least visible but often most decisive element. Senior legislators are briefed privately and agree not to press too hard. The behaviour is tacit bargaining. The implication is mutual protection: executives avoid embarrassment; legislators avoid responsibility for outcomes they cannot control.

Proxy warfare exploits these understandings. Support programmes are framed as limited, technical, or temporary. Legislators are reassured that risks are contained. Metrics are chosen carefully. "No boots on the ground." "No direct combat role." Each phrase narrows perceived accountability.

The quiet motif running through oversight is the blindfold. Not ignorance, but partial sight. Legislatures see enough to claim involvement but not enough to direct outcomes. The blindfold slips during crises. Then it is tightened again.

Comparing constrained and deferential systems reveals trade-offs. Strong oversight can slow decision-making and expose programmes prematurely. Weak oversight can enable drift, escalation, and moral hazard. Neither guarantees good outcomes. But the distribution of risk differs. In constrained systems, executives bear more political risk. In deferential ones, the risk shifts outward to proxies and civilians.

The implication for proxy warfare is sobering. As long as oversight relies on secrecy-bound processes, executives will retain the upper hand. Reforms tend to address yesterday's failures. New techniques emerge. Old habits return.

The unresolved test is whether oversight can adapt to the pace and opacity of modern proxy support. Cyber operations, deniable logistics, and transnational financing further complicate supervision. Can legislatures develop tools that match this complexity without becoming adjuncts of the executive? Or will oversight remain reactive, arriving only after programmes collapse into scandal?

The answer will shape not only how proxy wars are fought, but how democracies understand their own limits.

Chapter 6

Economics, Sanctions and Cost Imposition

In the spring of 2014, a small group of officials gathered around a spreadsheet that looked reassuringly modest. The figures represented a foreign support programme—training here, equipment there, some intelligence hours absorbed quietly into existing budgets. The numbers were low enough to pass unnoticed through parliamentary committees and newspaper columns alike. No divisions deployed. No flags raised. The conflict in question barely registered in opinion polls. By the end of the decade, however, that same programme had become synonymous with diplomatic isolation, sanctions retaliation, and a reputation for recklessness that proved far more expensive than the original outlay. The balance sheet had lied.

Proxy wars are often justified as bargains. They promise influence at a discount, leverage without liability, pressure without pain. Leaders speak of *cost-effective engagement*, of doing more with less, of avoiding the ruinous bills that accompany conventional war. Yet the economics of proxy conflict rarely obey these tidy assumptions. Costs do not disappear; they migrate. They surface later, in unfamiliar forms, and often in places far removed from the original battlefield.

This chapter begins from a simple but uncomfortable observation. States are not nearly as good at counting the costs of proxy warfare as they believe. They are adept at measuring expenditure—how much money flows out, how many weapons are shipped, how many advisers are deployed. They are far less comfortable accounting for political capital burned, alliances strained, reputations corroded, and adversaries emboldened. The apparent cheapness of proxy war is one of its most dangerous illusions.

The first task, then, is to disaggregate what "cost" actually means. Proxy conflicts draw on multiple currencies at once. Cash is the most visible, but often the least consequential. Equipment can be replaced; intelligence hours can be reallocated; even losses among proxy forces can be framed as tragic but distant. Political capital is different. Once spent, it is difficult to recover. A single exposed programme can poison relations with neutral states, energise domestic opposition, or harden an adversary's resolve. The paradox is that programmes designed to minimise exposure often maximise reputational vulnerability when they fail.

From this accounting problem flows a second, more strategic one. Proxy wars are not always fought to win. Frequently, they are designed to *impose costs*—to distract rivals, drain their resources, and force them into uncomfortable choices. A limited investment in one theatre can compel an adversary to commit troops, money, and attention far beyond the initial trigger. The logic is familiar from Cold War contests, but it has not lost its appeal. In an interconnected global system, distraction itself becomes a weapon.

Yet cost imposition is not a neutral act. It invites retaliation, often in asymmetric forms. A rival drained in one arena may respond elsewhere: through cyber operations, economic pressure, or its own proxy networks. What appears as a clever diversion can metastasise into a wider competition that neither side fully controls. The economics of proxy warfare are therefore relational. They cannot be understood in isolation from the opponent's balance sheet, patience, and appetite for risk.

Sanctions complicate this picture further. Once treated as a separate instrument of statecraft, economic sanctions have become deeply entangled with proxy strategies. They are used to weaken rival patrons, restrict access to finance and technology, and signal resolve to domestic and international audiences. At the same time, sanctions create incentives for adaptation. They encourage smuggling networks, alternative currencies, and new alliances. In proxy contexts, they often harden the very actors they are meant to constrain.

The interaction between sanctions and proxy warfare produces a distinctive form of economic conflict. Patrons seek to starve their adversaries' clients while keeping their own proxies solvent. They tighten controls on banks and exports while quietly facilitating workarounds for favoured groups. The result is a layered economy of enforcement and evasion, where legality and illegality blur. Understanding this ecosystem requires more than moral judgement. It demands attention to incentives, loopholes, and unintended consequences.

Money, however, does not always flow from treasuries. Diaspora communities, private donors, charities, and illicit trades form a dense financial undergrowth beneath official policy. These streams are harder to monitor and easier to deny. They also reshape accountability. A proxy funded primarily by a state budget answers, at least in theory, to state priorities. One sustained by private donations or smuggling answers to different pressures. Shifts in funding sources can transform a group's behaviour, ideology, and relationship with its patron.

This chapter treats these financial ecosystems not as side effects but as central features of proxy warfare. Who pays matters as much as how much is paid. The provenance of funds shapes discipline, loyalty, and strategic alignment. Patrons who lose sight of this often discover too late that their proxies have acquired independent means—and independent agendas.

All of this raises a final, uncomfortable question. How should success be measured? Battlefield outcomes offer one set of metrics, but they are often misleading. A proxy may win tactically while undermining broader strategic goals. Conversely, a campaign that achieves little on the ground may yield valuable intelligence, access, or alliance cohesion. States frequently declare success in public while privately acknowledging failure—or vice versa. The gap between these assessments reveals much about how proxy wars are valued.

This chapter does not offer a formula for perfect calculation. No such formula exists. Instead, it proposes ways of thinking more honestly about return on strategic investment. It asks readers to consider not only what was gained, but what was foregone; not only what was spent, but what was risked. It treats proxy warfare as an economic activity in the fullest sense: one that reallocates resources, redistributes risk, and reshapes incentives across borders.

The stakes of this analysis extend well beyond any single conflict. As military technologies become cheaper and financial networks more opaque, the temptation to fight by proxy grows stronger. The tools appear affordable. The entry barriers are low. The exits, however, are rarely cheap. Costs accumulate quietly, then suddenly.

By the end of this chapter, the reader will be equipped to look at a proxy conflict and ask sharper questions. Who is really paying? In what currency? For how long? And to whose benefit? These questions do not yield comforting answers, but they do offer clarity. In a century defined by indirect conflict, clarity is already a form of power.

Counting costs for patrons and clients

In March 2011, as the uprising in Libya slid into armed conflict, officials in Paris and London argued that supporting local forces would spare them the expense and risk of a ground war. The intervention would rely on air power, intelligence sharing, and local fighters. Muammar Gaddafi fell in October. The cash outlay looked modest compared with Iraq or Afghanistan. Yet by 2015, Libya had become a byword for state collapse, arms proliferation, and regional instability. The reputational cost—particularly for France and the United Kingdom—proved far higher than the initial balance sheet suggested.

Cheap wars are rarely cheap.

Proxy warfare sells itself on arithmetic. Fewer troops deployed means fewer salaries, fewer pensions, fewer body bags. Equipment transfers are booked as aid. Intelligence time is absorbed into existing agencies. Politicians speak of *limited exposure*. The visible behaviour is substitution: local fighters replace regular forces. The implication is savings. That implication deserves scrutiny.

The real cost structure of proxy war is layered. Money is only the first line item, and often the smallest. Patrons fund training programmes, stipends, weapons, logistics, and intelligence support. These expenses are tangible and, in principle, controllable. They are also easy to underestimate because they are dispersed across departments and fiscal years. A few million here. A quiet appropriation there. Individually trivial, cumulatively significant.

Consider intelligence time. Satellites do not fly for free. Analysts do not work in isolation. Every hour spent tracking a proxy's battlefield is an hour not spent elsewhere. The behaviour is prioritisation. The metric is opportunity cost. The implication is that proxy wars crowd out other intelligence tasks, even when cash expenditure appears low.

Equipment costs behave similarly. Older weapons are often shipped to proxies under the assumption that they are surplus. They are not costless. They require refurbishment, transport, and replacement in donor inventories. The United States Government Accountability Office has repeatedly noted in reports on security assistance programmes that replacement and sustainment costs often exceed the initial transfer values (GAO, various years). The savings are illusory.

Then there is political capital. This is the cost most often ignored because it resists quantification. Political capital is spent when allies are pressured to acquiesce, when neutral states are alienated, and when domestic trust erodes after exposure. Unlike money, political capital does not sit in reserve accounts. It accumulates slowly and evaporates quickly.

The Libyan case illustrates this imbalance. NATO members avoided a costly occupation, but the aftermath damaged their credibility. Critics argued that the intervention created a vacuum exploited by militias and traffickers. Russia and China cited Libya repeatedly in subsequent debates over Syria, using it to justify vetoes at the UN Security Council. The behaviour was reputational spillover. The implication was constraint: future interventions became harder to legitimise.

From the patron's perspective, the contrast with deploying regular forces is stark. Conventional wars impose immediate, visible costs: defence budgets spike, casualties mount, voters react. Proxy wars defer and diffuse costs. That deferral is politically attractive. It is also dangerous. Deferred costs compound.

Clients face a different calculus. For them, proxy war costs are existential. Fighters are drawn from communities. Casualties are personal. Infrastructure is destroyed locally. Even when patrons provide funding, clients absorb the human and social toll. The behaviour is risk concentration. The implication is dependency: clients accept unfavourable terms because the alternative is annihilation.

This asymmetry shapes bargaining. Patrons can exit. Clients often cannot. The cost structure reinforces control—until it does not. When clients believe they are bearing disproportionate costs, resentment grows. That resentment has strategic consequences explored elsewhere in this book.

A credible counter-example complicates the argument. In some cases, proxy warfare has delivered durable influence at relatively low cost. The United States' support for certain Kurdish forces against the so-called Islamic State in Iraq and Syria between 2014 and 2019 involved limited troop deployments and modest financial outlays compared with earlier campaigns. The territorial defeat of the group reduced immediate threats. Reconciling this does not invalidate the cost critique. It refines it. Success depended on narrowly defined objectives, time-bound engagement, and a clear exit strategy. Where those conditions erode, costs escalate.

Risk is another currency. Proxy wars reallocate risk rather than eliminate it. Patrons shift battlefield risk to clients. They retain escalation risk. When a proxy commits abuses or suffers defeat, patrons face reputational and strategic blowback without direct control. The behaviour is risk transfer. The implication is volatility.

The balance-sheet motif runs quietly through these dynamics. Proxy wars look profitable because liabilities are hidden. When they surface, they do so unevenly. A leaked programme here. A parliamentary inquiry there. Each revelation forces a reassessment of costs that were never formally booked.

Measuring reputational damage is difficult but not impossible. Indicators include shifts in alliance behaviour, voting patterns in international organisations, and domestic approval ratings. After Libya, surveys and elite commentary in Europe reflected growing scepticism about interventionism. That scepticism constrained later policy choices. The cost was strategic flexibility.

Another example underscores the point without precise figures. Pakistan's support for various militant groups during the late twentieth and early twenty-first centuries involved limited direct expenditure. The reputational consequences, however, included strained relations with the United States, periodic sanctions, and persistent suspicion from neighbours. The behaviour was denial coupled with partial cooperation. The implication was chronic distrust.

What of the claim that proxy wars save lives? They may reduce casualties among patron forces. They rarely reduce overall violence. Civilian harm often increases as accountability weakens. That harm feeds back into political costs through media coverage and legal scrutiny. The International Committee of the Red Cross and multiple UN reports have documented higher civilian exposure in fragmented conflicts. Cite those reports, and the abstraction dissolves into data.

Five words matter here: costs migrate, they accumulate.

For clients, the cost ledger includes moral injury and long-term instability. Fighters demobilised after proxy wars often struggle to reintegrate. Weapons circulate. Economies warp around conflict. Patrons may withdraw, but the bill remains. This imbalance fuels narratives of betrayal that echo for decades.

None of this implies that proxy warfare is always irrational. It does imply that the usual comparisons—proxy war versus conventional war—are misleading. The relevant comparison is between proxy war now and proxy war later, after deferred costs mature.

The unresolved tension is whether states can learn to price these conflicts honestly. Can political systems internalise reputational and opportunity costs before they explode into crisis? Or will proxy wars continue to be justified by narrow fiscal comparisons that ignore their wider balance sheet?

The answer lies not in better spreadsheets alone, but in a willingness to treat political capital as finite and fragile. Until then, proxy wars will continue to look cheap—right up to the moment they are not.

Cost imposition and distraction strategies

On 3 July 1979, President Jimmy Carter signed a presidential finding authorising covert assistance to Afghan opponents of the Soviet-backed government in Kabul. The place was Washington, DC; the organisation that would later administer much of the programme was the CIA; the conflict's centre of gravity soon became Afghanistan. By December 1979, the Soviet Union had intervened directly. Over the next decade it committed roughly 115,000 troops at peak presence and poured resources into a war it did not plan to make its defining quagmire. The initial American investment was small by superpower standards. The Soviet bill was not.

A secondary theatre can become primary.

Proxy wars are often discussed as contests for victory: a patron backs a client to seize a capital, defend a regime, or expel an occupier. Yet many proxy campaigns are not designed to *win* so much as to *cost*. Their aim is to impose burdens on an adversary—financial, political, military, and psychological—until the rival's strategic posture bends elsewhere. The battlefield becomes a lever, not a destination.

This is not a cynical footnote to grand strategy. It is, in many cases, the strategy.

Cost imposition operates on a simple principle. If you cannot defeat a stronger rival directly, you can force it to spend. You can make it deploy troops to protect a flank. You can make it devote intelligence assets to a secondary problem. You can make it absorb casualties that erode domestic support. You can make it divert funds from modernisation to counterinsurgency. Each of these behaviours is measurable. Each alters the rival's options.

The Afghan case shows the core mechanics in a way that has become emblematic. Before Soviet tanks rolled, the costs were not yet high. After the intervention, Moscow faced a choice it could not avoid: either commit enough to stabilise its client or accept humiliation. That is the moment cost imposition seeks. It is not enough to irritate an adversary; the aim is to trap it in a commitment. Once trapped, the adversary pays to avoid losing, and then pays again to manage the consequences of paying.

Five words belong here: make them chase, then bleed.

The decision to intervene is often driven by reputation. Great powers fear that abandoning a client will signal weakness. Cost-imposing patrons exploit that fear by raising the stakes just enough to compel action. In Afghanistan, the Soviet leadership believed a hostile outcome on its southern border would be intolerable. Once intervention began, the war's logic shifted from geopolitics to inertia. Withdrawal became a political and ideological problem. The longer the war continued, the more costly it became to admit that it had been a mistake.

Name the concept. This is overextension, engineered through a proxy theatre. Explain why proxy support is suited to it. It allows a patron to invest relatively small amounts—arms, training, safe havens, intelligence—while forcing the adversary to respond with expensive deployments, logistics, and long-term occupation. The implication is asymmetry. A dollar of proxy support can compel multiple dollars of counter-measures.

The most effective cost-imposition strategies target a rival's vulnerabilities. For a state dependent on conscript forces, casualties erode legitimacy. For a state with fragile alliances, distraction creates fractures. For a state reliant on high-tech modernisation, prolonged irregular conflict drains funds into maintenance and manpower. The behaviour is diagnostic: patrons choose proxy theatres where the adversary's weaknesses are likely to surface.

Yet cost imposition is not only material. It is cognitive. Rivals forced to manage a messy theatre experience strategic distraction. Senior leaders spend time on briefings rather than reforms. Intelligence agencies shift focus. Military planning cycles tighten around a persistent nuisance. The metric is attention allocation: budgets, leadership travel, diplomatic bandwidth. The implication is opportunity loss. Even if the adversary "wins" in the proxy theatre, it may lose elsewhere through neglect.

This logic is visible in more recent examples. In the 1980s, the Soviet Union's Afghan war consumed attention during a period when the country faced economic stagnation and political strain. Analysts disagree on the war's precise contribution to Soviet collapse, and that disagreement is itself instructive. Cost imposition rarely produces a single decisive collapse. It produces erosion.

A second checkable example shows the strategy in a different setting: the Iran–Iraq War (1980–1988). External actors supported both sides at different moments for reasons that included balancing and cost imposition. Iraq's invasion in September 1980 initiated a conflict that drained two regional powers for eight years. Gulf states provided significant financial support to Iraq; various channels supplied arms to both sides. The war's outcome was essentially a bloody stalemate, but its strategic effect was clear: both states emerged weakened and indebted, altering the regional balance. The behaviour was sustained financing and arms flows. The implication was mutual exhaustion, which benefited other regional actors by reducing immediate threats.

Cost imposition can also be pursued through *distraction by proliferation*. Multiple small proxy theatres can force an adversary to disperse resources, creating a strategic whack-a-mole. The behaviour is diffusion: the rival establishes advisory missions, bases, and surveillance in multiple locations. The implication is thinning. Forces and funds are spread, and response times lengthen.

A credible limitation must be taken seriously. Cost imposition often works best in hindsight. Patrons can misjudge an adversary's tolerance. They can underestimate how cheaply a rival can absorb pain, especially if the rival's regime structure suppresses dissent. They can also trigger escalatory responses that impose costs on themselves. Afghanistan did not only cost the Soviets; it contributed to long-term instability, radicalisation, and blowback that affected many states, including those that helped build the proxy capacity.

Reconciling this limitation clarifies the risk. Cost imposition is not cost-free. The patron is not merely an accountant of the rival's losses; it is also a participant in a system that produces second- and third-order effects. Weapons leak. Networks persist. Refugees move. Ideologies harden. The patron may achieve its immediate aim while creating a longer-term security problem.

This is why the concept of "limited investment" must be handled with care. Limited *budget* does not mean limited *liability*. A patron can spend little cash and still generate large downstream costs. The behaviour of proxy conflicts is not linear. Small inputs can produce large, unpredictable outputs.

Cost-imposing strategies also rely on time. They are rarely quick. They require patience, consistency, and the ability to maintain support despite fatigue. That patience is itself a resource, and not all patrons possess it. Democracies may struggle to sustain attention. Autocracies may find it easier, though they face their own legitimacy constraints. The implication is that cost imposition is as much a test of the patron's political endurance as the adversary's.

The quiet motif here is the side theatre. It begins as a footnote. It becomes a chapter. It can become the book.

How does a patron decide whether cost imposition is working? Not by asking whether the proxy is winning. The more relevant question is whether the adversary is *paying* in ways that matter strategically. Are its forces tied down? Is its budget diverted? Are its alliances strained? Is its leadership distracted? Those are observable behaviours: troop deployments sustained beyond initial plans, procurement delays, domestic unrest, diplomatic concessions.

But there is a moral and strategic discomfort in this logic. When a war is treated as a lever to burden an adversary, local lives become instruments. This is not an argument for sentimental restraint; it is an argument for honest accounting. Cost imposition externalises harm. It can also backfire politically when audiences perceive cynicism.

The forward test is sharp. Before a patron backs a proxy primarily to drain a rival, it should ask a diagnostic question that is rarely posed plainly: can we control the spillover once the adversary begins to bleed? Because that is the hidden wager. The patron seeks to make the rival overextend, yet overextension produces chaos that does not respect borders or budgets. The side theatre may remain a footnote—or it may become the place where empires learn, too late, what they have purchased.

Sanctions as tools of proxy warfare

On 15 May 2018, in Washington, President Donald Trump announced that the United States would withdraw from the Joint Comprehensive Plan of Action and reimpose sanctions on Iran. The statement was delivered as a matter of principle—pressure for better behaviour, leverage for a better deal—but it landed as something more operational. For Iran and for the groups tied to it across the Middle East, sanctions were not a background condition. They were a battlefield constraint. Within months, the contest over militias, missiles, and influence in places such as Lebanon, Syria, Iraq, and Yemen increasingly ran through banks, shipping registries, insurers, and export-licensing desks.

Money moves or it stops.

Sanctions and export controls are often described as alternatives to war. In proxy warfare, they are better understood as forms of war conducted through financial and technological choke points. They do not replace proxy strategies; they merge with them. Patrons impose sanctions to weaken rival patrons while sustaining their own clients, and rivals respond by re-routing finance, decentralising supply chains, and leaning harder on deniable actors. What looks like economic policy from a distance becomes, up close, a way of shaping who can fight, how long they can fight, and how visible their patrons must become.

The logic begins with a simple behaviour: restriction. When a state is sanctioned, its access to hard currency narrows, its ability to transact through reputable banks shrinks, and its procurement of high-grade technology becomes slower and riskier. That matters for proxies because proxy warfare consumes resources in a distinctive way. It requires continuous small payments, spare parts, logistics, and communications kit. It also requires risk tolerance among intermediaries. Sanctions are designed to reduce that tolerance by raising the cost of being caught.

The implication is that sanctions target the *plumbing* rather than the fighters. If weapons are the muscle of proxy war, finance and technology are its circulation. Cut circulation and even disciplined forces fatigue. Cut it badly enough and commanders spend more time managing shortages than managing strategy.

A quiet motif runs through this chapter of the story: the valve. Sanctions are valves on the flow of money and components. Turn them and the conflict changes shape.

Consider the Iran case as a long-running proxy contest in which restrictions on finance and technology reshaped behaviour without ending the underlying struggle. Iran's relationships with partners such as Hezbollah in Lebanon, various militias in Iraq, and the Houthi movement in Yemen have been central to its regional strategy for decades. Opponents—including the United States and various regional rivals—have repeatedly used sanctions to constrain Iran's ability to fund and equip those partners, while Iran has repeatedly adapted by changing payment methods, shifting procurement routes, and encouraging proxies to develop local revenue streams.

Sanctions do not need to reduce a state to poverty to matter. They need only to make the marginal transaction harder. In proxy war, marginal transactions are often the whole war: a transfer to a commander, a payment to a smuggler, a shipment of dual-use components, a replacement part for a missile guidance system. When restrictions bite, proxies experience it as delay, scarcity, and uncertainty.

One of the clearest examples of financial restriction shaping this contest came in March 2012, when SWIFT—the Brussels-based financial messaging cooperative—disconnected designated Iranian banks following European Union measures. The organisation was SWIFT; the place was Brussels; the date was March 2012; the consequence was practical. International payments became more cumbersome. Trade finance tightened. Even where transactions were technically possible, banks and firms grew cautious. The behaviour was de-risking: institutions refused exposure that might trigger penalties. The implication for proxy support was predictable. If a patron struggles to move money cleanly, it must either reduce support, take greater risks to sustain it, or push clients to find their own funding.

Export controls layer a different form of constraint. They limit access to specific technologies—advanced electronics, precision manufacturing tools, software, and certain industrial materials. In proxy war, export controls matter because modern weaponry often depends on dual-use components. Even crude rockets and drones can rely on specialised parts. Restrict the patron's access to those parts and you alter what proxies can field, how reliably they can field it, and how quickly they can replace losses.

This is the point at which sanctions stop being a moral gesture and become a design feature of warfare. A patron's proxy strategy can be weakened not by confronting the proxy directly but by starving the patron of the means to sustain the proxy's most strategically sensitive capabilities. Conversely, a patron that anticipates this will diversify, stockpile, and encourage local adaptation long before restrictions tighten.

It is tempting to treat sanctions as binary—either they work or they fail. Proxy warfare exposes how misleading that is. Sanctions can "work" in one dimension while "failing" in another. They may reduce a patron's ability to fund cash-intensive operations while leaving space for lower-cost harassment. They may slow the acquisition of sophisticated systems while encouraging proxies to innovate with cheaper alternatives. They may constrain formal procurement while expanding black-market networks that become harder to dismantle later.

A second, checkable example shows how sanctions can operate as a proxy instrument even when the target is not the proxy's patron but the proxy itself. Hezbollah has been subject to varied sanctions regimes and financial restrictions over many years, with the United States expanding measures through legislation such as the Hezbollah International Financing Prevention Act (2015). The place here is Washington; the date is 2015; the mechanism is financial pressure on networks suspected of facilitating funding and money laundering. The behavioural effect, documented in banking compliance practices across Lebanon, has often been heightened scrutiny and risk aversion. Lebanese banks, fearing exclusion from dollar clearing, tightened compliance. The implication is that sanctions can reshape the domestic political economy of a proxy by making certain relationships financially dangerous, thereby influencing which factions and institutions choose proximity to the proxy and which choose distance.

Sanctions, then, do not merely target actors; they reorganise incentives around actors. They pressure banks, insurers, shipping companies, and even charities to become unwilling participants in the contest. A patron imposing sanctions uses the market as a force multiplier. A patron under sanctions uses deniable networks as a substitute market.

This interaction produces a distinctive pattern: a formal economy and a shadow economy growing side by side. The formal economy is where enforcement is strongest. The shadow economy is where proxies learn to survive. The valve tightens; the shadow economy thickens.

There is, however, a credible limitation that any serious account must confront. Sanctions can punish civilians and weaken state institutions more than they weaken armed groups. When formal economic life contracts, proxies sometimes gain relative power because they can provide wages, protection, or access to scarce goods. This dynamic has been observed in multiple sanctioned environments: the state loses capacity, while armed networks gain leverage. Reconciling this limitation requires intellectual honesty. Sanctions are not a clean tool. They can constrain patron finance and procurement while simultaneously hardening the proxy's grip on local society.

That is why patrons applying sanctions in proxy contests often pair them with selective exemptions, humanitarian carve-outs, or parallel support to favoured clients. Yet carve-outs do not always translate into real access. Banks and firms may still avoid transactions that appear legally permissible but reputationally risky. The behaviour is over-compliance. The implication is that even "targeted" sanctions can have wide blast radii, which adversaries then exploit in propaganda and recruitment.

Sanctions also function as signalling devices. They tell allies and rivals how seriously a patron takes a contest. They demonstrate willingness to incur economic costs for strategic objectives. In proxy warfare, signalling matters because direct military confrontation is often avoided. Sanctions become a way to show resolve without firing a shot. The question is whether the signal is credible. If sanctions are announced but weakly enforced, they teach rivals that evasion is tolerable. If enforcement is aggressive, they teach intermediaries to disappear.

Enforcement is where the proxy logic re-enters the picture. A state may impose sanctions publicly while quietly tolerating certain flows to sustain a friendly proxy or preserve stability in a partner state. The behaviour is selective policing. The implication is that sanctions regimes often contain their own grey zones—spaces where enforcement discretion becomes another form of foreign policy.

Export controls create similar dilemmas. Tight controls can slow an adversary's technological progress, but they can also encourage substitution, reverse engineering, and local manufacture. Over time, the restricted actor may become less dependent on formal supply chains and more capable in its own right. The valve tightens; the pipe is rebuilt.

This is one reason sanctions rarely "end" proxy contests. They change the shape of the contest. They move it into different channels. They reward certain forms of organisational discipline: redundancy, decentralised logistics, and financial improvisation. They also reward political ruthlessness: the willingness to shift burdens onto civilians and to monetise scarcity through smuggling and taxation.

The strategic implication for patrons is uncomfortable. Sanctions can be most effective when paired with a theory of adaptation. If a patron assumes the rival will simply capitulate, it will misread the outcome. The more realistic question is how sanctions alter the rival's proxy strategy: do they force the rival to reduce support, or do they force the rival to change support in ways that are harder to detect and counter? Those are different outcomes with different risks.

For clients, sanctions create their own accounting. A proxy dependent on sanctioned finance may face delayed salaries, reduced equipment quality, and tighter discipline imposed by anxious patrons. Alternatively, it may be pushed to become self-financing—through taxation, coercion, or illicit trade—thereby changing its relationship with the population it claims to represent. The behaviour is institutional drift. The implication is moral and political transformation: a proxy that funds itself differently may govern differently.

The forward test is deceptively simple. When a patron turns to sanctions as a tool of proxy warfare, does it measure only the pressure placed on the rival—or does it measure the adaptations it is underwriting? Because sanctions are not merely barriers. They are incentives. They teach rivals and proxies what kinds of networks survive. And once those networks exist, they rarely dissolve politely when the policy mood changes.

Funding streams, donors, and illicit finance

In January 2006, Hamas won the Palestinian legislative elections in Gaza. The organisation was named; the place was Gaza; the date was January 2006; the outcome was immediate. Within weeks, key international donors suspended direct aid to the new administration, banks froze accounts, and formal budgetary transfers slowed to a trickle. Salaries went unpaid. Ministries stalled. What filled the gap was not a single substitute patron but a mosaic of private donations, charities, cash couriers, and informal taxation. Accountability shifted with the money.

Follow the money. Always.

Proxy warfare lives or dies on finance, yet its financial architecture is rarely singular or stable. Patrons and clients rarely rely on one stream for long. Instead, they assemble portfolios: state budget lines masked as aid, diaspora remittances routed through community networks, charities operating at the edge of regulation, and illicit trades that convert control of territory into revenue. The practical question is not whether money exists, but who controls its valves and under what conditions those valves can be tightened or loosened without leaving fingerprints.

Begin with the most legible stream: official state funding. When a patron uses its own budget to support a client, the behaviour is formal allocation. Funds move through ministries, intelligence services, or defence channels. The advantage is scale and predictability. Salaries can be paid on time. Equipment can be procured in bulk. The implication is leverage. A patron that pays regularly can demand discipline, reporting, and restraint. The risk, of course, is exposure. Parliamentary oversight, audits, and leaks turn budget lines into political liabilities. As scrutiny rises, formal funding becomes harder to sustain.

This pressure often pushes patrons towards the second stream: diaspora remittances. Migrant communities send money home for family support, reconstruction, or political causes. These flows are difficult to police without alienating voters or violating civil liberties. When a proxy taps into diaspora networks, the behaviour is decentralised fundraising. Contributions are smaller but numerous. The implication is resilience. Cut one channel and others persist. Yet resilience comes at a cost. Money raised from sympathisers is less conditional. Donors may demand ideological purity rather than strategic discipline, pulling clients away from patron preferences.

Charities sit at the boundary between legitimacy and suspicion. Many perform genuine humanitarian work. Some double as financial conduits. For patrons, charities offer deniability. Funds can be justified as relief rather than war support. The behaviour is re-labelling. The implication is ambiguity. Ambiguity protects patrons politically, but it complicates control. Once money is framed as charity, clawing it back or redirecting it becomes harder without public scandal.

Illicit finance completes the ecosystem. When proxies control territory or routes, they tax goods, traffic commodities, and exploit black markets. The behaviour is extraction. The implication is autonomy. A client that raises its own revenue is less dependent on patrons and less responsive to instruction. This autonomy can sustain a fight under sanctions, but it corrodes governance. Extortion and smuggling alienate civilians and entrench criminal interests that outlast the war.

The Hamas case illustrates how shifts between these streams alter accountability. Before 2006, much external support flowed through official or semi-official channels tied to the Palestinian Authority. After sanctions and diplomatic isolation, funding tilted towards private donations from the Gulf, local taxation in Gaza, and informal transfers. The immediate effect was survival. The longer-term effect was structural. With fewer formal donors to satisfy, the movement answered more to its base and its hardline supporters. Patron leverage weakened. Internal accountability narrowed.

This pattern is not unique. Hezbollah's financial ecosystem offers a second, checkable example. Since the 1980s, Hezbollah has combined state backing from Iran with extensive use of social institutions and charities in Lebanon. The organisation is Hezbollah; the place is Lebanon; the dates span decades, but a useful marker is 2015, when the United States expanded sanctions targeting its financial networks. Banks tightened compliance. Some charities closed or restructured. The behavioural response was diversification. Cash couriers increased. Overseas businesses carried more weight. The implication was adaptation rather than collapse. Pressure shifted practices without eliminating capacity.

Every abstraction here has a visible behaviour. *Control* appears as payroll timing. *Trust* appears as the willingness of intermediaries to move funds despite risk. *Risk* appears as the choice between bank transfers and cash. Measure these behaviours and the financial health of a proxy becomes legible.

Patrons try to steer these flows quietly. One method is selective tolerance. Authorities enforce regulations unevenly, signalling which channels are acceptable. Another is parallel funding: reducing official aid while encouraging "private" donors to fill the gap. The behaviour is orchestration without signatures. The implication is plausible deniability coupled with diminished control. Once private donors dominate, patrons can no longer calibrate support precisely.

A credible limitation complicates this account. Not all shifts towards private or illicit funding reduce accountability. In some cases, competition among donors forces proxies to professionalise, to publish accounts, or to demonstrate effectiveness to keep money flowing. The Taliban's taxation system in Afghanistan, for example, evolved into a relatively systematic revenue apparatus over time, tied to territory and enforcement. This does not make it benign, but it shows that illicit does not always mean chaotic. Reconciling this limitation requires distinguishing *who* enforces accountability. When enforcement comes from armed authority rather than civic institutions, the political consequences differ sharply.

Funding streams also shape internal politics. Units that control lucrative routes gain influence. Commanders who manage donors gain voice. Financial power becomes factional power. The implication for patrons is risk of fragmentation. Money meant to sustain a proxy can accelerate its splintering if not carefully channelled.

Technology has altered these dynamics without erasing old ones. Digital payments, cryptocurrencies, and online fundraising platforms have lowered barriers to entry while increasing traceability in some jurisdictions. Proxies experiment. Patrons watch. Regulators chase. The result is constant motion. A valve closes; another opens.

The quiet motif of the valve returns because it captures the strategic dilemma. Patrons want flows that are steady enough to sustain clients but narrow enough to control. Clients want flows that are resilient enough to survive pressure but flexible enough to avoid capture. Sanctions, oversight, and public scrutiny tighten valves. Diaspora enthusiasm and black markets widen them.

The unresolved tension sits at the end of this chain. When a patron nudges a proxy away from official funding towards private or illicit streams to reduce exposure, at what point does it trade deniability for loss of control? Because money that arrives without conditions rarely leaves without consequences.

Measuring return on strategic investment

On 15 February 1989, the last Soviet armoured column crossed the Friendship Bridge from Afghanistan into the Uzbek SSR. The Soviet Union had spent a decade fighting, arming local allies, and sustaining a war it could neither win outright nor abandon cheaply. The immediate outcome was clear: Moscow disengaged, Washington declared success, and the Afghan mujahideen stood victorious on the battlefield. The longer ledger told a different story.

Victory is not value.

Proxy wars tempt leaders with the promise of efficiency. Spend less, risk fewer lives, achieve strategic aims indirectly. Yet the question that lingers long after the fighting ebbs is whether the investment paid off in the ways that matter. Counting wins and losses on a map rarely answers it. Strategic return sits elsewhere: in access secured or lost, intelligence gained or poisoned, alliances strengthened or strained, and domestic politics stabilised or inflamed.

Begin with what patrons often measure first because it is easiest to see. Territorial outcomes. Did the proxy hold ground, topple a rival, or force an adversary to withdraw? In Afghanistan, the answer in 1989 appeared affirmative. The Soviet withdrawal was real and costly. The behaviour was retreat. The implication, widely assumed at the time, was strategic success for those who had backed the insurgents. Yet territory is a perishable metric. It decays when not anchored to governance, legitimacy, and long-term alignment.

A more demanding measure is strategic access. Access is not land but reach: basing rights, overflight permissions, ports, corridors, and influence over decision-makers. After 1989, the United States had little durable access in Afghanistan. Its investment had expelled a rival but secured no stable foothold. The proxy coalition fractured, and access evaporated. The return was negative not because the war was lost, but because the peace yielded no leverage.

Contrast this with a more modest effort that rarely features in triumphalist accounts. In northern Iraq after 1991, Western powers provided limited but sustained support to Kurdish groups, notably through the enforcement of a no-fly zone following the Gulf War. The organisations were the Kurdistan Democratic Party and the Patriotic Union of Kurdistan; the place was Iraqi Kurdistan; the period began in 1991. The immediate battlefield outcomes were uneven and often violent between the Kurds themselves. Yet over time, the arrangement produced enduring access: intelligence cooperation, local partners, and a region receptive to Western engagement. The investment was constrained. The influence lasted.

Show the behaviour. Limited air patrols. Political mediation. Selective aid. Name the concept. Strategic access. Explain the implication. A small, sustained presence can outperform a decisive but transient intervention when measured over decades rather than campaigns.

Intelligence gains form another axis of return. Proxies can act as sensors as much as fighters. They provide human intelligence, cultural insight, and early warning. But intelligence quality depends on alignment. In Afghanistan, competing factions fed patrons information shaped by local rivalries. Intelligence became noisy. Decisions followed bad data. The implication was strategic blindness at critical moments, including the rise of transnational jihadist networks that patrons neither fully anticipated nor effectively controlled.

Compare this with Colombia in the late 1990s and early 2000s. Under Plan Colombia, the United States supported the Colombian government rather than a non-state proxy, but the logic of indirect investment still applied. The place was Colombia; a key marker date was 2000, when the plan formally launched. The behaviour was institutional strengthening: training, intelligence sharing, and targeted assistance. The implication was improved intelligence fidelity. While the programme had costs and controversies, it produced usable, sustained intelligence partnerships that endured beyond immediate combat operations.

Alliance management is a quieter but decisive metric. Proxy campaigns often strain allies who must absorb refugees, endure spillover violence, or defend controversial policies at home. A campaign that succeeds militarily but fractures alliances can be strategically ruinous. During the Afghan war of the 1980s, Pakistan gained influence but also inherited instability, militancy, and long-term security costs. For the patron, reliance on a single conduit created vulnerability. When that ally's interests diverged, leverage collapsed.

Visible behaviour matters here. Who bears the burden? Who hosts bases? Who answers domestic critics? These questions determine whether alliances harden or hollow out. A proxy war that compels allies to defend actions they do not control often erodes trust faster than it weakens adversaries.

Domestic politics complete the accounting. Proxy wars are often chosen precisely to avoid domestic backlash. Casualties are low. Budgets are opaque. Yet political costs do not vanish; they shift in time. When outcomes sour or unintended consequences surface, earlier secrecy magnifies later outrage. In the United States, the narrative of success in Afghanistan curdled after 2001, when the same terrain became the staging ground for attacks against American targets. The earlier "cheap win" became politically expensive in retrospect.

Here the abstraction is legitimacy. The behaviour is narrative reversal. A campaign once defended as prudent is recast as reckless. The implication is loss of trust in institutions that championed indirect war as a low-cost alternative.

A credible counter-example tempers this analysis. Not all seemingly successful proxy campaigns backfire, and not all modest ones endure. The Soviet experience in supporting proxies elsewhere, such as in Angola during the Cold War, yielded mixed returns but did secure periods of influence and access aligned with broader strategic aims. Reconciling this requires attention to scope and ambition. Where objectives are limited and matched to resources, returns are more likely to hold.

This brings us to measurement itself. Patrons often fail not because they choose the wrong metrics, but because they choose them too late. Value is assessed after sunk costs accumulate and narratives harden. By then, course correction is politically difficult. The visible behaviour of successful patrons is early calibration. They compare costs not only to adversary losses but to alternative uses of attention and capital.

The quiet motif threading this analysis is the ledger. Proxy wars invite creative accounting. Costs are hidden. Gains are overstated. A proper ledger includes entries that do not fit neatly into columns: reputational damage, institutional distortion, and the opportunity cost of strategic distraction.

Return on strategic investment is therefore not a single figure but a profile. Does the proxy expand or contract future options? Does it clarify or cloud intelligence? Does it stabilise or strain alliances? Does it simplify or complicate domestic politics? Answering these questions requires patience and restraint, qualities often in short supply during war.

The unresolved test remains. If a proxy campaign delivers a battlefield success tomorrow but narrows strategic choice for a decade, was it worth the spend? And who decides when the ledger is closed?

Chapter 7

Escalation, Spillover and Risk

On the night of 24 November 2015, a Russian Su-24 strike aircraft was shot down near the Turkish–Syrian border. The missile was fired by a Turkish F-16. The aircraft crashed inside Syria; one pilot was killed by fighters on the ground. Within hours, Moscow accused Ankara of a deliberate provocation. Ankara insisted on self-defence. NATO convened emergency consultations. Hotlines lit up. For several days, two states with long memories, bruised pride, and incompatible narratives hovered uncomfortably close to direct confrontation.

The proximate cause was a proxy war.

Syria had already become a crowded theatre of militias, advisers, intelligence services, and competing patrons. What made the incident so unsettling was not its novelty but its familiarity. Proxy wars are meant to localise violence, to contain risk by displacing it onto others. Yet again and again, they behave like cracked vessels. Pressure leaks. Shockwaves travel. What begins as an indirect contest acquires a momentum of its own.

This chapter is about that momentum: how proxy wars spread, escalate, and occasionally escape the careful choreography designed to keep them limited.

At first glance, proxy conflicts appear bounded. The fighting happens elsewhere. The patrons insist on restraint. Public statements emphasise red lines that will not be crossed. And yet, almost every major proxy war of the past century has generated regional spillover. Borders harden, then blur. Refugees move faster than diplomats. Armed groups discover that neighbouring states offer sanctuary, recruits, or new enemies. A civil war ceases to be a domestic affair not through grand design, but through accumulation.

The mechanism is often banal. Families flee violence and settle across borders, carrying stories, grievances, and political claims with them.

Fighters pursue rivals into borderlands that states only partially control. Shared ethnic, sectarian, or tribal ties transform sympathy into mobilisation. What looks like a humanitarian problem becomes a strategic one. Camps become recruiting grounds. Corridors become supply lines. Neighbours are drawn in not because they planned to intervene, but because non-intervention becomes harder to sustain.

Consider how the Lebanese civil war, beginning in 1975, drew in Syria, Israel, Iran, and multiple Palestinian factions, reshaping the eastern Mediterranean for decades. Or how the Syrian uprising that began in 2011 metastasised into a regional struggle involving Turkey, Iran, the Gulf states, Russia, the United States, and a shifting constellation of non-state actors. Each step outward was justified as defensive, temporary, or exceptional. Each made the conflict harder to contain.

Spillover sets the stage for escalation, but escalation is not automatic. It follows patterns that policymakers understand well enough to name. The idea of escalation ladders—sequences of actions that carry progressively higher risks—has long been applied to nuclear strategy. In proxy wars, the ladders are less formal but no less real. Supplying small arms differs from supplying air defence systems. Intelligence sharing differs from targeting assistance. Advisers embedded at headquarters differ from advisers accompanying units into combat.

What matters is not only the action, but how it is read by others.

Signalling in proxy wars is a delicate craft. Patrons try to demonstrate resolve without triggering retaliation. They probe red lines through calibrated moves, often accompanied by back-channel messages that clarify intent. A convoy is struck, but not the command centre behind it. A base is shelled, but casualties are avoided. Silence itself can be a signal, as can an unusually loud public statement.

Yet signalling depends on shared assumptions. When those assumptions fray, the ladder becomes slippery. A single strike near a sensitive facility—a nuclear plant, an airbase hosting foreign personnel, a capital city—can be interpreted as a rehearsal for something larger. In such moments, leaders must decide quickly whether to climb, freeze, or step back. Proxy wars compress decision time even as they expand the number of actors involved.

Here the shadow of nuclear weapons looms large. Between nuclear-armed states, proxy wars have historically flourished precisely because direct war is so dangerous. Nuclear deterrence creates space for competition below the threshold of open conflict. It encourages risk-taking at the margins while imposing caution at the centre. This paradox is one of the defining features of the post-1945 international order.

The Cold War offers abundant examples. The Korean War, Vietnam, Afghanistan, Angola, and Central America all involved indirect clashes between nuclear-armed patrons. In each case, the presence of nuclear backstops constrained escalation at critical junctures. There were moments of intense danger—Berlin, Cuba, Able Archer—but they reinforced the lesson that some lines truly must not be crossed.

Contrast this with proxy conflicts where such backstops were absent. In regional wars without nuclear-armed patrons, escalation has often been more brutal and less predictable. The Iran–Iraq War of the 1980s, while not a proxy war in the narrow sense, demonstrated how absence of ultimate restraint can produce prolonged, high-intensity conflict with devastating human costs. Where no actor fears existential retaliation, the ladder stretches higher.

Nuclear deterrence, then, both enables and restrains proxy warfare. It lowers the probability of total war while raising the frequency of indirect contests. Understanding this duality is essential to grasping why proxy wars are so persistent—and why they are never as safe as their architects hope.

Even when intentions are cautious, accidents intrude. Intelligence is imperfect. Units on the ground act on partial information. Local commanders pursue tactical advantage without appreciating strategic consequences. Rogue actors exploit ambiguity to settle scores or advance agendas. In dense operational environments, misperception becomes a structural risk.

Modern militaries respond with crisis management tools designed to buy time and restore clarity. Hotlines link capitals and commanders. Deconfliction arrangements separate airspace or patrol zones. Agreed procedures govern encounters at sea and in the air. These mechanisms do not prevent conflict; they prevent spirals. They are safety rails on a narrow road.

Their importance becomes visible when they are tested. When an aircraft is downed, a ship is struck, or foreign personnel are killed, the question is not only how to respond, but how to communicate restraint while doing so. The speed with which leaders can reassert control over narratives and forces often determines whether a proxy war remains indirect.

Yet there are moments when patrons decide that indirection has failed.

The shift from proxy support to direct intervention is one of the most consequential decisions a state can make short of declaring war. It is usually framed as reluctant, necessary, and limited. The language emphasises advisers, trainers, or air support rather than ground troops. The triggers vary: a client's imminent collapse, the threat of reputational loss, domestic pressure to "do something", or fear that rivals will seize the initiative.

History suggests that once this threshold is crossed, the logic of involvement changes. Commitments deepen. Stakes rise. Exit becomes harder. What began as an effort to manage risk becomes a wager on control.

The American experience in Vietnam, where advisory missions expanded into full-scale intervention, remains the most cited example. But it is far from unique. Soviet escalation in Afghanistan in 1979 followed a similar pattern, as did Russian intervention in Syria in 2015. In each case, leaders believed that limited force could stabilise a proxy and secure interests at acceptable cost. In each case, the long-term consequences proved more complex.

This chapter does not argue that escalation is always a mistake. Sometimes direct intervention reshapes conflicts decisively. Sometimes restraint invites greater danger. The point is subtler and more troubling. Proxy wars create environments in which escalation is both easier to stumble into and harder to control. They distribute agency across actors with different incentives and perceptions of risk. They blur the line between signal and noise.

A recurring motif runs through the pages that follow: thresholds. Borders crossed. Lines tested. Decisions made under pressure. Proxy wars thrive on ambiguity, but escalation feeds on clarity—moments when ambiguity collapses and choices must be explicit.

As great power rivalry intensifies and conflicts continue to smoulder at the edges of the international system, the questions raised here grow sharper. How much spillover is tolerable before a proxy war becomes something else? Which signals stabilise, and which provoke? When does caution shade into paralysis, and when does resolve harden into recklessness?

The answers are rarely obvious in advance. They emerge, if at all, in crisis. And by then, the cost of misjudgement is no longer borne by proxies alone.

How proxy wars spread regionally

In March 2011, protests in the southern Syrian city of Daraa were met with live fire. Within months, tens of thousands of Syrians had crossed into Turkey, Lebanon, and Jordan. By the summer of 2012, armed groups were moving the other way, slipping across porous borders to fight, resupply, or regroup. What began as a domestic uprising had already acquired a regional geography. By 2014, Syria was no longer a single war but a mesh of overlapping campaigns involving Iran, Turkey, Russia, the United States, Gulf states, Kurdish movements, and transnational jihadist networks. Front lines shifted. Patrons multiplied. The conflict's centre of gravity dissolved.

Wars rarely stay put.

The spread of proxy wars across regions is not usually announced by formal declarations or grand strategy documents. It happens through motion: people moving, weapons moving, ideas moving. Borders that once served as political boundaries become logistical seams. Neighbours are drawn in not because they seek war, but because proximity erodes the distinction between involvement and exposure.

The first vector is human. Refugee flows are often treated as a humanitarian consequence of war, which they are, but they are also a strategic accelerant. Large-scale displacement alters the domestic politics of neighbouring states, strains budgets, reshapes labour markets, and sharpens identity debates. When Turkey hosted more than three million Syrian refugees by the late 2010s, the issue became inseparable from its security policy, border posture, and relations with Europe. Refugees carry not only trauma but information: accounts of atrocities, factional loyalties, and appeals for support. Camps become sites of recruitment and surveillance. Governments that initially promise neutrality discover that neutrality has costs.

Show the mechanism. In northern Lebanon's Tripoli in 2012, clashes erupted between Alawite and Sunni neighbourhoods as fighting intensified across the border in Syria. Name it. Sectarian affinity turned a neighbouring civil war into a local security problem. Explain it. Shared identity lowered the barrier to mobilisation; refugees and fighters blurred; external patrons funnelled money and arms through sympathetic networks. Implication: a conflict that crossed no formal border nonetheless destabilised a state already balancing on sectarian compromise.

The second vector is armed motion. Cross-border raids, hot pursuit, and sanctuary-seeking are among the oldest features of irregular warfare. When one side gains an advantage, its adversaries seek refuge just beyond reach. The border becomes less a line than a zone. States faced with incursions must choose between tolerating violations of sovereignty or escalating to stop them. Each choice carries risk.

The Afghan war of the 1980s offers a classic illustration. After the Soviet invasion in December 1979, millions of Afghans fled to Pakistan. Mujahideen groups used Pakistani territory as a rear area, while the United States, Saudi Arabia, and others channelled support through Islamabad. Soviet and Afghan forces occasionally struck targets near or across the border. Pakistan publicly denied belligerence while privately managing the war's logistics. Show. Arms convoys moved through the Khyber Pass. Name. The Inter-Services Intelligence Directorate became the principal intermediary. Explain. Geography and plausible deniability aligned. Implication: Pakistan was drawn deep into a proxy war whose aftershocks would shape its internal security for decades.

A third vector is identity. Shared ethnic, sectarian, or linguistic ties create corridors of sympathy that states cannot easily seal. These ties are not deterministic, but they are powerful. They lower transaction costs for mobilisation and raise the political price of indifference. When conflicts align with identity boundaries that straddle borders, regionalisation becomes likely.

The Kurdish question demonstrates this dynamic with particular clarity. Kurdish populations span Turkey, Syria, Iraq, and Iran. When conflict intensifies in one theatre, reverberations follow elsewhere. The rise of Kurdish armed groups in northern Syria after 2012 reshaped Turkey's security calculus, revived tensions with the Kurdistan Workers' Party, and complicated relations with the United States, which found itself supporting Kurdish forces against the Islamic State while managing alliance commitments to Ankara. Trust, here, was not abstract. It was measured in specific decisions: which units received weapons, which were excluded, which airstrikes were authorised. The implication was unavoidable. A local conflict activated a transnational identity network, pulling multiple states into overlapping proxy relationships.

Regional spread is rarely symmetrical. Some neighbours become staging grounds; others become battlegrounds. Some host quietly; others intervene loudly. These roles are shaped by regime type, state capacity, and perceived stakes. Jordan, bordering Syria, chose tight control and limited engagement, balancing alliance commitments with fear of domestic spillover. Lebanon, with weaker central authority and embedded non-state actors, experienced direct involvement through Hezbollah's intervention on behalf of the Syrian government. The same war produced different regional effects.

There are limits. Not every civil war regionalises. Sri Lanka's long conflict, despite Tamil populations in India, remained largely contained, in part because New Delhi imposed constraints after early involvement and Colombo reasserted control. This counter-example matters. It shows that regional spread is not inevitable. It depends on choices. Borders can harden. Patrons can restrain clients. Refugees can be managed without militarisation. The reconciliation lies in capacity and intent. Where neighbouring states possess strong institutions and clear red lines, spillover can be dampened. Where they do not, it accelerates.

Another mechanism operates through rival blocs. Proxy wars attract attention because they offer arenas to contest influence indirectly. As soon as one external patron commits, others reassess. A local conflict becomes a test of credibility. Standing aside risks conceding ground. Joining risks escalation. The result is often incremental involvement justified as balancing rather than expansion.

Yemen after 2014 illustrates this logic. The Houthi movement's seizure of Sana'a drew in a Saudi-led coalition concerned about Iranian influence on its southern flank. Iran's support for the Houthis was limited compared with the coalition's intervention, but perception mattered more than parity. Show. Airstrikes began in March 2015. Name. Operation Decisive Storm. Explain. Regional rivalry reframed a domestic power struggle as a proxy contest. Implication: front lines multiplied, humanitarian costs soared, and diplomatic exit narrowed.

A quiet motif runs through these cases: gravity. Conflicts generate their own pull. Actors orbit closer, drawn by fear, opportunity, or obligation. Once within range, they must expend energy to escape. This is why regionalisation is so hard to reverse. Each new entrant changes the incentives of the others.

Metrics make this visible. Count the number of patrons over time. Track refugee figures alongside troop deployments. Measure the distance from the original conflict zone to subsequent clashes. These are not metaphors. They are indicators of spread. When Syrian fighting produced clashes in Arsal,

Beirut, Reyhanlı, and later beyond the Levant through terrorist attacks and returning fighters, the arc of spillover could be traced geographically.

Information flows accelerate the process. Social media, satellite television, and diaspora networks compress distance. Images of violence circulate within minutes, shaping public opinion in neighbouring states and among patrons' home audiences. Leaders respond not only to events but to their portrayal. This interaction between narrative and movement will be taken up later in the book, but its role here is catalytic. Perception shortens the fuse.

The implications for patrons are sobering. Supporting a proxy in one theatre often commits a state to managing consequences elsewhere. Refugee policy becomes foreign policy. Border security becomes diplomacy. Internal cohesion becomes a strategic variable. The costs are unevenly distributed, which fuels resentment among neighbours who feel they bear burdens without influence.

For clients, regionalisation is double-edged. It can bring resources and allies. It can also fragment authority and dilute objectives. As more patrons enter, agendas multiply. Local actors become brokers rather than commanders. Battlefield success may depend less on local legitimacy than on alignment with external interests.

The unresolved tension is this: regional spread is often cited as a reason to intervene early, yet early intervention itself can accelerate spread. Delay invites spillover; action invites counteraction. The diagnostic question facing policymakers is therefore not whether a proxy war might spread, but how much spread they are prepared to manage, and at what cost, before the conflict ceases to be peripheral at all.

Escalation ladders and red lines

On 27 February 2022, artillery fire struck near the Zaporizhzhia Nuclear Power Plant in southeastern Ukraine. The International Atomic Energy Agency followed events in real time; so did defence ministries across Europe and beyond. For several hours, the world confronted a question that proxy wars are designed to avoid: could a conflict managed indirectly tip into catastrophe through a single misjudged action near a sensitive site? The plant did not suffer a radiological release, but the episode sharpened a truth that practitioners rarely state aloud. Escalation is not linear. It is a ladder with missing rungs.

This was a red line moment. Everyone knew it.

Proxy conflicts are often sold as safer than direct confrontation because they diffuse responsibility and distance principals from the battlefield. Yet this same distance complicates control. When clients act, patrons infer. When patrons signal, clients interpret. Each step up the escalation ladder is negotiated in ambiguity, and the most dangerous moments occur when one side believes it has remained on a lower rung while the other concludes the opposite.

Escalation theory provides a language for this instability. Thomas Schelling's work on deterrence described conflict as a process of bargaining through moves and countermoves, each calibrated to alter the other side's expectations without triggering uncontrolled violence. In proxy wars, that bargaining is indirect, conducted through airstrikes attributed to "unknown aircraft", cyber operations whose authorship is disputed, or weapons transfers framed as defensive. The ladder is climbed sideways.

Show the mechanism. A patron authorises a strike against a proxy's logistics hub. Name it. Limited escalation. Explain it. The action is intended to impose cost while signalling restraint by avoiding high-value targets. Implication: if the opponent interprets the strike as preparation rather than punishment, it responds at a higher rung, forcing both sides upwards.

Red lines are the ladder's guardrails. They are rarely written down. Some are public, declared for domestic or alliance audiences. Others are private, conveyed through back channels, intermediaries, or patterned behaviour. Their purpose is not to prevent all escalation, but to channel it away from thresholds that would compel direct intervention.

Consider the long-running contest between Israel and Iran in Syria. Since 2013, Israel has conducted hundreds of airstrikes against Iranian-linked targets, aiming to prevent the transfer of advanced weapons to Hezbollah. Iran has absorbed losses while avoiding direct retaliation against Israeli territory. The red lines are tacit but legible. Israel avoids striking Iranian senior leadership directly. Iran avoids responses that would force Israel into a broader war. The ladder holds, until it does not.

In February 2018, an Israeli F-16 was shot down after a strike near the Tiyas (T-4) airbase in Homs province. Israel responded with a larger wave of attacks, including against Syrian air defence systems. The incident did not trigger open war, but it revealed how quickly a familiar pattern can fray. Aircraft losses change domestic calculations. So do funerals.

Signals matter because they shape interpretation. In proxy wars, signalling is often designed to be ambiguous enough to allow retreat. A strike may be accompanied by a leak rather than an announcement. A weapons delivery may be confirmed by journalists rather than officials. Silence can be a signal too. When the United States refrained from striking Syrian regime forces after limited provocations in certain periods, it communicated priorities without speeches.

Back-channel warnings are the ladder's maintenance crew. During the Cold War, Washington and Moscow invested heavily in hotlines and diplomatic intermediaries to manage crises. Proxy conflicts inherited these tools. Deconfliction lines between militaries operating in the same theatre, such as those established between the United States and Russia in Syria after 2015, are not about cooperation. They are about preventing accidents from becoming messages.

Accidents still happen.

On 17 September 2018, Syrian air defences responding to an Israeli strike accidentally shot down a Russian Il-20 reconnaissance aircraft near Latakia, killing fifteen Russian servicemen. Moscow blamed Israel's tactics; Israel blamed Syrian operators. Russia responded by supplying Syria with the S-300 air defence system. Show. A proxy theatre produced a direct loss for a major power. Name. Accidental escalation. Explain. The absence of intent did not reduce the political cost. Implication: even well-understood ladders are vulnerable to noise.

Sensitive facilities occupy the highest rungs. Nuclear plants, major oil infrastructure, and command-and-control hubs compress decision time and magnify stakes. The September 2019 attack on Saudi Arabia's Abqaiq processing facility, attributed by Riyadh and Washington to Iran though claimed by Yemen's Houthi movement, temporarily knocked out roughly half of Saudi oil production. The response was restraint. No immediate military retaliation followed. This was not because the attack was minor, but because escalation calculations dominated. The red line had been touched without being crossed.

The paradox is instructive. Severe actions can be met with limited responses if leaders judge that retaliation would worsen their position. Lesser actions, misread, can provoke overreaction. The ladder is climbed in perception, not fact.

Counter-examples clarify the limits of the model. In conflicts where one side lacks credible escalation options, red lines are brittle. During the Sri Lankan civil war's final phase in 2009, the government faced international pressure over civilian harm but no realistic threat of external military intervention. Red lines were asserted rhetorically but not enforced. The ladder existed, but only one side could climb it. Reconciliation lies in symmetry. Escalation ladders stabilise when both parties believe the other can impose unacceptable costs.

Metrics help distinguish signal from noise. Frequency of strikes. Target categories. Casualty profiles. Public statements timed to military actions. These observable behaviours indicate where actors believe they are on the ladder. When patterns shift, so has the rung.

Trust is often invoked here, but it is better measured as predictability. In Syria, predictability emerged through repetition. Israel struck. Iran absorbed. Russia protested diplomatically. The sequence became familiar. Efficiency followed familiarity. Risk fell, until a deviation occurred.

Proxy clients complicate the picture. They may not share their patrons' appetite for restraint. A client facing existential threat has incentives to provoke escalation, hoping to drag its patron into direct intervention. Patrons respond by constraining weapons use, vetting targets, or withholding capabilities that could force their hand. Control is exerted through logistics, not lectures.

The unresolved tension sits here. Escalation ladders are meant to prevent disaster, yet they rely on shared understanding in environments designed to obscure intent. Each rung climbed without consequence encourages confidence. Each red line not enforced invites testing. The forward test is simple to state and hard to answer: how many ambiguous steps can a proxy war sustain before ambiguity itself becomes the trigger?

Nuclear backstops and great power caution

On 26 October 1962, a Soviet submarine commander in the Caribbean nearly authorised a nuclear torpedo launch. Vasili Arkhipov's refusal to consent, aboard B-59 near Cuba, is now a matter of record. The confrontation passed without catastrophe, but the lesson endured. Nuclear weapons do not merely raise the cost of war; they reorder how wars are fought. In the decades that followed, the United States and the Soviet Union collided repeatedly without engaging each other directly, from Angola to Afghanistan. The bomb hovered overhead, unseen yet decisive.

This shadow shapes proxy warfare. Nuclear deterrence encourages competition precisely because it forbids certain forms of confrontation. When direct war between nuclear-armed states promises mutual destruction, indirect conflict becomes the safest available instrument of rivalry. The paradox is stark. The most destructive weapons ever built make smaller wars more likely.

Yet the same backstop restrains escalation. Proxy conflicts between nuclear powers are bounded by caution, ritual, and an obsession with signalling. The ladder exists, but the highest rungs are radioactive. Actors climb carefully.

Show the pattern. In December 1979, the Soviet Union invaded Afghanistan, installing a client regime and committing its own forces. Name it. A nuclear power intervenes directly. Explain it. Moscow judged the theatre peripheral to American vital interests and calculated that Washington would respond indirectly. Implication: the response came through covert support to the mujahideen, not US divisions crossing borders. The war was brutal and long, but it remained contained within the proxy logic.

Contrast this with conflicts lacking nuclear backstops. In the Iran–Iraq War of the 1980s, neither side possessed nuclear weapons. External patrons provided arms, intelligence, and finance, but without the same fear of escalation between patrons themselves. The war ground on for eight years, featured mass mobilisation and chemical weapons use, and ended without decisive external restraint. The absence of a nuclear ceiling did not make the war bigger in geography, but it made it less disciplined.

Nuclear deterrence works through expectations. Leaders believe that certain actions will provoke responses too costly to bear. This belief shapes behaviour far from nuclear silos. In proxy theatres, it manifests as restraint in targeting, care in attribution, and a preference for deniable tools. When US and Russian forces operate in proximity, as in Syria after 2015, they avoid striking each other even while backing opposing sides. Aircraft fly, but flight paths are communicated. Bases are mapped mentally. Accidents are feared more than defeats.

Metrics reveal caution. No deliberate strikes on each other's personnel. Limited geographic expansion. Rapid diplomatic engagement after incidents. These are observable behaviours tied to nuclear backstops, not goodwill.

Trust is not the mechanism. Fear is.

The Cold War offers the canonical case, but the pattern persists. India and Pakistan, both nuclear-armed since 1998, have fought multiple proxy conflicts in Kashmir without escalating to full-scale war. After the Kargil conflict in 1999, where Pakistani forces and militants crossed the Line of Control, India limited its response geographically. Pakistan withdrew under international pressure. Nuclear weapons did not prevent fighting; they channelled it.

A credible counter-example sharpens the argument. North Vietnam and the United States fought a proxy war under the shadow of nuclear weapons, yet escalation still occurred through massive bombing campaigns. Reconciliation lies in asymmetry. Only one side possessed nuclear weapons. The backstop restrained Washington from invading the North with ground forces, but it did not protect Hanoi from airpower. Nuclear deterrence stabilises when it is mutual.

Mutuality encourages caution at the top while enabling violence below. This dynamic produces what strategists call the stability–instability paradox. Strategic stability at the nuclear level creates tactical instability at lower levels. Proxy wars thrive in the gap.

Visible decisions illustrate this paradox. During the Syrian civil war, Russia deployed airpower to support the Assad regime in September 2015. The United States adjusted its operations to avoid Russian assets, even as both sides continued to back opposing local forces. Deconfliction channels multiplied. Public rhetoric hardened, but battlefield interactions softened. Nuclear backstops did not eliminate rivalry; they professionalised it.

Time horizons matter. Nuclear-armed patrons think in decades. Proxy clients think in months. This divergence strains relationships. A client may seek decisive escalation to secure survival. A patron prefers endurance. Control mechanisms follow. High-end weapons are withheld. Rules of engagement are imposed. Intelligence is shared selectively. Each decision reflects awareness of the ceiling above.

Risk is often framed abstractly. It is better measured in behaviours such as target selection and response timing. When a proxy attack kills advisers from a nuclear-armed patron, the response is usually symbolic rather than escalatory. Strikes are calibrated. Statements are issued. Then activity resumes.

The absence of nuclear backstops produces different incentives. In Libya after 2011, external actors intervened without fear of confronting a peer nuclear power. Competing patrons backed rival factions openly. Airpower was used decisively. The war fragmented rapidly. Without a ceiling, escalation became opportunistic.

This does not imply that nuclear backstops guarantee control. Misperception remains dangerous. Leaders may misjudge an opponent's tolerance or misread signals. The downing of a Russian Su-24 by Turkish forces near the Syrian border in November 2015 prompted economic sanctions and sharp rhetoric but stopped short of military retaliation. Nuclear considerations influenced Moscow's restraint, but so did alliance politics and economic calculation. Backstops interact with other constraints.

The quiet motif running through nuclear-backed proxy wars is the invisible line. Everyone senses it. Few can draw it precisely. The line shifts with domestic politics, leadership changes, and technological developments. Cyber operations blur it further, offering new ways to impose cost below traditional thresholds.

The forward test remains unresolved. As more states acquire nuclear capabilities and as proxy warfare incorporates autonomous systems and cyber tools, does the nuclear backstop continue to restrain escalation, or does it merely push competition into domains where miscalculation is easier? The shadow still falls. Whether it cools or darkens the conflicts beneath it is the question patrons must answer before the next rung is climbed.

Accidents, misperceptions, and crisis management

On 24 November 2015, a Turkish F-16 shot down a Russian Su-24 near the town of Yayladağı on the Turkish–Syrian border. The pilot ejected; one was killed by fighters on the ground. Ankara said the aircraft had violated Turkish airspace despite repeated warnings. Moscow denied it and accused Turkey of a "stab in the back". Within hours, NATO met in Brussels, Russian officials promised consequences, and the Syrian war—already thick with competing patrons—suddenly felt like a contest between states rather than clients.

Then the phones began to ring.

Proxy wars are built on controlled ambiguity. Patrons supply, advise, and signal while insisting they are not parties to the fight. This architecture reduces certain kinds of risk, but it magnifies others. It multiplies actors, compresses decision time, and makes attribution harder. When something goes wrong—and it will—leaders must interpret events through imperfect information while domestic audiences demand certainty. Accidents become messages. Messages become ultimatums.

The path from proxy war to direct clash is rarely a deliberate march. It is more often a stumble: a radar operator misidentifies a track; a pilot crosses an invisible line; a militia fires a rocket it cannot aim precisely; a commander assumes approval that was never given. Show the behaviour. A trigger is pulled. A plane falls. Name it. Inadvertent escalation. Explain it. The immediate act is local; the political meaning is strategic. Implication: the patron is forced to respond not to an incident alone, but to its interpretation by allies, rivals, and voters.

Misperception is the oxygen of proxy crises. It thrives in environments where intent is hidden and information is contested. A patron may interpret a proxy's battlefield success as evidence of foreign direction. A client may interpret restraint as betrayal. An adversary may interpret silence as weakness. These are not philosophical problems; they are operational hazards. Leaders make decisions based on what they believe the other side believes. That recursive logic, described by Schelling and others, becomes unstable when the actors are not just states but armed networks with uneven discipline.

The Syrian theatre after 2011 became a case study in misperception precisely because so many actors operated with partial visibility. Russian aircraft, Turkish jets, US drones, Syrian air defences, Kurdish units, Islamist factions, Iranian advisers, and numerous militias all moved in proximity. The airspace became a crowded room. In crowded rooms, people bump.

The Su-24 incident illustrates how quickly a bump can harden into a shove. Turkey's behaviour was immediate: it publicised radar tracks and asserted sovereign rights. Russia's behaviour was punitive but calibrated: economic sanctions, travel restrictions, and a more assertive posture in Syria, including deploying the S-400 air defence system to Hmeimim air base. The implication was clear. Moscow would raise the cost of Turkish freedom of action without firing directly at NATO aircraft.

Crisis management tools exist to keep such episodes from becoming wars. The first is communication: hotlines, military-to-military contacts, diplomatic channels, and third-party intermediaries. These are not symbols of trust. They are mechanisms for preventing misinterpretation. When a state can clarify what it did and what it intends to do next, it can reduce pressure on the other side to assume the worst.

The second tool is deconfliction. Deconfliction arrangements are practical rules designed to prevent physical collision and accidental engagement. They can include shared air corridors, altitude separation, notification protocols, and agreed procedures for encountering each other's aircraft. In Syria, the United States and Russia established a deconfliction line after Russia's intervention in September 2015. The behaviour was procedural. The implication was strategic: even bitter rivals can cooperate tactically to avoid catastrophe.

A third tool is controlled response. In a crisis, leaders face domestic pressure to retaliate. Yet retaliation can be shaped. Target selection, timing, and public messaging can signal resolve without escalating further. The most skilful crisis responses treat retaliation as communication rather than catharsis.

A fourth tool is narrative management. In proxy wars, narratives are not decoration; they are operational constraints. If a leader publicly commits to a hard line, it becomes harder to climb down. If a leader frames an incident as an accident rather than an attack, it creates room for de-escalation. The behaviour is rhetorical calibration. The implication is political flexibility.

There is a temptation to treat these tools as technocratic fixes. They are not. They work only when leaders choose to use them and when institutions can implement them quickly. Some regimes have well-drilled crisis procedures. Others rely on improvisation, which magnifies risk.

A second, checkable example shows how a downed aircraft can force rapid coordination in a proxy environment. On 17 September 2018, Syrian air defences responding to Israeli strikes accidentally shot down a Russian Il-20 reconnaissance aircraft near Latakia, killing fifteen Russian servicemen. Israel had notified Russia shortly before the strike, but Russia claimed the warning was too late and accused Israel of using the aircraft as cover. The immediate danger was not only Israeli–Russian confrontation but a collapse of deconfliction mechanisms in Syria.

Moscow's response again demonstrated crisis logic. Russia did not strike Israel. It imposed diplomatic and military costs by supplying Syria with S-300 air defence systems and tightening operational coordination. Israel, for its part, continued strikes but adjusted tactics to reduce risk of Russian casualties. Show the behaviour. The deconfliction line remained active. Name it. Managed escalation. Explain it. Both sides absorbed the incident into a revised rule-set rather than allowing it to trigger direct war. Implication: crisis management can convert accidents into new tacit understandings.

Tacit understandings are a fifth tool, and they matter more than formal agreements in proxy theatres. These are unwritten rules derived from repeated interaction: "we strike here, not there"; "we avoid your personnel"; "we do not hit your embassy"; "we do not cross this border in force". They are enforced not by courts but by retaliation. Their advantage is flexibility. Their disadvantage is fragility. When a new actor enters, or when a domestic shock changes incentives, tacit rules can collapse without warning.

Rogue actors exploit this fragility. A militia may fire at foreign forces to force its patron's hand. A commander may stage an incident to gain prestige. A political faction may benefit from crisis to silence opponents. In proxy wars, agency is distributed. That distribution is itself a risk.

A credible limitation must be admitted. Crisis management is not always possible, and sometimes it can be counterproductive. Hotlines do not help if leaders refuse to answer. Deconfliction fails when parties suspect the other is using it to gain advantage. In some conflicts, communication becomes a channel for deception rather than clarity. Reconciliation lies in incentives. Crisis management tools work when both sides prefer containment to escalation. When one side believes escalation will improve its position, the tools become irrelevant.

Risk, then, is best measured not by the presence of hotlines but by the behaviour of leaders under stress. Do they communicate quickly? Do they issue narrow statements or broad threats? Do they punish subordinates for errors or reward defiance? Do they change operational procedures to reduce recurrence? These decisions reveal whether the system is stabilising or approaching breakdown.

The quiet motif in this section is the blink. Proxy wars rely on the hope that, in a crisis, someone blinks—slows down, asks for clarification, chooses a limited response. Yet blinking is politically costly. It can be framed as weakness. Leaders often prefer escalation they can control to restraint they cannot justify.

The forward test is therefore stark. When the next aircraft falls—or the next ship is struck, or the next sensitive site is hit—will crisis management mechanisms function as brakes, or will they act as mere witnesses to a slide already under way?

When patrons decide to intervene directly

On 8 March 1965, United States Marines came ashore at Da Nang in South Vietnam. The White House described the deployment as protective: the Marines would secure the air base. Advisers would continue to advise. The war would remain limited. By 1968, more than half a million US troops were in Vietnam, and the conflict had become the defining American trauma of the twentieth century. The line between assistance and intervention proved not a line at all, but a slope.

It starts small. It rarely stays small.

Proxy warfare rests on a bargain. The patron supplies money, weapons, intelligence, and political cover; the client supplies manpower, local knowledge, and the visible risk of combat. Direct intervention breaks that bargain. It means the patron has judged that the proxy arrangement can no longer deliver acceptable outcomes, or that the costs of continued deniability now exceed the costs of ownership. The moment is often framed as necessity. It is also a confession: indirect control has reached its limit.

The decision to intervene directly is usually triggered by a combination of pressures rather than a single shock. The first is client collapse. When a client begins to lose ground rapidly, or when its command structure fragments, the patron faces a choice between escalation and abandonment. Abandonment risks reputational damage, loss of strategic access, and the empowerment of rivals. Escalation risks entanglement. The behaviour is a forced choice; the implication is that proxy wars, though designed as flexible instruments, can produce rigid commitments under crisis.

In Vietnam, the collapse pressure was framed through a series of discrete events: the instability of the South Vietnamese government after the 1963 coup, the increasing effectiveness of the Viet Cong, and the vulnerability of US-backed infrastructure. Each step required a decision. Each decision created a new baseline. Direct intervention was not a single leap but an accumulation.

The second trigger is prestige. States do not like to be seen to lose, particularly when they have publicly invested in a client. Prestige is not an abstraction; it is measured in alliance confidence, deterrence credibility, and domestic narratives about competence. When a patron fears that retreat will embolden rivals elsewhere, it may intervene not because the theatre itself is vital, but because the theatre has become symbolic.

The Soviet invasion of Afghanistan in December 1979 shows how prestige and perceived credibility can harden into direct action. Moscow feared the collapse of a friendly regime on its southern flank and the broader implications for influence in the region. It intervened directly, assuming it could stabilise the situation quickly. The behaviour was decisive deployment; the implication was strategic overconfidence. What followed was a decade-long war that consumed resources and legitimacy.

The third trigger is domestic pressure, which often arrives as a paradox. Leaders choose proxy warfare partly to avoid domestic costs—body bags, visible spending, parliamentary debate. But secrecy and distance create their own political vulnerabilities. When images of atrocities circulate, when allies demand action, or when a perceived threat is framed as imminent, domestic audiences can push leaders from covert support towards overt force.

This pressure is not always hawkish. Sometimes it comes from humanitarian concern, sometimes from fear, sometimes from wounded pride after an attack. What matters is that domestic politics can convert a proxy commitment into a direct one by making restraint appear immoral or weak.

The fourth trigger is operational friction. Proxy warfare often fails at the level of competence. Clients may lack discipline, coordination, or the ability to integrate advanced weapons. Patrons discover that their investment is being wasted. The tempting solution is to add advisers, then add more, then add air power to compensate for tactical failures. This is not a psychological story. It is an institutional one. Military organisations tend to solve problems with the tools they know: additional personnel, better intelligence, more firepower.

Vietnam's advisory mission illustrates this escalation logic with painful clarity. In the early 1960s, the United States increased the number of military advisers. Advisers did not simply "advise"; they shaped operations, intelligence flows, and logistics. As the mission expanded, the distinction between advising and directing blurred. Helicopters, then aircraft, then combat units followed. The slope steepened.

Show the behaviour. Advisers accompany units. Name the concept. Mission creep. Explain the mechanism. Each incremental addition is justified as temporary and limited, but it changes the mission's purpose from enabling a client to substituting for it. Implication: the patron becomes responsible not merely for outcomes but for the conduct of war itself.

A fifth trigger is escalation by the adversary. When a rival patron increases involvement—deploying advisers, transferring sophisticated weapons, or intervening openly—it can force the other side to respond to avoid strategic defeat. This is not always symmetrical, but it is often contagious. Proxy wars can become arms races in slow motion. When one side breaks deniability, the other may feel compelled to follow.

Russia's intervention in Syria in September 2015 offers a modern illustration of direct patron action in a proxy-heavy environment. The Assad regime was under severe pressure in parts of the country, facing multiple armed opponents. Russia had long supplied weapons and diplomatic support. It shifted from support to direct air operations, deploying aircraft to Hmeimim and striking targets across Syria. The intervention stabilised the regime and altered the war's trajectory. The behaviour was overt air power; the implication was restored influence and strategic access, including long-term basing arrangements.

Yet even here, the line between limited and expansive proved mutable. Air power required ground coordination. Coordination required advisers. Advisers required force protection. The mission grew complex. It remained more limited than Vietnam, but the underlying dynamic—capability expansion to solve operational friction—was familiar.

There is a credible limitation that deserves attention. Direct intervention does not always expand. Sometimes it remains tightly bounded, either because leaders impose strict constraints or because the theatre allows a narrow use of force. The 1999 NATO air campaign in Kosovo, while not a proxy war in the same sense, demonstrates how air power can be used without ground invasion to achieve political objectives, albeit with its own controversies and reliance on local forces. Reconciling this limitation requires attention to objectives and geography. Missions expand when goals are vague, when clients are weak, and when adversaries adapt faster than expected.

Risk is often cited as the reason to avoid direct intervention. Yet paradoxically, patrons sometimes intervene precisely to reduce risk. They fear that an uncontrolled proxy war will spill over, empower extremists, or destabilise allies. Direct action is framed as containment. The behaviour is escalation for control. The implication is that "risk" is not a fixed quantity; it is a comparison between unpleasant alternatives.

Measurement matters. When patrons intervene directly, they change what can be measured and what must be justified. Casualties become political facts. Budgets become visible. International law becomes sharper. The patron's narrative shifts from "supporting" to "acting". This can strengthen resolve, but it also narrows exit options. Once a patron owns the war, leaving looks like defeat.

A quiet motif threads through these decisions: the mask. Proxy warfare is a mask that allows patrons to act without full recognition. Direct intervention is the moment the mask is removed—sometimes voluntarily, sometimes because it has already slipped. The face underneath may be stronger than expected. It may also be trapped by its own exposure.

The forward test is both strategic and moral. When a client begins to collapse, when prestige is at stake, when domestic audiences demand action, does the patron still have a choice? Or has the earlier decision to fight indirectly already written the script that ends with direct intervention?

Chapter 8

After The Guns Fall Silent

On a humid afternoon in May 2006, thousands of militiamen in southern Lebanon gathered to hand in their weapons under the gaze of politicians, clerics, and foreign observers. Cameras lingered on stacks of rifles and crates of ammunition. The ceremony suggested closure. Yet within weeks, many of those weapons had reappeared—some hidden, some transferred, some quietly replaced. The war had ended. The armed order it created had not.

The end of fighting is often mistaken for the end of conflict. In proxy wars, it rarely is. What follows is not peace but a reckoning with the structures built to fight without responsibility. Militias trained for survival must now learn restraint. Commanders rewarded for loyalty must accept compromise. Patrons accustomed to leverage must decide whether to dismantle it. The silence after the guns fall quiet is therefore not empty. It is crowded with unresolved bargains, unpaid debts, and memories that refuse to fade.

This chapter turns to what happens after proxy wars conclude—or appear to. It examines the afterlife of indirect conflict: the fighters who cannot be easily demobilised, the political settlements shaped by force rather than consent, and the long shadows cast across societies long after patrons have moved on. The core argument is simple and unsettling. Proxy wars do not end cleanly because they were never cleanly fought.

Disarming and demobilising proxy forces is often treated as a technical exercise: collect weapons, offer stipends, provide training. In practice, it is a political gamble. Fighters paid by outside patrons rarely trust promises made by fragile states. Commanders who survived war by hedging loyalties are reluctant to surrender their last insurance policy. Partial disarmament becomes common—not because actors misunderstand the risks, but because they understand them too well. When one group disarms while a rival remains armed, peace becomes a strategic liability.

The incentives are visible. Weapons mean bargaining power. Armed cohesion deters marginalisation. Even when patrons encourage demobilisation, their credibility is suspect. The very states that once paid for violence now ask for restraint, often without offering long-term security guarantees. The implication is corrosive: demobilisation fails not because fighters reject peace, but because the post-war order offers them too little reason to trust it.

Political settlements deepen this tension. Former proxies are frequently woven into new arrangements as parties, ministers, or security chiefs. The logic is pragmatic. Excluding armed actors risks renewed war; inclusion promises stability. Yet inclusion also rewards coercion. Militia leaders become power brokers not through votes but through force. Patrons may support such deals to preserve influence, secure allies, or freeze conflicts at tolerable levels. Peace becomes conditional, reversible, and uneven.

There are moments when this strategy works, at least temporarily. In Bosnia and Herzegovina after the Dayton Accords of 1995, former armed factions were absorbed into political structures under intense international supervision. Violence declined sharply. But the settlement also entrenched ethnic divisions and external tutelage, producing a state that survives but rarely governs. The guns fell silent. The war's logic remained embedded.

Where settlements fail or stall, darker paths emerge. Warlordism thrives on ambiguity. Fighters without salaries turn to extortion. Networks built for war adapt easily to smuggling, trafficking, and organised crime. The skills required—violence, secrecy, loyalty—transfer smoothly. In parts of West Africa, armed groups once backed by foreign patrons evolved into regional criminal enterprises, destabilising states long after the original conflicts faded from international attention. The behaviour is adaptation; the implication is generational instability.

These outcomes are not accidental. Proxy warfare encourages decentralised violence and rewards autonomy. When patrons withdraw, they leave behind actors trained to operate without oversight. States emerging from proxy conflicts inherit armed groups they did not create and cannot easily control. The social fabric frays under the strain of unresolved grievances, revenge killings, and informal justice. Peace agreements signed in capitals do little to restrain neighbourhood vendettas.

Displacement compounds the problem. Proxy wars are efficient producers of refugees. Those displaced rarely return quickly, if at all. Diasporas form political communities in exile, funding factions, lobbying foreign governments, and keeping narratives alive. These communities are not monolithic, but they are powerful. They shape how conflicts are remembered and when they are revived. Frozen conflicts persist not because fighting is inevitable, but because political mobilisation continues across borders.

Consider the Caucasus, where ceasefires halted large-scale violence but failed to resolve underlying disputes. Diaspora activism sustained claims, funded militias, and hardened positions. Patrons tolerated this ambiguity. Frozen conflicts offered leverage without responsibility. The human cost—decades of displacement and uncertainty—was treated as background noise.

This chapter also confronts the question of learning. Do states absorb lessons from proxy campaigns, or do they mythologise them? The record is mixed. Some institutions conduct after-action reviews, revise doctrines, and build oversight mechanisms. Others bury failures beneath narratives of success or necessity. Bureaucratic turnover erodes institutional memory. New leaders inherit old tools without understanding their consequences.

The contrast is instructive. One state, chastened by a proxy campaign that produced long-term instability, invested in clearer command structures, tighter financial controls, and explicit exit strategies. Another repeated the same pattern—arming clients, denying responsibility, disengaging abruptly—only to confront similar blowback years later. The difference lay not in intelligence or capability, but in willingness to remember.

A subtle motif runs through these post-conflict landscapes: inheritance. Proxy wars leave behind institutions, habits, and expectations. Fighters inherit weapons. Politicians inherit armed constituencies. Societies inherit mistrust. Patrons inherit reputations. None of these can be wished away by declarations of peace. They must be managed, or they will manage themselves.

The relevance is immediate. As contemporary conflicts grind on and new proxy relationships form, the question is not only how wars are fought, but how they end—and who lives with the aftermath. Disarmament programmes are being designed even as weapons flow. Political settlements are being sketched while front lines shift. Diasporas are mobilising in real time. The future is already taking shape.

This chapter does not offer comforting conclusions. It offers clarity. The afterlife of proxy war is long, contested, and morally fraught. The guns may fall silent. The consequences do not. The test that follows is stark. Can patrons accept responsibility for what they helped create, or will they once again mistake silence for peace?

Disarming and demobilising proxy forces

On 31 May 1991, in Lisbon, José Eduardo dos Santos and Jonas Savimbi signed the Bicesse Accords to end Angola's long war. The agreement promised a familiar sequence: ceasefire, demobilisation, a unified army, elections. The ink dried; the world exhaled. Yet the critical transaction—turning armed men into political citizens—never fully cleared. Weapons were hidden, units remained cohesive, and command chains endured behind the paperwork. After the September 1992 elections, violence returned with speed and ferocity. A peace that looked complete on paper proved dangerously incomplete in the field.

Five words mattered most then. *Who keeps the guns tonight?*

Disarmament, demobilisation, and reintegration are often presented as the administrative epilogue to war: a technical clean-up operation after the drama. In proxy conflicts, they are closer to the climax. Proxies are not ordinary combatants who simply happen to be armed; they are organisations structured around outside sponsorship, trained to survive shifts in patronage, and accustomed to treating the state as a rival rather than a home. When the shooting stops, they do not become neutral. They become uncertain. And uncertainty is a powerful reason to keep a rifle.

The difficulty begins with a simple asymmetry. A state or patron can announce a programme, sign a deal, set out eligibility rules. A fighter must decide whether to walk into a cantonment site and surrender what may be his only insurance against future betrayal. That decision is rarely ideological. It is actuarial. A weapon is not merely a tool; it is a *key*—to protection, to status, to bargaining power. The central challenge of demobilising proxy forces is persuading thousands of individuals and dozens of commanders to hand over their keys before they can see the locks they will be offered in return.

Show the behaviour. A commander delays registration, moves weapons across a river at night, keeps an elite unit "on standby". Name it. Hedging. Explain it. Proxy leaders learned during the war that promises expire, patrons shift priorities, and local rivals exploit moments of weakness. Implication: a demobilisation plan that assumes good faith will be gamed, not because the actors are uniquely deceitful, but because they are rational under threat.

This is why incentives matter, and why they so often disappoint. Stipends, vocational training, and reintegration packages are designed to make disarmament attractive. Yet these incentives are frequently small relative to the value of coercive capacity in shattered economies. A young man offered a brief allowance and uncertain training is being asked to trade certainty for hope. If his rival remains armed, hope looks thin.

Amnesties are another lever. They are controversial for good reason: they can offend victims and corrode legitimacy. But in proxy wars, amnesties often function less as forgiveness than as a bargaining chip to dismantle armed cohesion. When a commander believes he will be prosecuted or assassinated once disarmed, he is likely to spoil the peace. When he believes there is a credible exit from the battlefield, he may accept political constraints. The word "credible" is doing heavy work here. An amnesty that is politically contested, inconsistently enforced, or silently reversible may be worse than none at all, because it tempts actors into vulnerability and then punishes them for it.

Security guarantees are therefore the hard currency of demobilisation. Without them, incentives and amnesties are paper. Guarantees can take many forms: integrating fighters into national security forces, deploying neutral peacekeepers to monitor ceasefires, establishing verified cantonment zones, or creating reliable protection for former commanders. The United Nations' Integrated Disarmament, Demobilization and Reintegration Standards (IDDRS), issued in 2006, treats security and confidence-building as foundational rather than optional. That emphasis reflects bitter experience. Where the post-war state cannot protect those who disarm, the armed groups will protect themselves.

Angola's Bicesse process shows what happens when these guarantees are thin. The accords envisioned a unified national army, but integration was partial and distrust remained high. Both sides retained covert capabilities. The demobilisation process did not dissolve command networks; it merely relocated them. When political competition sharpened after the 1992 elections, armed structures were still intact enough to convert fear into violence almost immediately. The spoiler here was not a single rogue faction; it was the system's residual coercive capacity.

A second, equally instructive example comes from Lebanon after the Taif Agreement of 1989, which ended the Lebanese civil war. In 1991, the Lebanese government pursued the disarmament of militias, and many groups surrendered heavy weaponry or dissolved formally. Yet

Hezbollah, citing resistance to Israeli occupation in the south, retained its arms and organisational integrity. The result was a state with selective sovereignty: some factions disarmed into politics, while one major actor kept an autonomous military capability. This was not merely a domestic arrangement. It was entangled with external patronage, regional strategy, and the enduring logic of proxy warfare.

Show the behaviour. One group hands in weapons and registers as a party; another keeps a disciplined armed wing and a parallel command structure. Name it. Asymmetric demobilisation. Explain it. When disarmament is partial, the remaining armed actor gains leverage over both rivals and the state, because it alone retains the ability to coerce outside formal politics. Implication: even if violence declines, the political settlement remains hostage to the balance of force, and fragile peace can be spoiled not only by fighting but by threat.

This is where demobilisation collides with the moral economy of post-war societies. Fighters who disarm must return to communities that may fear or despise them. Victims demand justice. Commanders seek dignity. Politicians seek stability. Patrons seek plausible exit. These demands rarely align. The temptation is to treat DDR as an engineering problem: design the programme correctly and compliance will follow. But proxy forces are not machines; they are political organisms.

Their internal structure matters. A cohesive proxy with disciplined leadership can, in some cases, demobilise more effectively than a fragmented coalition, because orders travel down a chain of command and can be enforced. Yet that same cohesion also makes the group more capable of remobilising if it feels threatened. Fragmented proxies present the opposite challenge. Their commanders cannot reliably deliver compliance, and fighters may defect into criminal networks. Either way, the goal is not simply to collect weapons, but to dissolve the *social infrastructure* of armed power: payrolls, loyalties, clandestine supply lines, and the habit of settling disputes through force.

Weapons collection itself is a deceptive metric. A rifle turned in is a fact; the absence of a rifle is not. Proxies and their patrons have long mastered the art of inventory theatre—handing over obsolete arms while retaining modern ones, declaring caches destroyed while relocating them, registering some fighters while keeping others "unregistered" as a reserve. If the monitoring system is weak, the programme becomes performative. The peace is then built on a stage set.

A credible limitation must be faced. Some disarmament efforts succeed better than sceptics expect, including in environments where former rebels enter politics without returning to war. Mozambique after the 1992 Rome General Peace Accords is often cited as a comparatively successful case of demobilisation and reintegration, with the RENAMO movement transitioning into a political party. The reconciliation lies in two features that are easy to underestimate. First, external monitoring and support helped stabilise the process. Second, the principal parties accepted—however grudgingly—that political competition was safer than renewed war. Even there, later episodes of violence and remobilisation remind us that "success" is not permanence; it is a reduction of risk, sustained by continuing political management.

That insight matters because proxy wars distort the baseline. The patron's exit can be as destabilising as the patron's involvement. Fighters who have been paid and supplied externally often face a sudden loss of income and status when the pipeline shuts. Some will accept demobilisation if offered credible alternatives. Others will seek new patrons, new markets, or new forms of coercion. Reintegration becomes the hinge. If reintegration is treated as charity rather than as a security strategy, it will be underfunded, improvised, and politically sidelined. The consequences follow with grim predictability: armed labour becomes available to the highest bidder.

The concept of "spoilers", articulated forcefully by Stephen Stedman in 1997, is useful here not as a label for villains but as a diagnostic for incentives. Spoilers are actors who believe peace threatens their power or safety. Proxy forces, especially those with strong external ties, often have spoiler potential because peace can mean marginalisation. If a settlement is designed in a way that offers them only surrender without security, the programme will manufacture spoilers even where none existed.

This brings us back to the motif of keys. In a functioning state, the key to safety is the law, the police, the courts. In a shattered state, the key is often a gun. Demobilisation asks people to exchange keys. It works only when the new keys reliably open doors.

The most consequential decisions are therefore not technical but political. Will the state integrate former proxy fighters into a reformed security apparatus, or will it treat them as an inconvenience to be dispersed? Will patrons provide long-term support for reintegration, or will they fund only the visible moment of weapons collection? Will rival factions disarm in parallel, or will one be permitted to retain arms for "special reasons"? Each choice shapes whether demobilisation consolidates peace or plants the seeds of the next conflict.

The closing tension is unavoidable. A proxy war can be ended by a ceasefire, but the proxy force created by the war often survives the ceasefire as a latent institution. The forward test is stark and practical: when the patron withdraws and the cameras leave, what, exactly, persuades a former proxy to hand over the last key?

Political settlements and power-sharing deals

On 24 December 2003, under the bright lights of Accra's conference halls, Liberian faction leaders signed the Comprehensive Peace Agreement that ended fourteen years of civil war. In August 2003, Charles Taylor had resigned and gone into exile; by October, a transitional government began to take shape. Within months, men who had commanded militias—some backed by external patrons, some financed through the trade in timber and diamonds—were allocated ministerial posts and seats on transitional bodies. It was a striking reversal. Those who had broken the state were now invited to run it.

Peace, here, was not a moral reward. It was a transaction.

Power-sharing deals sit at the most uncomfortable junction of proxy warfare's aftermath. They are designed to stop fighting by turning commanders into stakeholders: to convert coercive capacity into political participation. Yet they also risk teaching a brutal lesson—that violence is an efficient route to office. In proxy conflicts, where armed groups have often been equipped and legitimised by outsiders, this tension intensifies. The settlement must satisfy local factions, reassure anxious civilians, and accommodate patrons who still wish to shape outcomes. A power-sharing agreement is therefore less a social contract than a balancing act carried out on a narrow ledge.

The logic begins with a pragmatic observation. After a proxy war, the winners are rarely able to govern alone, and the losers are rarely so defeated that they cannot spoil. The battlefield produces stalemate more often than surrender. In such contexts, political settlements are not the opposite of coercion; they are coercion rearranged into institutions. Posts, budgets, and security roles become the new terrain.

Show the behaviour. A militia leader demands the Ministry of Defence or a lucrative revenue agency. Name it. Spoils bargaining. Explain it. In transitional settings, ministries are not merely administrative units; they are sources of patronage, access to arms, and control over appointments. Implication: portfolios are chosen for power, not policy, and the state becomes an arena for factional security rather than public service.

Liberia's 2003 settlement provides a vivid example of how power-sharing can stabilise violence while institutionalising armed leverage. The agreement allocated positions across the transitional government to representatives of the main factions—former regime elements, rebel groups, and political parties—under international supervision. Several senior faction figures entered government. The immediate outcome was a reduction in large-scale fighting and the creation of a pathway to elections in 2005, which brought Ellen Johnson Sirleaf to power. The deeper implication was more ambiguous. The transition relied on the co-option of warlords as a means to stop warlordism.

This is not an aberration. It is a recurrent pattern in post-proxy settlements precisely because patrons and mediators often prefer a flawed peace to a continued war. The calculus is visible. A cabinet post is cheaper than a renewed military campaign. A security force role is easier to monitor than an insurgency. Yet what is gained in short-term stability can be lost in long-term legitimacy. Citizens learn that the ballot follows the gun.

Why do patrons support such deals? Often because they stabilise a client state without requiring direct occupation or indefinite aid. A patron that invested in a proxy has an interest in ensuring that its preferred actors are not purged. Power-sharing provides insurance. It locks influence into institutions—ministries, parliaments, security forces—where it can be maintained through funding and advice rather than through constant resupply. It also offers diplomatic cover. Supporting a "unity government" sounds less cynical than continuing to arm a faction.

But patrons do not always want settlements. Sometimes they prefer frozen conflicts—ceasefires without resolution, institutions without integration. A frozen conflict keeps leverage alive. It allows a patron to pressure a rival, block unwanted alliances, or maintain a security buffer. The cost is borne locally: stalled economies, militarised politics, permanent displacement. The benefit accrues strategically: influence without responsibility.

Show the behaviour. A patron discourages disarmament, insists on "security concerns", continues low-level funding. Name it. Conflict maintenance. Explain it. When unresolved disputes keep a client dependent, the patron can extract concessions—basing rights, diplomatic alignment, economic access. Implication: peace becomes a variable to be managed, not an objective to be achieved.

A second, contrasting example illuminates the stakes. The Dayton Accords of December 1995 ended the Bosnian war by creating a complex power-sharing system between Bosniaks, Croats, and Serbs. The settlement halted large-scale violence and established institutional mechanisms that have endured for decades, supported by extensive international oversight. Yet Dayton also entrenched ethnic vetoes and produced a state whose political logic often rewards obstruction. Here, power-sharing prevented renewed war, but it also fossilised the conflict's identity divisions inside the machinery of government.

The juxtaposition with Liberia matters. Liberia's power-sharing was explicitly transitional, designed to lead to elections and a new constitutional order. Bosnia's was designed as a durable constitutional architecture. Both stabilised violence. Both also carried long-term costs. The implication is that power-sharing is not a single instrument but a family of arrangements, varying in purpose and effect. What they share is a willingness to trade normative purity for immediate containment.

The mechanisms by which former proxies are woven into the state are more concrete than the language of reconciliation suggests. There are three common pathways, each with its own hazards. One is political party transformation: armed groups register parties, contest elections, and accept the discipline of campaigning. This can work when the group has a coherent constituency and when electoral competition is credible. Another is ministry allocation: leaders receive executive posts and access to state resources. This can stabilise their incentives but risks turning ministries into fiefdoms. The third is security integration: fighters are incorporated into national armed forces, police, or special units. This can reduce the number of autonomous guns, but it can also militarise the state and embed factional loyalties within it.

Pair abstraction with metric. "Integration" sounds uplifting; the metric is whether units accept unified command and whether disciplinary systems function. "Representation" sounds democratic; the metric is whether posts translate into service delivery or into patronage extraction. "Legitimacy" sounds philosophical; the metric is whether citizens trust courts and police enough to settle disputes without armed intermediaries.

The patron's role in these pathways is often decisive, even when it is discreet. Patrons can underwrite salaries to keep integrated units from fragmenting.

They can provide training that professionalises security forces. They can condition aid on anti-corruption measures. They can also, deliberately or not, reinforce factionalism by channelling resources through preferred individuals rather than through institutions. When a patron treats a ministry as a conduit for influence rather than as an engine of governance, it teaches local actors to do the same.

There is a further tension, less discussed because it is so uncomfortable: justice versus stability. Power-sharing commonly involves compromises that limit prosecutions or dilute accountability. For civilians, this can feel like betrayal. For armed actors, it can feel like survival. The trade-off is not merely ethical; it has strategic implications. When victims believe peace requires impunity, they may withdraw from politics, radicalise, or support revenge. When commanders believe peace brings prosecution, they may spoil.

A credible limitation is that some settlements avoid co-opting warlords and still achieve stability, particularly where one side wins decisively or where international forces impose security. Sierra Leone's war ended with a combination of military pressure, British intervention in 2000, and UN deployment, followed by the Special Court for Sierra Leone. Yet even there, elements of bargaining and reintegration were present. Reconciliation lies in recognising that the degree of co-option varies with the balance of force. When coercive capacity is broken, power-sharing is less necessary. When it is intact, power-sharing becomes the price of peace.

The quiet motif threading through these arrangements is the chair. Who sits in the chair—ministerial, parliamentary, command—matters because chairs signal permanence. A chair turns a commander into an official. It changes how outsiders deal with him. It changes how his followers imagine their future. It also changes the state itself, because the chair carries with it access to budgets, appointments, and licences. In post-proxy politics, chairs are often the most valuable terrain.

The hardest question is whether power-sharing deals can be designed to erode coercion over time rather than entrench it. The answer depends less on constitutional elegance than on enforcement and sequencing. If armed actors enter government while retaining autonomous forces, the state becomes hostage. If security integration is credible and gradual demobilisation follows, coercive power may slowly migrate into institutions. If economic opportunities expand, armed recruitment becomes less attractive. If not, violence remains a career path.

The forward test for patrons and peacemakers is therefore not simply whether a deal stops shooting next month. It is whether the deal changes the incentives that made proxy warfare rational in the first place. When a militia leader sits in a ministerial chair, does he begin to fear elections more than rivals with guns—or does he use the chair to keep the guns and win the election too?

Revenge, warlordism, and criminalisation

In June 1999, as NATO troops entered Kosovo and Serbian forces withdrew, fighters of the Kosovo Liberation Army began dismantling checkpoints and rebranding themselves as guardians of order. Within months, some of those same networks were controlling fuel depots, border crossings, and protection rackets across western Kosovo and northern Albania. By 2001, Europol and the United Nations Interim Administration Mission in Kosovo were warning that former KLA-linked figures dominated organised crime routes running from the Balkans into Western Europe. The war was over. The business had begun.

Peace did not disarm power. It redistributed it.

This is the dark afterlife of proxy warfare, where armed groups that once served strategic purposes for patrons mutate into private authorities, criminal syndicates, or engines of revenge. The transition is rarely abrupt. It unfolds through familiar mechanisms: unpaid fighters seek income; commanders retain weapons "just in case"; local grievances settle into vendettas; external funding dries up and illicit revenue fills the gap. What emerges is not chaos but order of a particular kind—coercive, transactional, and resilient.

The first step in this trajectory is revenge. Proxy wars fracture societies along lines that persist long after ceasefires. Families remember who manned checkpoints. Neighbourhoods recall who collaborated. When formal justice is absent or distrusted, retaliation becomes personalised. Show the behaviour. A former fighter targets a rival clan, not for territory but for memory. Name it. Vendetta violence. Explain it. In the absence of credible courts, violence substitutes for adjudication. Implication: insecurity persists even without strategic objectives, eroding confidence in the post-war state.

Revenge alone, however, does not explain longevity. Warlordism does. When armed groups retain command structures and weapons, they become alternative providers of security and arbitration. They collect "fees" to resolve disputes, guard convoys, or protect businesses. The metric is visible: checkpoints turn into tolls; uniforms turn into branded insignia; commanders move from trenches to offices. This is not anarchy. It is governance without accountability.

Afghanistan after 2001 offers a sobering illustration. Numerous militias, some empowered by external patrons during the anti-Taliban campaign, were folded nominally into state structures while retaining de facto autonomy. As Antonio Giustozzi documented in *Empires of Mud* (2009), many commanders leveraged their wartime status to dominate local economies—controlling land, smuggling routes, and reconstruction contracts. The implication was clear. When proxies are rewarded with authority but not constrained by institutions, they professionalise coercion rather than abandon it.

Criminalisation completes the arc. Once ideology fades and security markets saturate, illicit trade provides scale. Drugs, arms, people, antiquities—whatever moves reliably across borders becomes attractive. The organisational skills honed in war—logistics, secrecy, violence—translate efficiently. Pair abstraction with metric. "Opportunity" means a border post that processes trucks without inspection. "Risk" means a bribe-to-profit ratio that remains favourable. "Efficiency" means fewer intermediaries between source and market.

Return to the Balkans. By the mid-2000s, investigations by the Council of Europe and reporting by journalists such as Misha Glenny linked networks associated with former KLA figures to heroin trafficking along the Balkan route. The groups were not mere remnants. They had adapted. Political influence shielded them from prosecution; diaspora ties facilitated laundering; legitimacy from the war muted scrutiny. The transformation from proxy force to criminal enterprise was not a betrayal of wartime ideals so much as a continuation of power by other means.

This pattern recurs beyond Europe. In Colombia, the demobilisation of the United Self-Defence Forces of Colombia in 2006 was incomplete. Many fighters reconstituted themselves as *bandas criminales*, controlling cocaine corridors and illegal mining. The state dismantled an organisation but not the incentives. The implication is uncomfortable: partial demobilisation can reduce battlefield violence while expanding criminal governance.

A credible limitation must be acknowledged. Not all former proxies become criminals. Some reintegrate successfully, particularly where disarmament is comprehensive, economic opportunities are real, and justice mechanisms function. Mozambique after the 1992 Rome Accords offers a partial counter-example, where former RENAMO fighters entered politics and rural life with comparatively limited criminal spillover. Reconciliation lies in recognising that outcomes depend on sequencing and enforcement. Where weapons remain plentiful and livelihoods scarce, criminalisation outcompetes reintegration.

The role of patrons in this descent is often indirect yet decisive. Patrons withdraw attention once strategic goals are met. Funding stops. Oversight fades. Local commanders, accustomed to external support, seek substitutes. Illicit economies rarely provoke the same diplomatic costs as renewed fighting, at least initially. This creates perverse tolerance. A proxy turned smuggler is less embarrassing than a proxy turned insurgent. Until it isn't.

The quiet motif threading through these cases is the ledger. During war, ledgers track supplies and casualties. After war, they track debts and profits. When a commander opens a ledger to record extortion payments rather than ammunition, the nature of violence shifts but does not disappear. It becomes quieter, more selective, more enduring.

Criminalisation also corrodes political settlements. Warlords with illicit revenue can finance parties, intimidate rivals, and capture regulators. This blurs the line between state and syndicate. Citizens experience governance as extraction. Trust erodes. Migration follows. Diasporas then become funding sources, sometimes willingly, sometimes through coercion. The conflict's footprint expands geographically even as it contracts militarily.

There is a further implication for international security. Criminalised former proxies do not respect borders. They link conflicts. Weapons from one war arm gangs in another. Money from trafficking launders through global financial systems. The residue of a local proxy war becomes a transnational problem. Measuring this is possible. Seizure data, arrest networks, and price convergence across markets reveal integration. These are not anecdotes; they are indicators.

The unresolved tension at the end of this path concerns responsibility. When a proxy group mutates into a criminal network, does culpability end with the ceasefire? Or does it linger with those who armed and legitimised the group without ensuring its dismantlement? The answer shapes future choices. If patrons treat criminal afterlives as externalities, they will recur. If they are treated as deferred costs, the calculus of proxy warfare changes.

The forward test is stark. When the guns fall silent and ledgers open, who closes the accounts—and who is willing to pay the bill?

Refugees, diasporas, and frozen conflicts

On 15 May 1948, as the British Mandate ended and war spread across Palestine, hundreds of thousands of Palestinians fled or were expelled from their homes. In the following years, the United Nations Relief and Works Agency for Palestine Refugees in the Near East—UNRWA—was created in 1949, and refugee camps solidified into a political geography stretching from Gaza to Lebanon and Jordan. By the late 1960s, in places such as Amman, Beirut, and the camps of southern Lebanon, exile had become more than a humanitarian condition. It had become an organising principle for politics, mobilisation, and war.

Exile has a long memory.

Proxy wars displace people at scale, but their distinctive after-effect is what displacement *does* to politics. When a conflict is shaped by patrons and clients—by supply lines, covert support, and strategic narratives—refugees become more than victims. They become constituencies. They are counted, courted, and sometimes coerced. A displaced population can confer legitimacy, generate funding, and create international pressure. It can also freeze a conflict in place by making compromise feel like betrayal, particularly when return is the central demand and the patron's leverage depends on keeping that demand unresolved.

Show the behaviour. Families keep keys to houses that no longer exist, teach children the names of villages they have never seen, and organise commemorations that function as political meetings. Name it. Exile politics. Explain it. Displacement transforms personal loss into collective identity, and collective identity becomes a resource that leaders can mobilise. Implication: even when front lines stabilise, the conflict continues in memory, in law, and in lobbying.

The first mechanism is demographic shock. Refugee flows alter the political balance of neighbouring states, sometimes destabilising them and pulling them into the original conflict. In Lebanon, the arrival and long-term presence of armed Palestinian factions, combined with Lebanon's own sectarian structure, became one ingredient in the civil war that erupted in 1975. The point is not to reduce that war to a single cause; it had many. The point is that displacement is not merely a humanitarian overflow. It is a strategic spillover. A proxy contest displaces people; those people reshape the states that receive them; those states then become arenas, corridors, or patrons in the same contest.

The second mechanism is institutionalisation. Refugee camps, once established, become semi-permanent. They develop governance systems—formal and informal—because daily life requires order. Where host states restrict employment, movement, or political participation, camps can become separate political worlds. Patrons and armed groups understand this quickly. Camps offer recruits, shelter, and legitimacy. They also offer a narrative: *we are the dispossessed; therefore we may fight.* Pair abstraction with metric. "Legitimacy" becomes a rally that fills a stadium; "capacity" becomes an armed wing that controls a camp gate; "leverage" becomes the ability to disrupt host-state stability.

The third mechanism is the diaspora's distance advantage. Diasporas are often safer, richer, and better connected than those who remain near the front. Distance reduces immediate fear, which can harden preferences. A person living under shelling may accept compromise to stop the killing; a person living abroad may refuse compromise because the cost is borne elsewhere. This is not a moral judgement. It is a structural tendency. When the personal risks of continued conflict are low, the political appeal of maximal demands can rise.

Show the behaviour. A diaspora organisation raises funds for "humanitarian relief" that is diverted into political mobilisation, purchases media time, hires lobbyists, and frames legislation. Name it. Remote mobilisation. Explain it. Diaspora networks convert economic and civic power in host countries into influence over the conflict's narrative and, sometimes, its material capacity. Implication: the conflict's centre of gravity can move abroad, where the incentives for settlement differ sharply from those at home.

A second, checkable example demonstrates how diaspora funding can help sustain armed struggle, prolonging war long after the initial grievances have become politically soluble. During Sri Lanka's civil war, the Liberation Tigers of Tamil Eelam (LTTE) drew support from sections of the Tamil diaspora, particularly in Canada and parts of Europe, through fundraising and coercive collection methods documented by multiple governments and researchers over the years. The details varied by country and period, and diaspora communities were never uniform. Yet the broader pattern was visible: a movement facing military pressure at home could still draw resources from abroad, allowing it to sustain operations and resist political compromise.

Show the behaviour. A diaspora donor channels money through informal networks, attends commemorations that double as recruitment events, and shares propaganda videos that elevate martyrdom. Name it. Transnational sustainment. Explain it. Armed movements can survive local setbacks if they maintain external revenue streams and narrative control among supporters abroad. Implication: demobilisation becomes harder, because the war is no longer financed only by local extraction or patron state budgets; it is partly financed by identity itself.

This is where frozen conflicts take on their peculiar durability. A frozen conflict is not a peaceful conflict; it is a conflict whose violence has been reduced without resolving its political core. Ceasefires create a new normal: checkpoints, de facto borders, unrecognised authorities, and a generation raised on stalemate. Displaced communities, especially those prevented from returning, become living evidence that the conflict is not settled. Patrons may find this useful. Frozen conflicts keep rivals constrained and clients dependent. Diasporas may find it intolerable. Frozen conflicts turn their lives into waiting rooms.

The interaction between patrons and diasporas is more complex than the cliché of "diasporas fuel war". Patrons do not simply exploit diaspora sentiment; they sometimes fear it. A patron seeking a settlement may confront diaspora organisations that lobby against compromise. Alternatively, a patron seeking to prolong leverage may amplify diaspora narratives of irreconcilable grievance. Media outlets, cultural institutions, and advocacy groups can become nodes in a wider strategic contest. The result is an uncomfortable truth: what looks like grassroots activism can, at times, operate in parallel with state strategy—without formal coordination, but with mutual benefit.

A credible limitation must be stated. Diasporas can also be engines of peace. They can fund reconstruction, support moderation, and pressure armed groups to accept political solutions. The Irish-American role in supporting the Northern Ireland peace process offers a partial counter-example, where diaspora influence, at key moments, helped legitimise negotiation rather than sabotage it. Reconciliation lies in distinguishing between diaspora engagement that broadens political options and diaspora engagement that narrows them. The difference is often visible in behaviour: funding schools and clinics versus funding armed wings; lobbying for prisoner releases tied to ceasefire compliance versus lobbying for maximal territorial claims without compromise; supporting truth recovery versus glorifying violence.

What, then, turns displacement into a long-term political force rather than a transient tragedy? Three conditions recur. First, sustained denial of return or meaningful integration. When refugees are trapped between a lost home and an unwelcoming host state, mobilisation becomes one of the few available forms of agency. Second, the presence of organisations—armed or political—that can convert grievance into structure. Third, the continued usefulness of the unresolved issue to patrons, local elites, or both. When these conditions align, the suitcase becomes permanent furniture.

The motif of the suitcase matters because it captures the paradox. A suitcase suggests movement. Frozen conflicts produce immobility. People live for decades with packed belongings they rarely use, narratives they constantly revisit, and documents that substitute for citizenship. In such settings, identity hardens around loss. Politics becomes custodianship of memory. That custodianship is not merely symbolic; it shapes voting blocs in host countries, influences foreign policy debates, and can deliver funds that outlast a patron's direct interest.

For the societies that receive refugees, the stakes are equally high. Host governments may instrumentalise refugee populations for domestic politics, restrict rights to avoid permanent settlement, or exploit camps as bargaining chips in regional diplomacy. These decisions create feedback loops. Restriction breeds resentment; resentment breeds radicalisation; radicalisation invites securitisation. The original proxy conflict thus reproduces itself in new forms across borders.

The most difficult implication is temporal. Proxy wars are often justified as limited engagements with controllable costs. Displacement exposes the lie. Refugee politics extends the conflict across decades, embedding it in the institutions of multiple states and in the emotional lives of people far from the original battlefield. Even if guns fall silent, the politics of return and recognition can keep the conflict alive—sometimes peacefully, sometimes violently, often in a state of suspended resolution that suits patrons better than it suits refugees.

The forward test is deceptively simple. When a ceasefire holds and a frozen conflict settles into routine, does anyone still have an incentive to make refugees whole—not rhetorically, but materially, legally, and politically? Or will the suitcase remain packed, generation after generation, because too many actors benefit from keeping it that way?

Lessons learned and institutional memory

On 1 October 2015, Russian aircraft began flying combat missions over Syria, marking a decisive shift from covert support and advisers to overt air power. Within weeks, the intervention stabilised Bashar al-Assad's position, reshaped the battlefield, and signalled Moscow's return as a regional military actor. In official Russian narratives, the campaign quickly became a model: precise, effective, limited. Yet it also drew on an older lineage—Soviet experience in Afghanistan, hard lessons about overreach, and a determination to avoid certain failures while repeating others in new forms. The question was not whether Russia had learned. It was what, exactly, it had learned *to do*.

Memory is policy's hidden infrastructure.

States fight proxy wars through agencies and intermediaries, but they remember them through institutions. After a proxy campaign ends, leaders change, files are classified, and veterans leave government. The record becomes a contest: between after-action review and myth, between sober assessment and the political need to claim success. In that contest, institutional memory either accumulates into capability or dissolves into repetition.

The first thing to grasp is that "lessons learned" is not a natural outcome of experience. It is a bureaucratic achievement. A state can fight ten proxy campaigns and remain ignorant if it lacks mechanisms to record, debate, and enforce hard conclusions. Conversely, a state can fight one disastrous campaign and improve rapidly if it builds processes that convert embarrassment into reform. Show the behaviour. A ministry commissions an internal review, changes procurement rules, and creates a standing unit to manage partner forces. Name it. Institutionalisation. Explain it. A lesson becomes real only when it changes budgets, authorities, and incentives. Implication: learning is measurable in organisational change, not in speeches.

After-action reviews are the cleanest route to this kind of learning, and they are also politically fraught. A proper review asks dangerous questions: Were our aims coherent? Did we understand the client's agenda? Did our weapons leak? Did our deniability collapse? Who benefited? Who paid? Such questions threaten careers. They also threaten narratives. Proxy wars, by design, are often conducted in the shadows; the less public oversight, the fewer compulsory reckonings. A state that relies heavily on proxies is therefore structurally tempted to avoid learning, because learning requires exposure.

Even when reviews occur, they can be neutered by classification. Secrecy protects capabilities and keeps allies calm, but it also prevents genuine institutional diffusion. A lesson locked in a safe is not a lesson; it is a secret. The consequence is familiar: the small circle that ran the last programme knows its pitfalls, but the next circle—staffed by new officials, facing a new crisis—rediscovers them at full cost. Bureaucratic turnover is not merely a human-resources issue. It is a security risk.

Here, the distinction between *myth-making* and learning becomes decisive. Myth-making takes the complexity of a proxy campaign and compresses it into a story that flatters the state: we were clever, deniable, economical; the client did what we wanted; any failure was someone else's fault. Myth-making is seductive because it performs political work. It justifies budgets. It preserves reputations. It reassures the public that chaos abroad is manageable. But it also creates doctrine by folklore—an inherited set of assumptions that shape future decisions.

One five-word sentence matters here. *Myths survive bureaucratic churn.*

A second, equally important sentence follows. Lessons often do not.

The United States provides an instructive case of both tendencies—serious institutional learning alongside recurrent repetition. After the Iran–Contra scandal broke in late 1986, revealing the clandestine sale of arms to Iran and diversion of proceeds to support the Contras in Nicaragua, Washington faced a rare moment of forced transparency. Investigations followed, including the Tower Commission (1987) and congressional inquiries. Procedures tightened. Legal and oversight frameworks gained attention. Yet the broader appetite for covert action did not disappear; it adapted. Later proxy-heavy efforts, in different theatres and with different justifications, still struggled with familiar problems: divergent client agendas, arms leakage, reputational blowback, and mission creep.

Show the behaviour. A covert programme expands without clear political end-state, relies on local partners with opaque loyalties, and becomes harder to terminate than to initiate. Name it. Policy inertia. Explain it. Proxy relationships create dependencies—political, operational, reputational—that persist even when the strategic rationale weakens. Implication: without institutional brakes, proxy programmes drift towards permanence.

Contrast this with a state that, over time, built more formalised mechanisms to manage proxy risk as a matter of doctrine and force design. Israel's experience with proxy relationships—most notably with the South Lebanon Army (SLA) from the late 1970s to 2000—offers a stark lesson in the consequences of exit. When Israel withdrew from southern Lebanon in May 2000, the SLA collapsed rapidly; many of its members fled into Israel, and Hezbollah consolidated control in the south. The episode exposed the fragility of client forces once patron protection ends and underscored the long-term reputational and security costs of creating local auxiliaries without a sustainable political settlement.

Israel's subsequent approach to irregular partners and border security became more cautious in some respects and more technologically mediated in others. It invested heavily in intelligence, surveillance, and rapid strike capabilities designed to reduce reliance on local proxies for territorial control. The shift was not absolute; states rarely abandon useful tools. But it illustrates institutional adaptation: replacing a proxy-dependent model of control with a different architecture of force. The lesson was written not in a report alone, but in procurement choices and operational doctrine.

Now consider a state that repeatedly struggled to internalise proxy lessons because political incentives favoured short-term gains and blurred accountability. Pakistan's relationship with militant proxies, particularly in Afghanistan and Kashmir, is widely discussed in scholarship and policy analysis. Over decades, elements of the Pakistani security establishment supported certain militant groups as instruments of regional strategy. The blowback was severe: domestic insurgency, international pressure, and cycles of violence that did not respect the boundary between "external" and "internal" assets. Yet the pattern proved persistent, shaped by strategic fears, organisational culture, and competing power centres within the state.

Show the behaviour. A proxy network originally justified for external leverage becomes embedded in domestic politics, resists dismantlement, and generates splinter groups. Name it. Asset entrenchment. Explain it. Once a proxy becomes part of an establishment's identity and informal toolkit, dismantling it threatens internal cohesion and perceived strategic depth. Implication: the state repeats the same risky behaviour because the cost of change appears higher than the cost of continuation—until the bill arrives.

This comparison is not moral theatre. It is organisational analysis. One state, chastened by a client collapse, reorients force design to reduce dependence on unreliable local auxiliaries. Another, confronted with blowback, struggles to uproot the proxy logic because internal incentives reward its continued use. Both face security dilemmas. The difference lies in the machinery of learning.

A credible limitation must be acknowledged. Sometimes repetition is not stupidity; it is constraint. States may continue proxy relationships because alternatives are worse: direct intervention is too costly, diplomacy is blocked, and withdrawal invites hostile domination. In such cases, "learning" may mean not avoiding proxy warfare but managing it with clearer guardrails. Reconciliation lies in distinguishing between *unavoidable use* and *avoidable negligence*. The former accepts imperfect tools under constraint; the latter refuses to measure risk.

Measurement matters. What does institutional memory look like in practice? It looks like vetting protocols that evolve after betrayal. It looks like tighter end-use monitoring after diversion. It looks like clearer chains of command for advisers embedded with partners. It looks like exit criteria tied to political objectives rather than to battlefield indicators alone. It looks, crucially, like records that survive personnel changes—training curricula, doctrine manuals, oversight routines, and dedicated offices that outlast any single crisis.

The quiet motif threading through this is the archive. Proxy wars generate archives—some literal, some informal: files, cables, intelligence assessments, budget lines. An archive can be a library or a tomb. When it becomes a library, new officials can learn without repeating old disasters. When it becomes a tomb, the dead facts stay buried and the living make the same mistakes with a new vocabulary.

The unresolved tension is immediate for any state tempted by proxy warfare's apparent economy. Can a government build institutions that tell the truth about its own covert behaviour—truths awkward enough to change policy—without exposing everything it seeks to keep secret? Or will it continue to rely on myths that flatter, soothe, and ultimately mislead, until the next proxy becomes the next problem it insists it did not create?

Chapter 9

Private Military Companies And Marketised Force

On 16 September 2007, armed contractors working for Blackwater opened fire at Nisour Square in Baghdad, killing seventeen Iraqi civilians. The incident detonated international outrage, legal confusion, and years of argument over who, precisely, bore responsibility. The men involved were not soldiers in uniform, yet they were carrying out security tasks inseparable from a war. They were not proxies in the classic sense, yet their actions reshaped a conflict and constrained a patron's political room for manoeuvre. The episode exposed a paradox that sits at the heart of modern warfare: states increasingly outsource violence, yet struggle to control the consequences of treating force as a service.

War has entered the marketplace.

Private military companies did not emerge from a vacuum. They arrived at the intersection of shrinking conscript armies, expanding expeditionary commitments, and a political appetite for distance—distance from casualties, from legal scrutiny, and from the moral weight of direct intervention. Where earlier chapters examined proxy militias bound by ideology, ethnicity, or survival, this chapter turns to actors bound by contract. The difference matters. A proxy believes, obeys, or depends. A contractor invoices.

That distinction reshapes everything.

The core idea running through this chapter is simple but unsettling: when force is bought and sold, incentives change. Loyalty becomes conditional. Risk acquires a price. Success is measured not only in territorial control or political outcomes, but in contract renewal, deliverables met, and losses avoided. The market does not abolish strategy, but it refracts it through spreadsheets, insurance clauses, and corporate structures that blur neatly into state power while denying formal responsibility.

To understand why private military companies are neither merely mercenaries nor just another proxy, it helps to begin with how they coexist alongside traditional clients. In several contemporary conflicts, states have deliberately used both models in parallel. One local militia provides manpower, local legitimacy, and political cover. A PMC supplies training, logistics, technical expertise, or protection for critical assets. Each does a job the other cannot. The militia absorbs casualties and embeds itself socially. The company delivers speed, professionalism, and deniability with a commercial sheen. Together, they form a layered force architecture that allows patrons avoids choices they would rather not make.

This coexistence is not accidental. It reflects a strategic calculation about control. Ideological proxies can drift, radicalise, or defect. PMCs, in theory, can be fired. Contracts can be terminated. Payments can be withheld. Yet this apparent control conceals a deeper vulnerability: when the relationship is commercial, the logic of the battlefield is filtered through the logic of profit. Contractors are not rewarded for reconciliation, restraint, or political compromise unless those outcomes are explicitly priced in. More often, they are rewarded for visible stability—secure perimeters, guarded convoys, suppressed threats—whether or not those achievements translate into durable peace.

Follow the money, and behaviour follows.

Business models matter more than rhetoric. A firm that prices contracts by personnel deployed will favour presence over exit. One paid per incident prevented may favour aggressive deterrence. One rewarded for short-term calm may suppress symptoms while deepening structural grievances. These are not moral judgements; they are incentives. Understanding them is essential to understanding why marketised force often produces tactical competence alongside strategic fragility.

Ownership structures complicate matters further. Many prominent PMCs present themselves as apolitical service providers, yet their operations frequently track the geopolitical interests of their home states. This alignment may be explicit, informal, or mutually convenient. Resource concessions, preferential access, intelligence sharing, and diplomatic protection can bind company fortunes to state strategy without any formal chain of command. When that happens, the distinction between public policy and private enterprise becomes performative. The firm appears autonomous. The state appears distant. Both benefit from ambiguity.

Ambiguity, in this domain, is currency.

Legal frameworks lag behind practice. Jurisdictions overlap. Regulations vary by country, contract, and theatre. Enforcement is uneven. When abuses occur, responsibility fragments across corporate entities, subcontractors, host states, and patrons who deny control. Accountability, when it comes, is often narrow and retrospective: a trial years later, a settlement, a rebranded firm. The market survives. The lesson absorbed is not restraint, but risk management.

This chapter does not argue that PMCs are uniquely malign. Nor does it romanticise state control. Regular armed forces have their own pathologies, and proxy militias have inflicted immense harm. The point is analytical. Marketised force introduces a different set of trade-offs, ones that reward efficiency and flexibility while corroding clear lines of authority. It allows states to project power without mobilisation, to sustain operations without public debate, and to experiment with coercion below the threshold of war. It also introduces actors whose incentives are only partially aligned with any political end-state.

The future sharpens these questions. As warfare becomes more technical, the services most in demand—drone operation, cyber intrusion, intelligence analysis, secure communications—are increasingly provided by specialists who move easily between public and private roles. The contractor of tomorrow may never carry a rifle. They may sit behind a console, thousands of miles from the target, offering capabilities that are both deniable and indispensable. At that point, the line between a PMC and a standing proxy force dissolves almost entirely, replaced by a spectrum of paid auxiliaries embedded in state strategy yet shielded by corporate form.

The quiet motif running through this chapter is distance. Distance from the battlefield, from accountability, from political risk. PMCs thrive because they create distance while promising control. Whether that promise can be kept is the question that follows.

As the guns of earlier chapters fade, the contracts begin. Who signs them, who benefits from them, and who bears their costs will shape conflicts long after headlines move on. The pages ahead examine how private military companies fit into the architecture of proxy warfare, how markets reshape violence, and why the privatisation of force is not a technical detail but a political choice explained through balance sheets rather than banners.

What makes PMCs different from proxies

On 16 September 2007, at Nisour Square in Baghdad, armed employees of Blackwater fired into traffic while escorting a US diplomatic convoy. Seventeen civilians died. Within hours, American officials insisted the men were not soldiers and not under military command. Yet the incident occurred in a war zone created, sustained, and politically owned by the United States. The killings forced congressional hearings, diplomatic strain with the Iraqi government, and years of litigation that ended without a clear line of state responsibility. It was not a proxy failure in the usual sense. It was a contractual one.

Force had been outsourced.

The episode matters because it captures, in a single scene, what distinguishes private military companies from traditional proxies. Both fight in the shadow of state power. Both extend a patron's reach while softening accountability. But they are animated by different logics. A proxy militia is bound by belief, fear, patronage, or survival. A PMC is bound by a contract. That difference reshapes loyalty, discipline, risk tolerance, and political effect.

Money sets the terms.

Traditional proxies emerge from local soil. They recruit from communities, draw legitimacy from identity or grievance, and fight for causes that often predate the patron's involvement. When a state backs such a group, it enters an existing political ecosystem and tries to bend it. Control is partial, negotiated, and always fragile. Orders travel through intermediaries. Compliance is shaped by incentives, but also by pride, ideology, and internal factionalism. The patron manages a relationship.

A PMC offers something else entirely: a service menu. Training, site security, convoy protection, logistics, intelligence analysis, technical support. Each is priced, scheduled, and defined in advance. Personnel are hired for skills, not allegiance. If the mission changes, the contract changes. If the risk increases, the price rises. The relationship is managerial rather than political. That is the promise.

The implication is seductive. In theory, PMCs give patrons precision. They can be switched on and off. They can be scaled up without mobilisation and withdrawn without ceremony. Casualties do not appear on military rolls. Losses do not demand public explanation. The state appears present enough to shape events and distant enough to deny ownership. For leaders wary of domestic backlash, this is not a marginal advantage.

Yet the same features that make PMCs attractive also limit their strategic utility. Contractors are not invested in end-states unless those end-states are contractually defined. A proxy militia may accept losses to secure political dominance in its home territory. A PMC calculates exposure against remuneration. When conditions deteriorate, a proxy digs in. A contractor renegotiates or leaves. This is not cowardice. It is alignment with incentives.

The contrast becomes clearest when states use both models simultaneously.

In Syria after September 2015, Russia backed a patchwork of local militias aligned with the Assad regime while also deploying private military contractors linked to the Wagner Group. The militias provided manpower, local knowledge, and political anchoring in contested areas. Wagner units, operating around Latakia and later near resource sites in central and eastern Syria, focused on training, offensive operations, and the protection of strategic assets. The division of labour was explicit. One set of fighters absorbed casualties and maintained territorial presence. The other delivered specialised force where speed and plausible deniability mattered most. Moscow could calibrate exposure by shifting weight between the two.

This dual-track approach reveals the structural difference. Proxies anchor influence. PMCs shape margins.

Consider command and control. Proxy leaders bargain. They interpret guidance through their own priorities. When patrons push too hard, proxies may stall, defect, or pursue parallel agendas. PMCs operate under a clearer hierarchy. Orders flow through contractual authority, backed by pay and the threat of termination. Compliance is higher. Initiative is narrower. The battlefield becomes procedural.

That procedural quality carries consequences. Proxies often escalate conflicts unpredictably, dragging patrons into deeper commitments. PMCs tend to cap escalation. They avoid actions that threaten their legal position, insurance coverage, or future business. This can restrain violence. It can also freeze conflicts in place, producing tactical calm without political progress. Stability becomes a metric. Resolution does not.

The distinction also shapes accountability. When a proxy commits abuses, patrons can plausibly claim ignorance or loss of control. When a PMC does the same, the defence is legalistic: jurisdictional ambiguity, subcontracting chains, host-state responsibility. Both routes diffuse blame, but in different registers. Proxy deniability is political. PMC deniability is bureaucratic.

Neither is clean.

A credible counter-example complicates the picture. Some proxies, particularly those deeply dependent on a single patron for survival, can behave with a discipline that rivals contractual forces. Hezbollah's relationship with Iran, especially in Lebanon after 2006, shows how ideological alignment and institutional support can produce a proxy that acts with strategic restraint when required. Such groups may accept guidance on escalation, targeting, and timing in ways that resemble command relationships. The line between proxy and auxiliary blurs.

The reconciliation lies in time horizon. Ideological proxies with long-term political projects internalise patron preferences because their future depends on them. PMCs do not internalise. They comply. When the contract ends, so does the relationship. Memory does not carry over. Lessons are not absorbed unless written into new agreements. The state must relearn control each time.

Metrics expose the difference. Proxy effectiveness is often judged by territory held, rival groups neutralised, or political leverage gained. PMC performance is assessed through deliverables: sites secured, personnel trained, incidents reduced. A militia may tolerate chaos if it advances dominance. A contractor may suppress visible disorder even if it entrenches underlying conflict dynamics. Each produces a different war.

The quiet motif running through this comparison is loyalty. Proxies offer unreliable loyalty grounded in belief. PMCs offer reliable service grounded in payment. Patrons choose between them not because one is morally superior, but because each solves a different problem. When influence must be embedded, proxies matter. When exposure must be managed, contractors appeal.

The unresolved question is strategic. As conflicts become more fragmented and politically sensitive, will states increasingly prefer actors who can be fired over those who must be persuaded? Or will the absence of rooted commitment make marketised force a brittle substitute for genuine political alignment? The answer determines whether PMCs remain supplements to proxy warfare or quietly become its dominant form.

Business models for selling force

In 2004, the United States State Department signed a contract with Blackwater USA to provide personal security for diplomats in Baghdad. The setting was Iraq, the date was June 2004, and the outcome was immediate: armed contractors, not uniformed soldiers, became the most visible guardians of American power in the capital. The contract rewarded rapid deployment, uninterrupted movement, and the absence of high-profile attacks on convoys. It did not reward political reconciliation, local trust, or long-term stability. The incentives were clear. So were the consequences.

Force had a price.

That moment crystallised a shift that had been building for years. Private military companies were no longer marginal providers of guard services or training support. They were selling force as a bundled product, priced by risk, shaped by contract language, and judged by metrics that rarely aligned with the political end-states patrons claimed to want. To understand how PMCs behave on the battlefield, one must begin not with ideology or doctrine, but with invoices.

Risk is the core commodity. Everything else follows.

PMCs price risk through a mix of hazard premiums, insurance costs, personnel pay scales, and contingency clauses. A contract to guard an embassy in a relatively stable capital looks very different from one to escort convoys through contested territory. The visible behaviour that follows is predictable. Routes are chosen to minimise exposure. Engagement rules err towards overwhelming force to deter interference. Time on the ground is compressed. These are not tactical quirks; they are rational responses to cost curves.

Name the model and the logic sharpens. Most PMCs operate on cost-plus or fixed-price contracts with performance benchmarks. Cost-plus arrangements reimburse expenses and add a margin, encouraging expansion of activity and equipment. Fixed-price contracts reward efficiency, pushing firms to limit personnel, rely on technology, and avoid prolonged engagements. In both cases, the firm's survival depends less on winning a conflict than on managing liability.

The implication is subtle but profound. When stability is defined as the absence of incidents during the contract period, PMCs optimise for visibility rather than durability. Streets appear calm. Underlying grievances remain untouched.

Bundling deepens this effect. Modern PMCs rarely sell a single service. Training is paired with logistics. Site security comes with intelligence analysis. Communications support is folded into convoy protection. This bundling allows firms to lock in clients and cross-subsidise riskier activities with steadier revenue streams. It also concentrates influence. A company that trains a local force, supplies its equipment, and guards its headquarters shapes behaviour at every level without ever holding formal authority.

Consider DynCorp's role in Afghanistan after 2003. Tasked with police training, logistics support, and advisory functions, the company operated under contracts that prioritised numbers trained and facilities refurbished. The visible metric was throughput. The result, documented by the US Special Inspector General for Afghanistan Reconstruction in reports published between 2010 and 2015, was a police force that expanded rapidly but struggled with corruption, retention, and legitimacy. The business model delivered outputs. The political system absorbed costs.

Financial incentives also shape escalation. PMCs have little interest in battles that threaten contract termination or reputational damage in key markets. They avoid actions that could provoke direct confrontation with state forces or rival patrons. This restraint can dampen violence. It can also entrench stalemate. A proxy militia may gamble on escalation to force negotiations. A contractor rarely will.

The quiet motif here is the contract itself. It appears neutral. It is anything but.

Contracts translate political ambiguity into operational clarity. They specify what counts. They exclude what does not. When reconciliation is not billable, it is invisible. When visible calm is rewarded, deeper disorder persists beneath the surface.

A brief case makes the point starkly. In southern Iraq between 2006 and 2008, private security firms hired by energy companies and coalition agencies were rewarded for keeping facilities operational and attacks off the news cycle. Payments were tied to uninterrupted production and incident-free reporting periods. Local power brokers learned quickly. Violence shifted away from guarded sites into surrounding neighbourhoods. Stability was purchased. It was also displaced.

There are limits to this logic. A credible counter-example comes from UN-contracted security providers in Sierra Leone after 2000, where contracts were paired with political benchmarks and integrated into broader peacebuilding efforts. Firms operating under tighter oversight and clearer political guidance showed greater alignment with long-term goals. The reconciliation lies not in the market itself, but in how it is governed. When contracts encode political priorities, behaviour follows.

Yet governance is uneven. Jurisdictions differ. Enforcement is patchy. Firms arbitrage regulation as readily as they price risk. A company restricted in one market shifts focus to another. Personnel rotate. Institutional memory thins.

Metrics tell the story. Casualty rates among contractors are often lower than among local forces. Incident reports decline. Budgets remain contained. Meanwhile, measures of trust, legitimacy, and political integration lag. These are not accidental gaps. They reflect what the business model sees.

The implication for patrons is uncomfortable. By outsourcing force, states also outsource judgement. They replace political risk with financial risk and then act surprised when outcomes follow spreadsheets rather than strategy. The market does not misbehave. It performs as designed.

This does not mean PMCs are inherently destabilising. It means their incentives must be read with care. When contracts reward short-term calm, short-term calm is delivered. When they reward capacity-building with accountability, different behaviours emerge. The challenge is that the latter are harder to specify, slower to measure, and politically costly to enforce.

Five words suffice here. Incentives decide behaviour always.

The unresolved tension is strategic. As conflicts become more complex and politically constrained, will patrons accept the true costs of aligning contracts with long-term goals? Or will they continue to purchase the appearance of order and call it success? The answer will determine whether the market for force matures into a tool of statecraft or remains a mirror reflecting the limits of political will.

Blurring corporate and state interests

On 7 February 2018, near Khasham in Syria's Deir ez-Zor governorate, a force aligned with the Assad government advanced towards a position held by the US-backed Syrian Democratic Forces. US aircraft and artillery struck back. Reports soon circulated that Russian private military contractors—widely described as linked to the Wagner Group—were among those hit. Moscow denied that regular Russian troops were involved. The outcome was not only tactical; it was political. A potentially escalatory clash between nuclear-armed states was reclassified as something murkier: an incident involving "volunteers", "contractors", and a war nobody quite owned.

The paperwork mattered.

That is the point of marketised force at the strategic edge. Private military companies, in their purest commercial form, sell protection and training to whoever pays. Yet some of the most consequential firms are not "pure" in any meaningful sense. Their ownership structures, informal ties, and operational patterns make it hard—sometimes deliberately hard—to separate corporate activity from state policy. The result is a hybrid instrument: a company that behaves like an arm of national strategy while preserving the deniability and transactional flexibility of the market.

Follow the share register.

A state that uses such firms gains two advantages at once. First, it acquires a tool for coercion that can operate below the threshold of formal war, allowing leaders to test reactions, move faster than diplomats, and absorb setbacks without the domestic reckoning that accompanies uniformed casualties. Second, it can fuse violence to commerce: contracts, concessions, and political favours become the logistics of influence. In that fusion, the battlefield is no longer merely a theatre of war. It becomes a marketplace for access.

The mechanism begins with ownership and ends with behaviour. Show the behaviour: a firm appears in the same theatres as its home state's strategic concerns; it secures resource infrastructure; it trains local forces aligned with the patron's diplomatic agenda; it withdraws or advances in tandem with shifts in official policy. Name it: strategic synchronisation. Explain it: even without a formal chain of command, shared networks of elites, security services, and political protection can align a firm's choices with state priorities. Implication: the company becomes a semi-official instrument—useful precisely because it is not, on paper, official.

Resource concessions are the most visible clue to this alignment. When a security provider's revenue depends on access to oil fields, mines, or transport corridors, its operational logic changes. It does not simply keep clients safe; it shapes political outcomes to secure commercial rights. The patron, meanwhile, gains a self-financing auxiliary that can sustain operations without constant budgetary exposure. This is not a theoretical risk. It has been a recurring pattern wherever weak governance meets strategic competition.

In Syria, the Wagner-linked model has repeatedly been described in terms of protecting or advancing towards energy assets, with associated commercial entities reportedly seeking a share of proceeds in exchange for securing and recapturing infrastructure. The details of these arrangements are often contested and obscured by front companies, shifting contracts, and the fog of war. Yet the pattern itself is intelligible. A state pursues influence; a firm pursues revenue; both converge on the same targets. The motif of the share register returns, this time as a map of coercion.

A second example, in a different register, shows how corporate-state interest can blur even within formal legal systems. In the 1990s, the US-based Military Professional Resources Incorporated (MPRI) provided training and advisory services to the Croatian Army. Croatia's Operation Storm in August 1995 became a decisive military event in the Croatian War of Independence, with profound political consequences and enduring controversy over civilian displacement and war crimes committed during and after the offensive. Debates have persisted about what, precisely, foreign contractors contributed and how closely their work aligned with US strategic aims in the Balkans. The point here is not to settle that debate. It is to note the structure: a private firm operating in a conflict zone, offering capabilities consistent with a broader geopolitical orientation, while allowing official actors to maintain distance from the operational edge.

Distance is not absence. It is design.

When corporate and state interests blur, intelligence sharing becomes both lubricant and accelerant. A company that receives privileged access to imagery, signals intercepts, or operational deconfliction channels is no longer merely a private actor. It is plugged into state capacity. Conversely, a state that relies on a company's on-the-ground reporting gains a stream of intelligence without formal deployment. The relationship can be mutually reinforcing, and therefore mutually corrupting. Each party begins to depend on the other's information, and dependence shapes choices. A patron may hesitate to discipline a firm whose networks provide valuable access. A firm may shade reports to preserve patron protection.

Political favours complete the triangle. Licences, diplomatic support, legal shielding, and access to transport corridors can be traded for services that would be politically costly if performed by regular forces. This is where the market does more than sell force. It sells plausible deniability. The patron can say, with some legal plausibility, that a contractor is an independent actor. The contractor can say, with equal plausibility, that it is merely fulfilling a contract. The public gets a fog of explanations.

Yet fog does not eliminate causation. It merely complicates attribution.

One can measure the blurring through decisions that are hard to justify on commercial grounds alone. When a firm accepts unusually high-risk deployments without transparent compensation, or persists in a theatre despite reputational damage, the explanation often lies outside the balance sheet. It lies in political insurance: future contracts, state protection, access to privileged markets. Conversely, when a firm's operations track a state's strategic priorities with uncanny consistency—appearing where the patron seeks leverage and fading where the patron seeks de-escalation—the alignment is not accidental. It is structural.

A credible limitation must be faced. Not all private security or military firms function as shadow arms of state policy. Many operate in comparatively mundane roles: guarding ships against piracy, protecting corporate compounds, training local police under international programmes, or providing logistics support in permissive environments. They may be heavily regulated, subject to audits, and constrained by reputation in competitive markets. For these firms, the "blur" is less sinister than simply functional: private capacity serving public needs.

The reconciliation is to distinguish *market provision* from *market capture.* Market provision occurs when firms compete to provide services within clear legal frameworks and oversight. Market capture occurs when political power selects favoured firms, grants them privileged access, and uses them as instruments of strategy while insulating them from normal accountability. The latter is where corporate and state interests fuse, and where proxy logic re-enters through commercial form.

This fusion changes the patron's risk calculations in ways that can be dangerously misleading. A leader may assume a contractor's actions are containable because they are "private". Yet if the contractor's actions trigger retaliation, scandal, or escalation, the state will be pulled towards ownership regardless of initial denials. The deniability is therefore time-limited. It works until it doesn't. The Khasham episode in 2018 is instructive precisely because it shows both the utility and fragility of the model: plausible deniability prevented immediate escalation, but the incident also demonstrated how quickly contractors can become tripwires.

The blurring also changes the client's politics. Host states, militias, and local elites learn to bargain not only with diplomats and generals, but with corporate representatives who can offer security and resources. Power fragments. Accountability disperses. Corruption becomes more difficult to track because it is routed through contracts rather than ministries. The state patron may prefer this fragmentation because it weakens rivals and increases dependence. The long-term cost is institutional decay in the theatre of operations, and a legacy of armed entrepreneurship that outlasts any single conflict.

There is a moral hazard here, and it is measurable. When force is tied to commercial reward, violent success can generate revenue directly through access to assets. That creates an incentive to prolong insecurity just enough to justify continued presence, while preventing chaos so large that it threatens the business itself. Visible stability becomes the product; political settlement becomes a threat to revenue. Even when individual contractors behave professionally, the structure can still reward outcomes at odds with peace.

The motif returns: the share register as a strategic document. Who owns, who profits, who protects—these questions become inseparable from who fights and why.

The forward test is stark. When a patron's preferred company is simultaneously a security provider, an access broker, and a beneficiary of resource concessions, what exactly is the state purchasing: a service, a policy, or a disguised form of empire by contract? And when the next crisis erupts, will decision-makers still be able to claim they merely hired help—or will the ledger reveal, too late, that they outsourced violence but not responsibility?

Legal accountability and plausible deniability

On 16 September 2007, at Nisour Square in Baghdad, contractors working for Blackwater USA opened fire during a convoy operation. Iraqi civilians were killed. The incident detonated politically within hours. The United States government moved to distance itself from the shooters while affirming the legitimacy of its diplomatic mission. Blackwater asserted that its personnel had acted in self-defence. Iraq demanded accountability. Years later, after investigations, trials, convictions, appeals, and presidential pardons, the episode had produced a strange equilibrium: some legal consequences, a great deal of anger, and a private security market that survived intact.

The law did not fail outright. It bent.

That bending—elastic, selective, and uneven—is the legal condition that makes marketised force viable. Private military companies operate in a thicket of overlapping jurisdictions: the law of the hiring state, the law of the host state, the nationality of the contractors, the terms of the contract, and the fragments of international humanitarian and human rights law that may or may not apply. Each layer offers obligations. Each also offers exits. The resulting ambiguity is not merely tolerated. It is cultivated.

Plausible deniability is the quiet motif. It appears in statutes, contracts, and courtroom strategies, then returns as policy.

Begin with behaviour. Contractors move through conflict zones carrying weapons, conducting security operations, training forces, and sometimes engaging in combat-like activity. Name the claim: legal ambiguity structures conduct. Explain it: when actors know that attribution is uncertain and enforcement inconsistent, risk calculations shift. Implication: states gain flexibility; firms gain market access; victims gain uncertainty.

The foundational distinction is formal status. Contractors are not members of a state's armed forces. They are civilians accompanying the force, employees of a corporation, or subcontractors several layers removed from the original client. That status matters because the most robust bodies of war law—combatant immunity, military justice systems, clear chains of command—attach to uniforms and flags. Remove the uniform, and the law becomes conditional. This is not accidental. It is a design choice that allows states to externalise risk.

Consider jurisdiction first. A contractor may be hired by a state A, operate in state B, be a national of state C, and be employed by a firm incorporated in state D. If a violent incident occurs, which court has authority? State B may assert territorial jurisdiction, but practical access to the accused can be blocked by status-of-forces-like agreements or diplomatic pressure. State A may claim jurisdiction, but domestic prosecutors must decide whether the conduct fits existing statutes. State C may lack interest or capacity. State D may offer only corporate remedies. The gaps are predictable.

In the United States context, the Military Extraterritorial Jurisdiction Act (MEJA) was designed to close some of these gaps by extending federal criminal jurisdiction to certain crimes committed abroad by contractors supporting US missions. MEJA has been used. It has also been criticised for narrow scope, uneven application, and reliance on political will.

The Blackwater prosecutions—complex, protracted, and ultimately overshadowed by executive clemency—illustrated both the existence of tools and their fragility.

This is not merely an American story. In Iraq, after years of limited control over foreign contractors, the government moved in 2011 to require licensing and greater oversight. Enforcement remained difficult. In Afghanistan, a patchwork of regulations attempted to rein in private security providers, including efforts to disband or integrate them. Outcomes varied. The pattern holds: regulation expands after scandal, then recedes as operational demands return.

The second mechanism is contractual design. Show the behaviour: contracts specify tasks, rules of engagement, reporting requirements, and indemnities. Name it: risk allocation through paper. Explain it: liability can be shifted through clauses that place responsibility on the individual contractor, the subcontractor, or the local partner, while insulating the principal. Implication: when violence occurs, blame is pre-distributed.

Indemnification clauses, arbitration provisions, and confidentiality requirements are not legal curiosities. They are operational enablers. A firm that knows it will be defended by its client, or at least not aggressively prosecuted, prices risk differently. A state that knows a contractor bears initial liability can deploy capabilities it would hesitate to use directly. The market responds. Behaviour follows.

A second, checkable example sharpens the point. In September 2012, in Kabul, an incident involving G4S personnel—one of the world's largest security companies—led to Afghan scrutiny and temporary suspension of operations following allegations related to misconduct and corruption. Investigations resulted in fines and reforms, not criminal trials that threatened the firm's existence. G4S continued to operate globally, adjusting compliance frameworks while retaining contracts. Accountability occurred. It was bounded.

Bounded accountability is the compromise that keeps the market alive.

The third mechanism is enforcement capacity. Even where laws exist, host states emerging from conflict often lack the institutional strength to investigate, prosecute, and enforce judgments against foreign firms. Evidence collection is weak. Witnesses fear reprisal. Courts are politicised. States that hire PMCs know this. Firms know it too. The imbalance becomes a feature of the business environment, not a bug.

A credible counter-example must be acknowledged. Some states have moved towards tighter regulation and enforcement. Switzerland's Montreux Document of 2008, while non-binding, clarified existing international legal obligations related to private military and security companies and encouraged good practices. Several European states have strengthened licensing regimes, reporting requirements, and penalties for violations. The United Kingdom's approach, though criticised for restraint, has included export controls and corporate law mechanisms that can, in theory, be activated.

Reconciliation lies in incentives. Where PMCs serve primarily defensive, low-profile roles within stable legal systems, enforcement is feasible and reputational pressure matters. Where PMCs operate as instruments of state power in contested theatres, incentives reverse. States prioritise flexibility over enforcement. Firms prioritise access over restraint. The same legal framework produces different outcomes because political context changes the cost of action.

International law offers no simple rescue. Mercenary conventions exist, but their definitions are narrow and rarely fit contemporary firms that emphasise training, security, or logistics. International humanitarian law applies to conduct in armed conflict, but classification disputes—international or non-international, direct participation or not—complicate application. Human rights law may apply extraterritorially in some circumstances, but enforcement mechanisms are slow and indirect. Each regime gestures towards accountability. None delivers it consistently.

The motif returns: plausible deniability as architecture. States deny control; firms deny agency; law circles the perimeter.

One sees this architecture clearly in how scandals are managed. Show the pattern: an incident occurs; an investigation is announced; individuals are suspended; a report is issued; contracts are rebranded; the market stabilises. Name it: containment through process. Explain it: procedural responses absorb political pressure without altering the underlying model. Implication: learning is shallow.

Metrics help ground the abstraction. When firms face fines rather than licence revocation; when executives avoid personal liability; when states renew contracts after "reforms", the signal is clear. The system tolerates failure so long as it is episodic and deniable. Trust, in this context, is not moral confidence but predictability of consequences.

There is a deeper strategic effect. Legal ambiguity allows patrons to calibrate escalation. If a contractor's actions provoke backlash, the state can disavow and de-escalate. If they succeed quietly, the state can enjoy the gains. This optionality is valuable. It is also corrosive. Over time, it erodes the norm that the use of organised violence should be clearly attributable and politically accountable.

Victims, meanwhile, navigate a maze. Civil suits may be blocked by jurisdictional hurdles or immunities. Criminal complaints may stall. Compensation, if offered, is often ex gratia rather than adjudicated. Justice becomes a negotiation, not a right. That reality feeds resentment and undermines post-conflict stabilisation—the very outcome many contracts claim to support.

The unresolved tension is structural. Tighten the law too much, and states lose a tool they clearly want. Leave it loose, and the market continues to operate in a grey zone that rewards opacity. The forward test, then, is not whether accountability can be improved in principle, but whether any major patron is willing to accept the loss of deniability that real accountability would entail. When the next incident occurs—and it will—will the paperwork again absorb the shock, or will a state finally choose to own what it hires?

Future of marketised security provision

In September 2020, the Wagner Group appeared openly alongside Malian forces in Bamako, marking a visible shift in how outsourced force presents itself. The organisation was neither a rebel proxy nor a conventional private security firm. It operated through contracts, political understandings, and denials layered thickly enough to confuse attribution while shaping outcomes on the ground. By December 2021, Western governments were publicly naming Wagner's presence in Mali, even as Moscow denied command responsibility. The effect was paradoxical: exposure did not end the practice; it normalised it.

Markets learn quickly.

The future of marketised security provision is not a question of whether private military companies will persist, but how they will mutate. The quiet motif is substitution. Where states once substituted proxies for troops, they increasingly substitute firms for proxies, and technology for both. Each substitution promises control with distance. Each creates new risks.

Begin with behaviour. States contract regional security firms staffed by veterans with local language skills and cultural familiarity. Name the trend: regionalisation. Explain it: firms rooted in a region offer deniability and plausible competence at lower political cost than deploying foreign nationals. Implication: marketised force becomes harder to distinguish from local armed actors, blurring accountability further.

African security markets illustrate this shift. Firms such as STTEP, active in Nigeria in 2015, recruited regional fighters to advise and support operations against Boko Haram. Their short-term impact was tactically significant, but the arrangement collapsed once political winds shifted and contracts ended. The lesson absorbed by the market was not restraint, but adaptation: localise ownership, fragment branding, shorten chains of command. Regional firms now pitch themselves as capacity-builders rather than combatants, even when the boundary is thin.

Technology accelerates this process. Show the behaviour: contractors operate drones, manage surveillance feeds, and provide cyber security from secure facilities far from the battlefield. Name it: tech-heavy contracting. Explain it: as warfare becomes data-driven, the most valuable services are no longer boots but bandwidth, analysts, and algorithms. Implication: the physical presence that once anchored legal responsibility fades.

Consider a second example. In 2018, the United Arab Emirates reportedly employed contractors linked to the firm Reflex Responses to support operations in Yemen, including surveillance and targeting assistance. Publicly, the work was framed as security and training. The strategic effect was leverage without fingerprints. As aerial platforms and cyber tools proliferate, similar arrangements become easier to scale and harder to detect.

Metrics replace ideology here. Contractors are judged on uptime, response speed, and system availability. Trust becomes a service-level agreement. Risk is priced per hour, not per life. Decisions that once demanded political debate are reframed as procurement choices. This is not abstraction. It is a procurement logic that shifts how violence is authorised.

A credible counter-example tempers the picture. Some states are pulling capabilities back in-house. France's recalibration after Operation Barkhane, including greater reliance on national forces and multilateral frameworks, reflected discomfort with outsourcing core security functions. The reconciliation lies in scope. States retreat from outsourcing when strategic stakes are existential or when reputational costs spike. They outsource when objectives are limited, deniable, or peripheral.

Mixed public-private coalitions represent the next iteration. Show the behaviour: uniformed forces operate alongside contractors, NGOs, and tech firms within a single theatre. Name it: coalition outsourcing. Explain it: complexity diffuses responsibility and complicates attribution. Implication: escalation management becomes harder as more actors control critical functions.

Drone operators exemplify this future. A contractor flying an unmanned system from a third country can collect intelligence, cue strikes, or defend infrastructure without crossing borders. Cyber contractors extend this logic further. Attribution in cyberspace is contested by design. When offensive cyber operations are conducted by firms under contract, states gain deniability while retaining influence. The line between espionage, sabotage, and warfare blurs.

The motif returns: substitution. Each layer substitutes distance for responsibility.

Legal and ethical frameworks lag. Existing regulations focus on physical presence and kinetic action. They struggle to encompass algorithmic targeting, autonomous systems, and data-driven warfare. Firms respond by rebranding: "risk management", "resilience services", "digital defence". The language sanitises capability. Behaviour remains consequential.

One five-word sentence belongs here. Control without visible commitment.

The unresolved tension is strategic. As PMCs begin to resemble standing proxy forces—persistent, specialised, and politically aligned—states must decide whether the benefits of deniability outweigh the erosion of control. Markets will continue to offer solutions. The forward test is whether governments will accept the accountability that comes with the force they hire, or whether substitution will deepen until ownership of violence becomes irretrievably diffuse.

Chapter 10

Measuring Success And The Next Proxy Century

On 15 December 2011, as the last United States combat troops crossed the border out of Iraq, President Barack Obama declared that America was leaving behind a "sovereign, stable and self-reliant" country. The ceremony was crisp, the language confident. Less than three years later, fighters of the so-called Islamic State were driving captured American-made vehicles through Mosul, while Iraqi units trained and equipped at great expense collapsed or defected. Public victory had not prevented strategic unravelling. The war was over. The proxy struggle was not.

Success, in proxy wars, rarely announces itself honestly.

This chapter begins with a problem that sits quietly beneath every preceding one. If proxy warfare is chosen precisely because it lowers costs, blurs responsibility, and stretches outcomes over time, then by what standard is it judged to have worked at all? Victories are proclaimed, budgets closed, medals awarded, yet instability persists, rivals adapt, and civilians endure consequences that sit uncomfortably with official narratives. The language of success becomes elastic, stretched to cover contradictions.

The core insight is simple but unsettling: proxy wars are almost never fought to *win* in the conventional sense. They are fought to manage risk, shape environments, and postpone worse outcomes. That logic demands a different way of measuring results.

The first task of this chapter is to unsettle the battlefield reflex. Territorial gains, body counts, and regime change dominate headlines because they are visible. They photograph well. Yet patrons frequently value other outcomes more highly: keeping an ally in power, denying influence to a rival, maintaining alliance cohesion, or preventing domestic political fallout. These goals are harder to measure and easier to disguise. They explain why leaders can stand at lecterns declaring success while internal assessments catalogue strategic disappointment.

A recurring image threads through what follows: the scoreboard. Public scoreboards show one set of numbers. Private ones show another. The gap between them is where proxy wars live.

From there, the chapter turns to perspective. Success looks different depending on where one stands. For patrons, it may mean limited expenditure and plausible deniability. For clients, it may mean survival today at the cost of autonomy tomorrow. For civilians, success may be the absence of violence rather than the triumph of any side. These measures are often incompatible. A campaign celebrated in capitals can register as catastrophe on the ground. That tension is not accidental; it is structural.

Historical comparison sharpens the point. Cold War proxy conflicts in Korea, Angola, and Afghanistan reveal patterns that reappear today despite new technology and faster information flows. Patrons still overestimate control. Clients still adapt agendas. Local dynamics still outlive foreign attention. Drones, surveillance platforms, and autonomous systems compress timelines and amplify visibility, but they do not dissolve the underlying dilemmas. If anything, they multiply audiences and harden narratives, turning evidence into propaganda at the speed of upload.

Technology therefore complicates measurement rather than simplifying it. Drone footage can prove tactical effectiveness while simultaneously fuelling political backlash. Precision can coexist with strategic drift. The tools change. The accounting problem remains.

The final movement of the chapter looks forward. Power is diffusing. Non-state actors are better armed, better networked, and more financially independent than their predecessors. Proxy wars are likely to start faster, spread wider, and end messier. The question is no longer whether another proxy century is coming, but whether states are learning how to judge what they are actually achieving when they fight this way.

The chapter closes not with predictions but with tests. When the next local clash draws in outside patrons within weeks, when success is declared early and often, when footage circulates before strategy solidifies, the reader will be equipped to ask harder questions. Whose scoreboard is being shown. Whose costs are being counted. And whether what is called success today is merely the deferral of failure tomorrow.

Defining outcomes beyond battlefield wins

On 15 December 2011, at Fort Bragg in North Carolina, President Barack Obama announced that the United States was ending its war in Iraq. The language was decisive. The outcome, he said, was "a sovereign, stable and self-reliant Iraq". Combat operations had ceased. Casualties were down. The scoreboard, at least the public one, showed a win.

Three years later, Islamic State fighters were parading through Mosul in captured American equipment. Iraqi units trained at vast expense dissolved under pressure. Washington's internal assessments, later reflected in Congressional testimony and Special Inspector General reports, were far less sanguine than the speech. The war had ended. The proxy contest had merely changed shape.

Five words mattered. The scoreboard still lied.

The habit of judging proxy wars by battlefield outcomes persists because it is comforting. Territory can be mapped. Enemies killed can be counted. Flags raised can be photographed. Yet proxy wars are rarely designed around such metrics. They are instruments for managing exposure, shaping regional balances, and navigating domestic politics. Victory speeches are therefore not deceptions so much as translations, converting messy realities into usable narratives.

The first step in defining outcomes beyond battlefield wins is to observe how patrons behave once the cameras are gone. In Iraq after 2011, the United States did not dismantle its regional posture, abandon intelligence coverage, or withdraw diplomatic pressure. It shifted effort from combat units to advisers, from overt operations to partner management. That behaviour reveals the true metric: not conquest, but influence under constraint.

Name that outcome, and it clarifies much. Regime survival, not transformation. Regional positioning, not pacification. Alliance cohesion, not local harmony. Domestic political stability, not distant order.

Consider regime survival. In Syria, Russia announced "mission accomplished" moments in March 2016 and again in December 2017, each time framing battlefield momentum as strategic success. Publicly, the intervention was limited and effective. Privately, Russian military journals and budgetary data showed sustained deployments, casualty concealment, and escalating financial commitments. The core outcome was not the defeat of all opposition forces but the survival of the Assad government and the preservation of Russia's naval and air facilities at Tartus and Khmeimim. By that measure, the campaign worked, even as violence persisted and reconstruction stalled.

The implication is uncomfortable. A proxy war can succeed while failing locally.

Regional influence operates on a similar logic. Influence is not measured by kilometres held but by options denied to rivals. In Yemen, Iran's support for the Houthi movement did not require a decisive military victory. It required sustained pressure on Saudi Arabia's southern flank, missile and drone capabilities that imposed political and economic costs, and a bargaining chip in wider regional negotiations. Saudi-led coalition forces captured territory repeatedly. Iran's outcome lay elsewhere, visible in Saudi defence spending, diplomatic recalibration, and eventual negotiations in Beijing in March 2023. The scoreboard showed stalemate. The influence ledger told a different story.

Alliance cohesion is an even quieter metric. Proxy wars strain alliances precisely because they distribute risk unevenly. In Afghanistan, NATO allies publicly echoed American success narratives for years, even as national caveats multiplied and domestic support eroded. A 2018 SIGAR "Lessons Learned" report noted that US objectives shifted repeatedly, while allies adapted rhetorically to maintain political cover at home. The battlefield did not collapse overnight. The alliance did, gradually, as cohesion frayed under the weight of incompatible narratives.

Domestic stability completes the picture. Patrons fight proxy wars partly to avoid domestic costs. Casualty sensitivity, budgetary scrutiny, and electoral cycles shape declarations of success. When President François Hollande announced the end of major French combat operations in Mali in July 2014, the security situation remained volatile. What had changed was domestic tolerance. The outcome was framed to stabilise opinion at home, even as Operation Barkhane expanded regionally. The behaviour matched the metric.

At this point, a limitation deserves attention. Not all proxy wars can be written off as narrative victories masking strategic failure. There are cases where battlefield outcomes aligned with broader goals. The British campaign in Oman's Dhofar rebellion during the 1960s and early 1970s combined local forces, political reform, and limited external support to suppress an insurgency without regional spillover. The outcome endured. The difference lay in coherence: objectives were stable, client incentives aligned, and post-conflict governance addressed. This counter-example matters because it shows that broader metrics do not excuse poor strategy; they expose it.

Reconcile the cases, and a pattern emerges. Where patrons define outcomes clearly and align means accordingly, battlefield success can translate into strategic gain. Where outcomes remain implicit or politically convenient, victory speeches substitute for assessment.

The recurring motif of the scoreboard sharpens this analysis. Public scoreboards track visible wins. Private scoreboards track survivability, leverage, and risk. In Iraq, the public scoreboard closed in 2011. The private one stayed open. In Syria, Russia kept both running simultaneously, adjusting which one it displayed. In Yemen, Iran never bothered with the public version at all.

Metrics make this visible. Regime survival can be measured by continuity of leadership and control over core institutions. Regional influence shows up in basing rights, arms transfers, and diplomatic access. Alliance cohesion is reflected in voting patterns, troop contributions, and the language of joint communiqués. Domestic stability reveals itself in polling, budget votes, and media framing. These are behaviours, not abstractions.

Why, then, do patrons persist in declaring success amid disorder? Because proxy wars are fought as much against time as against enemies. Declaring success freezes a moment, allowing disengagement or recalibration without admitting failure. It is a political technology.

This brings us back to the paradox at the heart of proxy warfare. If success is defined broadly enough, almost any outcome can be claimed as a win. If defined too narrowly, none can. The art lies in choosing metrics that discipline decision-making rather than excuse it.

The unresolved tension remains. As proxy wars accelerate and visibility increases, will patrons continue to rely on elastic narratives, or will private scoreboards begin to leak into public debate faster than they can be managed? The next declaration of victory will test that balance. The scoreboard will be raised. The question is which one.

Indicators for patrons, clients, and civilians

On 1 May 2015, the Saudi-led coalition announced the end of *Operation Decisive Storm* over Yemen, declaring that its objectives had been achieved. Riyadh spoke of degraded enemy capabilities and restored deterrence. In Sana'a and Taiz, the war intensified. By December 2016, the United Nations Office for the Coordination of Humanitarian Affairs reported that more than 80 per cent of Yemen's population required humanitarian assistance (OCHA, 2016). Two scoreboards, same war.

Metrics decide reality.

That divergence was not accidental. It was the predictable result of measuring success through different lenses, each shaped by incentives and exposure. For patrons, indicators privilege control, reputation, and risk management. For clients, survival, autonomy, and leverage matter most. For civilians, success is painfully concrete: safety, access to food, schools that open, roads that work. Proxy wars force these measures into collision.

The first task is to show how patrons measure outcomes when they believe nobody is watching. In Yemen, the coalition's public indicators centred on air sorties flown, targets struck, and statements of resolve. Privately, indicators shifted to border security incidents, missile interception rates, and the diplomatic posture of allies. Show the behaviour, name the metric, explain the choice, and the implication becomes clear: patrons value controllable indicators that translate into domestic reassurance and bargaining power, even when they say little about local conditions.

Name this logic patron-centric success. It rests on three visible behaviours. First, the selection of metrics that can be briefed quickly to ministers and legislatures: sorties, sanctions imposed, partners trained. Second, the emphasis on alliance signalling: joint statements, votes at the UN, defence cooperation agreements. Third, the management of escalation risk, visible in rules of engagement and deconfliction channels. Each behaviour maps to a metric: political cover, coalition cohesion, and exposure containment. The implication is stark. A campaign can be judged successful even as the society in which it unfolds collapses.

Clients read the same battlefield differently. Their indicators track survival and bargaining leverage. In Afghanistan, local militias aligned with Kabul judged success by continued access to funding streams, weapons, and political appointments. When those flows faltered after the February 2020 US–Taliban agreement in Doha, client indicators flashed red despite continued fighting. The Afghan government's public messaging stressed resilience. Client behaviour told another story: defections increased, local ceasefires multiplied, and commanders hedged. Success, for clients, meant assurance of backing tomorrow, not territory today.

Pair abstraction with behaviour. Client *trust* appears as commanders staying put rather than negotiating exits. Client *efficiency* shows up in recruitment and tax collection. Client *risk* is measured by the speed with which leaders move families abroad. These are not metaphors. They are decisions.

Civilians inhabit a different universe of indicators altogether. In Aleppo in 2016, Russia and the Syrian government framed the recapture of eastern districts as liberation. International organisations recorded something else. According to the World Health Organization, only six hospitals remained partially functioning in east Aleppo by November 2016 (WHO, 2016). Civilian success metrics are unforgiving: casualty rates, displacement figures, school attendance, price inflation. When bread prices triple, success collapses into meaninglessness.

This creates the central tension of proxy warfare measurement. Indicators that reassure patrons often worsen civilian outcomes. Indicators that empower clients may entrench coercion. Indicators that reflect civilian wellbeing rarely align with patron timelines.

A brief case sharpens the point. In southern Lebanon after 2006, Hezbollah declared victory over Israel, pointing to survival and continued rocket capability. Israel's government, after initial hesitation, framed the war as a strategic warning delivered. Both narratives found audiences. Civilians experienced prolonged displacement, infrastructure damage, and the consolidation of an armed actor within the state. By 2008, UNIFIL reported relative calm along the Blue Line, an indicator patrons welcomed. Civilian indicators improved slowly, unevenly. The war was a success in capitals and a burden in villages.

At this juncture, a credible limitation deserves acknowledgement. There are cases where indicators align across stakeholders. The end of the civil war in Mozambique in 1992 produced improvements in security, economic recovery, and political participation that satisfied patrons, clients, and civilians. Why include this counter-example? Because it demonstrates that misalignment is not inevitable. Where incentives converge and post-conflict institutions function, indicators can reinforce one another. The reconciliation lies in governance, not goodwill.

The motif of the scoreboard returns, now multiplied. Patrons maintain dashboards optimised for political survival. Clients watch gauges of loyalty and leverage. Civilians count days without shelling. None is illegitimate. All are partial.

Technology complicates this further. Drone footage offers patrons immediate visual indicators: strikes executed, targets hit. Clients use the same footage for recruitment and intimidation. Civilians see their neighbourhoods reduced to pixels. The indicator is shared; the meaning diverges. This asymmetry widens the gap between declared success and lived experience.

Indicators also shape behaviour through incentives. When contracts or aid packages reward visible stability, actors perform stability. Checkpoints proliferate. Patrols increase. Meanwhile, reconciliation stalls. The behaviour is rational. The metric is flawed.

What follows is an uncomfortable implication for analysts and policymakers alike. If indicators remain siloed, proxy wars will continue to generate declarations of success alongside enduring instability. Bridging the gap requires at least acknowledging the multiplicity of measures at play.

That acknowledgement raises a final, unresolved test. When the next proxy campaign is hailed as a triumph, which indicators should observers consult first: the patron's briefing slides, the client's movements, or the civilian ledger of loss and recovery? The answer will determine whether the victory holds—or dissolves the moment the scoreboard is switched off.

Comparing historical and contemporary cases

In April 1961, Cuban exiles trained and equipped by the United States landed at Playa Girón, better known as the Bay of Pigs. Within seventy-two hours the operation collapsed. Washington denied direct involvement, Havana proclaimed imperialist aggression, and Fidel Castro emerged stronger. Fifty-eight years later, in October 2019, US-backed Syrian Democratic Forces watched as American troops withdrew from parts of north-eastern Syria, opening space for Turkish intervention. The technologies were different, the language more cautious, the media cycle relentless. The dilemma was unchanged.

Proxy wars repeat themselves.

The value of comparison lies not in nostalgia but in discipline. By placing Cold War proxy conflicts alongside contemporary interventions, patterns emerge that resist novelty. Patrons still overestimate influence, clients still adapt incentives to their own survival, and technology still promises control while delivering friction. The names change. The logic endures.

Begin with patron behaviour. During the Vietnam War, the United States framed its support for South Vietnam as containment, measured through body counts and territory held. The visible behaviour was escalation by increments: advisers became combat units, bombing campaigns expanded, metrics multiplied. Show the behaviour, name the pattern, explain the logic, and the implication follows. The pattern was *metric substitution*: when political goals proved elusive, military indicators filled the gap. According to the Pentagon Papers (US Department of Defense, 1971), internal assessments questioned progress even as public briefings remained upbeat. Success was narrated forward.

Now place this alongside Afghanistan after 2001. The United States and its allies again adopted proxy-heavy approaches, relying on local militias and a central government sustained by external finance. Behaviour repeated. Metrics shifted from Taliban casualties to districts controlled to Afghan forces trained. The Special Inspector General for Afghanistan Reconstruction documented how indicators improved on paper while institutions hollowed out (SIGAR, 2018). Technology enabled better reporting, not better outcomes. The implication is sobering. Improved data does not correct flawed incentives.

Clients evolve predictably across eras. In Angola during the 1970s and 1980s, movements such as UNITA and the MPLA adapted their ideologies to court patrons. Behaviour was visible in diplomatic travel, media messaging, and shifts in military posture timed to aid deliveries. Name this *adaptive clienthood*. The explanation is straightforward. Clients depend on patron flows; survival requires responsiveness. The implication is corrosive. Over time, local agendas bend around external expectations, often at the expense of legitimacy at home.

Fast-forward to Iraq after 2003. Shi'a militias initially supported to counter insurgents evolved into political actors embedded in the state. Their behaviour—contesting elections, controlling ministries, maintaining armed wings—mirrors earlier client trajectories. Technology altered recruitment and propaganda, not the incentive to hedge. When patrons reduced support, militias diversified funding and alliances. Client evolution followed a familiar arc: dependency, adaptation, partial autonomy.

Civilians appear as constants rather than variables. In Guatemala's civil war during the 1980s, US-backed counterinsurgency campaigns displaced hundreds of thousands. The Commission for Historical Clarification later documented systematic abuses (CEH, 1999). Public indicators during the war stressed stability and communist containment. Civilian indicators told another story. Compare this with Yemen after 2015. Coalition briefings highlighted degraded capabilities. Civilian metrics—cholera cases, malnutrition rates—spoke of collapse (WHO, 2017). The abstraction of *stability* becomes concrete in hospital admissions and migration flows.

Thread the motif of the scoreboard again. Cold War scoreboards were slow, curated, and secretive. Contemporary scoreboards update in real time. The number of scoreboards has increased; alignment has not.

Technology deserves particular attention, not as a rupture but as an amplifier. In the Korean War, air power promised decisive leverage but produced stalemate. In Libya in 2011, precision strikes and real-time intelligence enabled rapid regime collapse. Yet the post-conflict pattern echoed earlier cases. Armed groups proliferated, patrons disengaged selectively, and instability persisted. The behaviour—rapid intervention followed by ambiguous commitment—mirrors earlier episodes. Name this *compressed intervention.* The explanation lies in political appetite. Technology shortens timelines but does not sustain settlements. The implication is risk deferred, not resolved.

A mid-twentieth-century war set beside a recent intervention clarifies this. Consider the Soviet Union's experience in Afghanistan beginning in December 1979 and Russia's intervention in Syria from September 2015. In Afghanistan, Moscow backed a client regime with advisers, air power, and material support. Metrics focused on securing cities and supply lines. Clients defected. Costs mounted. Withdrawal followed. In Syria, Russia applied lessons selectively: limited ground exposure, decisive air support, and political bargaining. The outcome differed tactically. Strategically, core dilemmas persisted. Client dependence remained high. Civilian suffering continued. The difference lay in scale and visibility, not structure.

A credible counter-example complicates the picture. The Marshall Plan and subsequent security arrangements in Western Europe after 1945 did not produce the pathologies associated with proxy warfare. Why? Because clients possessed legitimacy, institutions, and shared threat perceptions. Patron behaviour aligned with reconstruction rather than control. This limitation matters. It shows that history does not trap outcomes; conditions do. Reconciliation lies in recognising when proxy logic applies and when it does not.

Abstractions sharpen when paired with metrics. *Trust* appears as basing agreements honoured or broken. *Efficiency* shows up in the ratio of aid delivered to forces retained. *Risk* is visible in escalation incidents per month. Replace slogans with numbers, and patterns clarify.

The persistence of patterns challenges claims of a fundamentally new era. Cyber operations, drones, and social media alter tactics but not incentives. During the Cold War, pamphlets and radio broadcasts shaped narratives.

Today, footage circulates instantly. Clients still perform for patrons. Patrons still curate narratives for domestic audiences. Civilians still bear costs that rarely enter official tallies.

Comparison also exposes myth-making. In the United States, the memory of Vietnam shaped restraint in the 1990s, then faded. In Russia, the trauma of Afghanistan informed caution until Syria reframed confidence. Institutional memory oscillates. Patterns repeat when lessons decay.

This leads to an unresolved test. When analysts confront a new proxy conflict, which comparison should guide judgement: the novelty of tools or the recurrence of incentives? If history is consulted only for colour, patterns will surprise again. If it is used as a diagnostic, repetition becomes visible early.

The question remains open. Are contemporary patrons prepared to accept what history keeps showing—that proxies solve tactical problems while reproducing strategic ones—or will each generation rediscover the dilemma under a different name?

Technology, drones, and autonomous systems

On 27 September 2020, the Azerbaijani Ministry of Defence released a steady stream of drone footage from Nagorno-Karabakh. The videos, filmed from Turkish-made Bayraktar TB2 unmanned aircraft, showed armoured vehicles destroyed, air defences suppressed, and positions exposed. Within weeks, Armenian forces withdrew from large swathes of territory. The outcome was concrete. Territory changed hands. The images travelled faster than the units they depicted. Control looked effortless.

The footage did more than document a campaign. It shaped it. It reassured patrons, intimidated opponents, and framed international commentary. Deniability thinned. Attribution sharpened. Technology spoke for policy.

Five words mattered most. *The sky never blinked.*

Drones and autonomous systems sit at the centre of contemporary proxy warfare because they promise two things patrons crave: control at distance and political insulation. Armed drones, persistent surveillance platforms, and algorithmic targeting systems appear to compress risk while extending reach. The question is whether they actually do. Show the behaviour, name the effect, explain the mechanism, and the implication follows. What looks like tighter control often produces wider exposure.

Begin with surveillance. Persistent intelligence, surveillance, and reconnaissance alters the patron–client relationship by reducing informational asymmetry. In theory, patrons see more and guess less. During the US campaign against the Islamic State in Syria between 2014 and 2019, coalition ISR platforms provided near-continuous coverage of partner forces. Behaviour changed. Clients adjusted movements to remain camera-friendly. Metrics multiplied: targets identified, strikes approved, footage archived. Name this *sensor-driven oversight*. The explanation is simple. When data flows increase, patrons substitute video for trust. The implication is double-edged. Tactical discipline improves, but strategic autonomy erodes. Clients become performers.

Armed drones intensify this dynamic. Their relatively low operating cost and political palatability lower thresholds for use. According to the Bureau of Investigative Journalism (2021), US drone strikes expanded rapidly in the 2010s precisely because they reduced domestic political exposure. Transfer that logic to proxy contexts and the pattern holds. Patrons authorise strikes executed by partners or contractors using shared platforms. Control appears granular. Responsibility blurs.

Nagorno-Karabakh provides the first named example. Azerbaijan combined drones, loitering munitions, and local ground forces to overwhelm Armenian positions. The visible behaviour was sequencing: drones exposed targets, artillery finished them, footage followed. Name this *kill-chain compression*. The explanation lies in integration. Platforms shortened the time between detection and effect. The implication reaches beyond the battlefield. Because systems were supplied, trained, and in some cases advised by external actors, attribution followed supply lines. Deniability narrowed even as distance grew.

A second example lies in Yemen. Between 2015 and 2022, Houthi forces used Iranian-supplied drones and missiles to strike targets deep inside Saudi Arabia, including the Abqaiq oil processing facility in September 2019. The attack temporarily disrupted roughly five per cent of global oil supply, according to Saudi Aramco statements at the time. Behaviour mattered. The Houthis demonstrated reach disproportionate to their resources. Name this *proxy amplification*. The explanation is technological leverage. Cheap systems imposed strategic costs. The implication for patrons was acute. Support for proxies equipped with such tools risks uncontrolled escalation.

Autonomy complicates matters further. Fully autonomous weapons remain limited, but semi-autonomous functions already shape proxy control. Target recognition algorithms, automated navigation, and swarming concepts reduce the need for skilled operators. This lowers barriers to entry. It also lowers accountability. When a loitering munition selects a target based on pre-programmed parameters, the chain of decision fragments. Name this *responsibility dilution*. The explanation is organisational. Decision authority disperses across code, operator, and sponsor. The implication is legal and political ambiguity that can protect patrons while undermining restraint.

Pair abstractions with visible behaviour. *Efficiency* becomes sorties per operator. *Risk* becomes attribution incidents per month. *Trust* becomes rules of engagement enforced through software locks. These are not metaphors. They are design choices.

Yet technology does not only empower patrons. It empowers clients. Drones and surveillance platforms provide clients with independent intelligence streams, reducing reliance on patrons. In Ukraine after 2014, volunteer and state forces alike used commercial drones to map positions and document engagements. Behaviour shifted. Units filmed their own actions. Name this *client visibility*. The explanation is access. Commercial systems democratise reconnaissance. The implication is leverage. Clients can bargain with evidence.

A credible counter-example tempers the argument. In Mali after 2013, French forces deployed advanced ISR and strike assets alongside local partners. Despite technological superiority, control over outcomes remained limited. Insurgents adapted. Civilian harm incidents persisted. The limitation matters. Technology amplifies incentives; it does not replace politics. Reconciliation lies in recognising that tools magnify structures already present.

The motif of the camera returns. Drones turn battlefields into stages. Footage functions simultaneously as evidence, deterrent, and propaganda. During the 2020 Karabakh war, Azerbaijani releases shaped international perceptions of inevitability. Armenian counter-narratives struggled to compete. The behaviour—curated transparency—deserves naming. Call it *selective exposure*. The explanation is informational warfare. What is shown becomes what is believed. The implication is strategic. Patrons may lose control of narratives once footage circulates beyond intended audiences.

This feeds back into denial. Traditional proxy warfare relied on opacity. Drones erode it. Persistent surveillance leaves digital traces. Satellite imagery, open-source analysis, and social media triangulate events rapidly. In Syria, strikes attributed to Israel, Iran, Russia, or local actors were often identified within hours by independent analysts using imagery and flight data. Deniability now requires coordination across technical domains. It is harder.

Metrics confirm this shift. According to research by the Stockholm International Peace Research Institute (SIPRI, 2022), the number of states operating armed drones has increased significantly since 2010. With each transfer, attribution chains lengthen but do not disappear. The more common the technology, the easier comparison becomes. Patterns emerge.

Technology also alters escalation ladders. Drones occupy ambiguous rungs: more than surveillance, less than manned strikes. Patrons exploit this ambiguity to test boundaries. Clients sometimes climb faster than intended. In January 2024, a drone strike in Jordan killed US personnel at Tower 22, prompting direct retaliation. The behaviour—proxy action triggering patron response—illustrates risk migration. Name it *threshold miscalculation*. The explanation is signalling failure. The implication is that autonomous or semi-autonomous systems can accelerate crises by compressing decision cycles.

Civilians remain central. Surveillance can reduce harm by improving targeting. It can also normalise constant presence. In Gaza, persistent aerial observation has been described by human rights organisations as psychologically damaging, irrespective of strike frequency (Amnesty International, 2014). Pair the abstraction *security* with the metric *hours under observation*. Control has a human cost.

Does technology make proxies easier to manage? Tactically, yes. Patrons can monitor, cue, and restrain clients with unprecedented precision. Strategically, the answer is less comforting. Control breeds dependence. Dependence breeds resentment. Resentment finds outlets once constraints loosen. Technology tightens the leash while lengthening the reach.

The future points towards mixed human–machine teams. Regional security firms already operate drones for border monitoring in Africa and the Middle East. Cyber contractors provide intelligence effects without physical presence. These trends suggest a convergence: marketised force adopting proxy characteristics, proxies adopting corporate tools. The boundary blurs.

End with a test rather than a claim. When the next proxy campaign unfolds under constant aerial gaze, will patrons measure success by targets struck or by restraint maintained? The cameras will record both. The harder question is which outcome will matter when the footage stops.

Scenarios for the next proxy century

On 19 March 2011, French aircraft struck Libyan air defences outside Benghazi as part of Operation Unified Protector, authorised days earlier by United Nations Security Council Resolution 1973. Within months, Muammar Gaddafi was dead, NATO declared its mission complete, and foreign leaders spoke of a limited intervention with decisive effect. The concrete outcome was regime collapse. The longer-term consequence was fragmentation, militia rule, and a decade of proxy competition involving Turkey, Russia, the United Arab Emirates, Egypt, and others. What looked like closure became prologue.

This is the paradox at the heart of the next proxy century. How can conflicts that begin with narrow mandates, modest means, and local actors metastasise so quickly into arenas of global rivalry? The answer lies less in intent than in structure. Power is diffusing. Non-state actors are stronger. Entry costs are falling. Exit costs are rising.

The future of proxy warfare will not unfold along a single path. It will be shaped by recurring scenarios, each with its own logic, tempo, and risks. Show the pattern, name it, explain why it recurs, and the implication becomes a tool for judgement rather than prediction. Scenarios do not forecast outcomes. They discipline attention.

Begin with diffusion. The first scenario is the *resource ignition spiral.* A local dispute over land, water, or minerals triggers violence between armed groups whose grievances are parochial but whose connections are not. Consider a hypothetical but plausible case: in the Sahel, a clash over access to a lithium deposit escalates between a local militia and a regional security force. Within weeks, the behaviour changes. One side seeks external backing to offset numerical disadvantage. A neighbouring state supplies arms. A distant power offers training through a private contractor. Diaspora groups fundraise. Metrics accumulate: shipments intercepted, advisers spotted, sanctions debated. Name this *horizontal pull.* The explanation is opportunity. Resources attract capital, and capital attracts patrons. The implication is speed. What once took years can now happen in weeks.

A second scenario is the *denial race.* As surveillance improves and attribution sharpens, patrons compete to maintain plausible distance while retaining influence. This produces layered involvement: cyber support without troops, intelligence sharing without strikes, financing without signatures. During the conflict in eastern Ukraine after 2014, multiple states navigated this terrain, calibrating aid to avoid formal escalation while shaping outcomes. Behaviour mattered. Uniforms were unmarked. Systems were familiar but not standard issue. Name this *graduated invisibility.* The explanation is risk management under scrutiny. The implication is fragility. Small disclosures can unravel carefully balanced positions.

A third scenario centres on *client capture.* Non-state actors, empowered by technology and finance, begin to dictate terms to their patrons. The Taliban's negotiations in Doha in 2020 illustrate the dynamic. Despite years of support to the Afghan government, the United States found itself bargaining directly with its adversary to secure an exit. The behaviour was inversion. The proxy outlasted the patron's political will. Name this *endurance leverage.* The explanation is asymmetry. Clients often measure time differently. The implication is caution. Short-term savings can buy long-term constraints.

Counter-examples refine the picture. Not all proxy engagements spiral. In the Balkans after 1995, sustained international presence and clear settlement terms limited re-proxying despite deep grievances. The limitation matters. Strong institutions and credible guarantees can arrest diffusion. Reconciliation lies in recognising that scenarios describe tendencies, not destinies.

Technology accelerates every scenario. Drones, encrypted communications, and digital finance compress distances. In a future *algorithmic escalation* scenario, an autonomous system misclassifies a convoy near a contested border, prompting a proxy strike that kills foreign advisers. Within hours, footage circulates. Statements harden. Forces mobilise. The behaviour is automaticity. Name it *machine-paced crisis.* The explanation is decision compression. The implication is that human judgement has less time to intervene.

Another scenario is *market saturation.* As private military companies, regional security firms, and cyber contractors proliferate, competition lowers prices and raises availability. A coastal state facing insurgency contracts multiple firms for overlapping tasks. Accountability blurs. Rival patrons invest through commercial fronts. Behaviour fragments. Name this *outsourced ambiguity*. The explanation is commodification. Force becomes a service with uneven oversight. The implication is diffusion without coordination.

History provides a baseline. Compare the Angolan civil war of the 1970s and 1980s with the Syrian conflict after 2011. In Angola, Cold War patrons backed rival movements over decades, constrained by logistics and ideology. In Syria, patrons entered and exited fluidly, constrained more by media cycles and sanctions. Technology changed the details. The dilemma endured. How to influence outcomes without owning them.

Thread a quiet motif through these scenarios: *the widening circle*. Each intervention draws another actor to the edge, then inside. Refugee flows pull in neighbours. Energy markets pull in consumers. Norms pull in institutions. Circles widen even when intentions narrow.

Questions matter more than answers. When assessing a future crisis, ask who benefits from delay. Measure who can absorb costs longest. Compare public statements with logistical commitments. Pair abstractions with behaviours. *Influence* becomes basing rights secured. *Stability* becomes checkpoints manned. *Commitment* becomes rotations sustained beyond headlines.

A final scenario returns to the local. In a river basin shared by three states, a drought displaces communities. Armed groups tax water access. One state backs a militia to secure its interests. Another responds. A third offers mediation while supplying surveillance. Within a month, external naval patrols appear offshore to protect trade. The original dispute remains unresolved. The circle widens again.

The unresolved tension is this. As proxies become easier to create and harder to control, will future patrons learn to stop earlier, or will the next proxy century be defined by ever-faster escalation from small causes to large consequences? The answer will not announce itself. It will emerge, quietly, in the first weeks of the next local clash that no one thinks will matter.

About the Author

Viktor Romcev writes about the hard edges of power: how states, movements, and markets turn resources into organised violence. His work focuses on the messy space between open war and formal peace, where deniable operations, covert aid, and commercial security actors quietly reshape entire regions. Drawing on years of close study of conflicts from the mid-twentieth century to the present, he is interested less in slogans and more in how incentives, logistics, and institutions actually work. A long-standing fascination with the imperial rivalries of Central and Eastern Europe gives his writing a historical depth that resists easy narratives of novelty. Across his books and essays, his aim is simple: to give readers clear, durable tools for thinking about force, so that they can see through official stories and recognise who is really bearing the costs of modern warfare.

www.ingramcontent.com/pod-product-compliance
Lightning Source LLC
Chambersburg PA
CBHW021215250926
51852CB00006B/26
* 9 7 8 8 1 9 9 7 8 6 8 3 7 *